Life in
Double Time
*Confessions of an
American Drummer*

||

Mike Lankford

CHRONICLE BOOKS
SAN FRANCISCO

Text copyright © 1997 by Mike Lankford

Library of Congress Cataloging-in-Publication Data
    Life in double time : confessions of an American drummer /
by Mike Lankford.
       p.   cm.
    ISBN 0-8118-0683-9
    1. Lankford, Mike.   2. Drummers (Musicians)—United States—
Biography.   I. Title.
ML419.L29A3   1997
786.9'092—dc20
    [B]   96-5946
                                                                CIP
                                                                MN

Jacket design by Pete Friedrich
Text design by Brenda Rae Eno
Printed in the United States of America.

Lyrics from "Tossin' and Turnin' " by Richie Adams and
Malou Rene reprinted with permission of Warner Brothers.

Distributed in Canada by Raincoast Books
8680 Cambie Street
Vancouver, B.C. V6P 6M9

10 9 8 7 6 5 4 3 2 1

Chronicle Books
85 Second Street
San Francisco, CA 94105

Web Site: www.chronbooks.com

Dedication

For

JAMES ALAN MCPHERSON

Acknowledgments

Margot, for being at home and near the phone for years at a time.

Joe, for his cartoon mind.

Dr. Wayne, for his wise friendship and occasional editing gigs.

All the folks in various bands I worked with while living cheap
and writing the book. If any of you wondered what
I was thinking about back there, this is it.

And first of all, John, bass player extraordinaire who got me back to
playing and then encouraged the book every inch of the way.

contents

"Hell is full of amateur musicians."

G. B. Shaw

|| PART ONE:

APPRENTICE

In the Beginning Was Elvis

In the early fifties, when I was growing up in Oklahoma, rock 'n'roll existed somewhere "out there" but I was only vaguely aware of it. Occasional reports of its existence would filter in but they would generally be dismissed. Even less occasionally it might be heard over the car radio, but like most young kids, I followed my parents' lead and thought of it as monkey music. Around our house, Lawrence Welk was considered "Mr. Party." And he had to be taken in moderation, and only on Saturday nights. As frequently happens when one is young and ignorant and unable to appreciate things, I had an enormous stroke of good luck. And didn't know it. I met Elvis Presley one night and didn't know it was Elvis Presley. He was just some guy dressed like a circus performer outside the Old South Club in Lawton, Oklahoma.

The Old South Club was a dinner establishment five days a week, with weekends reserved for live entertainment. We never went to the live entertainment. We did, however, go one Friday evening for dinner and I remember seeing a large bus parked in front and four or five men carrying boxes from it into the club. At the time I was much more interested in the bus than who might be inside it. It was as big as a house and I hadn't seen many buses before. As we came up along-side we saw two men standing and several speaker boxes on the side-walk. I remember only that the men were disagreeing about something and didn't care who heard them. One of the men bent over and picked up a box, still talking over his shoulder, and carried it inside. That was Elvis. That was Elvis before he was famous, back when he used to help unload his own equipment. We followed him inside and then met him again in the dining room on his return trip to the bus. Elvis was sweat-ing and still pissed off. The club owner introduced my father and mother. I was not actually introduced by name but I still consider the meeting to have taken place. I looked at him so closely I remember he glanced down at me once or twice and tried to smile. Even though he was dressed in neon colors and had a shirt collar that rose over six inches high, he was actually more remarkable for his haircut than for his clothes. I'd seen gangsters and other nightclub types on TV dressed up in flamboyant outfits and was fairly used to it; it was his hair that seized my attention. I'd never seen so much hair on a man, especially viewed from down low like that. It seemed to rise a straight foot above his head and I wondered if he might not have a large bump underneath to hold it up. I remember his name on the marquee inside, and I remember asking my mother what an "Elvis" was. She told me he was a musician and that's the end of the story. We sat down and ate and forgot all about it—except that ten years later a synapse fired and I suddenly remembered the incident, but by then couldn't get anybody to believe me.

I Hear My First Live Band

Many years would pass, probably seven or eight, before I began waking up to what was going on in the world around me. I was thirteen before I actually experienced in my own body what the rest of America already knew as rock'n'roll. In my town there was a place called the "Teen Club." I'd never been there before. It may have been that thirteen was the minimum legal age for getting in the door. More than likely it was my mother waiting for my resistance to evil to become sufficiently strong before allowing me to go in. With the sophistication of years, I can look back and know the place was nothing but a dark box of a room with a coke bar against one wall and a nothing little bandstand up against the other, but to me it looked like a posh nightclub. There were adult chaperons who kept an eagle eye on all the proceedings. There was dancing in the crude, unpracticed form you would expect, and it was mostly fast dancing. Slow dances were looked upon as rare opportunities to commit crime and ordinarily you would only try that with girls you knew. Because I didn't know any girls, I didn't try it. The notion of asking a strange girl to slow dance was more than most boys would consider. To try it would risk her going to tell the chaperon. At that age I was tender and sensitive about being thrown out of places, so I mostly watched and tried to convert slow dancing to an imaginative experience.

Which didn't work. Before long I had drifted over to the bandstand, where most of the single boys were, and began watching the musicians. There were four of them, and I'm sure—looking back—they weren't very good. But that was not my impression that night.

It took me the longest time to find a spot to stand so I could see clearly. The twenty or thirty boys in front refused to budge. Standing in the back all I could see were the singers' heads. I worked my way around the edges of the crowd until I was at one side of the stage, able to see only the back side of the band because of a speaker. But the part I saw included the drummer.

For the first three or four seconds I stood gazing, my composure remained intact; after fifteen seconds my breathing had slowed quite a bit but I was still able to draw air; then somewhere near the half minute mark I felt my foundations begin breaking up as the drummer executed a fancy fill and twirled his stick. I can't be sure, but I think my eyeballs rolled out and dangled at the end of their springs. To call it 'astonishing' would be to weaken the effect. I'd never seen such behavior in a person before. From the side I could see every tiny movement he made. I could see his feet moving in quick flurries, completely independent of each other, driving pedals on the floor; and then the hands punching through the air, like someone boxing with a swarm of bees. His face was a picture of inspiration: sweaty, wild-eyed, slack jawed, drooling, looking towards heaven. Around every movement he made, hinging on each note he played, was the song itself. If he hit a cymbal, guitars went off like fireworks. Maybe if I could've seen the front of the band I might have felt differently, but I doubt it.

The drum set itself was a majestic instrument, unlike anything else on the stage, large and chrome-plated with a hundred shiny parts, cymbals floating in the air around the drummer's head and a two-sided wall of drums around his waist. It seemed to me all of an enormous single piece: a sprawling and gaudy hunk of sculpture molded around his body, something he'd have to unbuckle himself from. Melody ceased to exist for me that night. Everything in the songs seemed done for the sake of the drummer. Every verse, chorus, bridge and ending was written so the drummer could do something else remarkable. He seemed a combination conductor, lead instrument, chief source of inspiration and spark plug for the whole band. Even when he stopped playing during breaks in the songs—pauses where he would slowly twirl one of his sticks and look nonchalantly around the room—it was only so he could make a dramatic reentry and remind everyone he was there. I had never seen such a flood of raw flowing talent in my whole life.

The next day I was like a moth circling a flame. My mind was in a fluttery state, fixed but uncertain. I was unable to concentrate on anything for longer than a minute. Try as I might, I could not yet imagine myself as a rock'n'roll drummer. And yet I could think of nothing else. I was not an awesome person to myself so it was quite difficult at first to figure out how I could sit behind a full set of drums and do anything respectable. Some conceptual leaps are just hard to make. But that difficulty lasted only for a while. Three days at most. I overcame my modesty. My imagination finally engaged. During solitary moments of complete abandon, I eventually did sneak up to the bandstand in my mind and play a song or two. And I felt I was quite impressive. I incorporated some special effects the other drummer had left out. Lightning bolts and things like that.

I began to live a secret life. I became a mystery to my family and friends. Things would occur which I had no words for and could not explain. Riding in the car with the radio on, the occasional rock'n'roll song would come over the air, and by the second verse I would be in a cold sweat improvising effects, all the while twirling my sticks like airplane propellers. In my mind I'd already become the world's most amazing drummer. My breathing would jerk up and I probably had a fixed look in my eye. I might even have twitched occasionally, although I tried not to. This was noticed eventually by my mother who thought I was having a fit and turned loose the wheel in heavy traffic, creating a lot of unnecessary panic, when she might've just turned off the radio. That night my temperature was taken and I was interrogated on everything from bowel movements to lunch money. That was the start of my becoming a suspicious person.

I also became a regular at the Teen Club. It was the only place in town I could hear a band. Some Saturday nights they played records and I was sorely disappointed to arrive and find the music was canned, but usually there was a living, breathing rock'n'roll band from somewhere in Oklahoma or Texas. I suspect groups were still somewhat rare in those days. We did not have much variety at the Teen Club. I do not believe our little medium-sized town had yet sprouted any bands of its own. The talent had to be imported from Oklahoma City or Wichita Falls or even as far away as Dallas. The Dallas bands were always a great event. Not only did they come from further away, but they had more equipment, including spot lights. Colored lights, I discovered, added immeasurably to the overall effect and were the easiest way to distinguish the amateur bands from the more "professional."

Everyone knew that a band from Dallas would be better than a band from Oklahoma City, and that a band from Oklahoma City would be better than a band from Wichita Falls. And any band from New York City (if we'd heard one) would naturally be better than any other band in the rest of the country. It was all simply a matter of size: big towns had the best bands. This innocent notion cannot stand up to much scrutiny but shows my development at the time. If a band was coming a hundred and fifty miles from Dallas, it became known weeks ahead and the buzzing would begin. If possible, I would arrive at the Teen Club early and begin analyzing the equipment. The presence of an extra drum or an amp that stood higher than two feet would convince me that I was about to experience genius. If I found an amp that had more than the usual number of knobs, or an amp that had an extra light, or even an impressive jumble of wires and cords, my mind was made up.

I would count the number of mic stands and assess the vocal talent. I would try and get a glimpse of the drumsticks laying on the bass drum and if they were sufficiently scarred, then I knew the drummer was good. Why, I don't remember.

Dilapidation was also favored when it came to speaker boxes. In general, the more beat up the speaker boxes, the better the band had to be. This was a difficult call to make and shows my growing subtlety. Bad equipment that was beat up counted for nothing, so you had to know the difference. Quality equipment that was sufficiently complicated looking and impressively scraped and bruised showed me road miles, and this was a sure indicator of talent. I did not know about pawnshops yet, so it never occurred to me that equipment could be bought used and that I might be deceived. I was young and honest and on matters as important as band equipment I expected honesty as well.

There was a group of us boys who stood around the stage before the music started, discussing various questions we had, comparing tiny bits of knowledge. There were endless questions to be answered and we discovered them one at a time. There was Charlie the bean pole who felt responsible for asking most of the questions; Bruce, who considered himself a human database, and who usually answered the questions; Chico, who had strong opinions of his own but didn't like to fight; and then me, the guy with his mouth slightly open. The four of us would speculate on the purpose of different amps and how things hooked together, explain knobs to each other and give names to instruments we only half understood. Charlie would contend that you could tell who the lead singer was by his microphone; Bruce would dispute this. Chico would finally weigh in and an argument would ensue and then die away before attention shifted to some other important subject, like which instrument was the hardest to play.

Looking back, I think we assumed that if a person played music, then he was somehow a "natural" at it, had an inborn ability, a gift for his particular instrument. We believed that if you looked closely enough, you could almost see the thumbprint of God on a really good musician's forehead. To my mind, it was similar to the gift of flight: you were either an eagle or an ostrich. All of us ostriches believed in inspiration. That was the whole point in admiring musicians. The ability of a guitar player to cock his head back and then throw open the floodgates of his creativity, filling the room with his very soul, we found nourishing in the extreme.

We'd arrive early and scan the room for the band members, and usually had no trouble locating them. If it was a band no one had heard before, we would speculate on which instrument each one played, based solely on his looks. This is an activity guaranteed to bring out the prejudice in a person, and arguments again ensued. We were passionately and perfectly ignorant. Little miracles of stupidity. Once the band finally started its set and relieved us of our anxiety, a knot of us boys would stand off to one side and stare as hard as possible for forty-five minutes, waiting for the break before resuming our analysis, taking apart everything we'd just seen and heard. Out of this little group of boys came, years later, two guitar players and one drummer, me.

My memory is absolute on a few points, and one of them is the first time I ever spoke to a musician. It took me several weeks of twisting up my courage before I actually walked over and tried to talk to one of these entities during his break. He was the bass player and lead singer. I wanted to talk to the drummer, of course, but he had a girlfriend who monopolized his free time so I had to approach the singer instead. I waited until he came down off the stage and then moved toward him in a timid fashion. Everything about his person was vivid in my eyes and larger than life. He had on musician clothes and a gold chain around his neck. He was sweating in a cool room and had his shirt sleeves rolled up to reveal a gorgeous tattoo on one arm: a twisted up, three color rattlesnake with over-sized head and fangs, stylishly wrapped around the word DIE. I said something to catch his attention, probably "Hey," and was so glad when he didn't walk right over me that I forgot the compliment I'd worked up. It had taken me most of ten minutes to get a really impressive compliment just right, one sure to get his attention and identify me as an astute fan. But I hadn't prepared myself to stand so close to him and still hang together. He was a foot taller but seemed to fill up four times more space. I started on my compliment, but then some key words disappeared on me, and I couldn't remember the punch line, and ended up with that timeless banality, "Ya'll sound real good." He was kind enough to act like he cared and even stood for a few moments chatting. I managed to ask him where they were playing next and he mentioned some Dallas ballroom I didn't recognize. Then I tried out another question on him and he tolerated that, and maybe two more compliments from me before he moved on and mingled with the crowd. I would've been sadly disappointed to learn he sacked groceries during the week, which was probably the case.

| | |

I became the Teen Club's most solid citizen. I never missed a Saturday night. As my observations piled up, I began to recognize differences among drummers. All drummers may be born equal but they quickly separate themselves into strata of varying ability. All drummers should keep the beat, and most of them do, but some drummers lay down a beat that is solid and punchy while other drummers seem to play the same notes in the same places and there's nothing reassuring about it.

It seemed to me there were two basic kinds of drummers: the tappers and the whackers. The whole world, really, is divided into these two camps. Tappers tend to work on precision while the whackers emphasized enthusiasm. I could see virtues in both methods but in my heart of hearts I knew that what mattered most was the energy. The songs would either jump, or they would sit politely on the bandstand and merely happen. Some drummers have a talent for energy and others treat it as an alien experience. This was the problem with the tappers. They were too reserved for my blood. While I admired the control and technique they sometimes showed, their playing was dry and timid and undeserving of respect. That was never a problem with the whackers. The worst of the whackers were sloppy and overbearing and sometimes drowned out the other instruments, but in general my sympathies were in their camp. Looking back, I believe that the best of the whackers refined their skills and went on to successful careers in music, while the tappers eventually abandoned their quest and moved to jobs in science or library arts.

I'm thinking of one guy in particular. The earliest whacker in my memory. He was Indian and played a big set with two bass drums, each a different color, pieces from various sets he'd patched together. He played the solo in "In A Gadda Da Vida" with his shirt off. He had Indian bracelets on both wrists and worked himself into a foaming lather, hammering his drums so hard he broke stick after stick. The sound was overwhelming. I remember him looking ugly and scowling at the audience during the solo, and I remember being transfixed by the beauty of it all. It was like watching a volcano erupt or some other force of nature; he spoke to me at a mythological level. The tappers never managed to do that.

Month after month my vision cleared and my mind grew. I became a budding musicologist. I learned new things each time I heard a band. I learned that beyond basic talent, there is the more important matter of style. Style is a gift. It cannot be taught, it can barely be imitated. I discovered drummers who were all style but only technically decent, and I saw drummers who were technical virtuosos with no more personality than a digital clock. The stylish drummer puts his initials all over the music he plays. A drummer with sufficient personality can be recognized off the barest scrap of music. This is true for any instrument but particularly true for drummers.

I first noticed style the night I heard Dewayne and the Belldettas. They were an Oklahoma City band and their drummer was some sort of state snare drum champion I'd heard about for months. His hair was red and he was a man possessed when he played. He had four acres of drums and enough cymbals for a Chinese parade. And he had this odd way of lifting his sticks very high. Where most people stay close to the drum, this fellow brought his sticks back past his ears, creating little fans in the air that moved around his head.

But what really accounted for his uniqueness, his style, was the *feeling* he brought to the songs. It was *personal*. He seemed to know things more deeply than other people. His accents were thoughtful and full of logic. His fills were pieces of art. He didn't just roll around the drums, he picked notes here and there and constructed elaborate figures punctuated by little explosions up on the cymbals. He must've played fifty beats and half of them I'd never heard before. I was convinced that Beethoven would play drums in much the same way—hardy, robust,

endlessly brilliant. The band around him shrank up and almost disappeared off the stage. Over the course of the evening, I experienced the
sort of deepening and widening of my mental horizon that you read
about in books. I felt I'd been touched by beauty and drenched in light.
That night I made the decision to become a drummer with style.

My Life Gains a Focus

Once I had resolved to begin this new and brilliant career, I
found myself immediately stymied by the problem all beginning
drummers have: how to get a drum set. I inquired into the matter and
discovered that a drum set was roughly as expensive as buying a car.
Up until this point in my life I'd not contemplated any major pur-
chases. At fourteen I had no credit history. When I approached the
salesman at the music store about maybe "borrowing" a drum set for
a few weeks and trying them out, he looked through me like I was a
glass window. I was at a complete loss as to what I should do. I decided
to go to my mother for help. She was my only parent and main cash
source and I'd have to talk to her sooner or later anyway. But that
night when I mentioned the problem to her, instead of things getting
easier, everything became four times as complicated.

"A drum set?!" she said, with an ugly look in her eye. It took
her a long minute to get over this wonder. "What do you want a drum
set for?"

"To play on," I said, full of truth.

She shook her head once, looked perplexed, stared off into empty
space a moment, and then closed the conversation by saying, "You
don't need a drum set."

This ancient conundrum I'd come up against before. It was the
biggest gun in her arsenal. I never had any easy way to get around this

notion of what she thought I "needed." As though the only items a person ever purchased around our house were those essential to group survival. The way I figured it, according to her logic, we didn't need her china cabinet either. I personally never used it at all. It seemed to me that ninety percent of what we had in the house wasn't "needed" in the strict sense of the term. I tried to point this out to her but she wouldn't catch my drift. It took me a while to figure out that maybe what she was saying was that *she* didn't need a drum set.

I let the issue cool for a few days and then came back with a different approach. I waited until she seemed relaxed and was eating her Post Toasties one morning when I asked, "What's wrong with a drum set?"

Her spoon stopped, her eyes glazed over again; suddenly she looked as old as Methuselah there in the morning sun. It took her another moment to reabsorb the question. Dropping her spoon and turning in my direction, she asked, very deliberately, "What's *right* about a drum set?"

The subject was finally open for conversation. Just as I was calling up the first of my hundred reasons, she cut me off. "They're loud. You'd be banging on it day and night. We have no place to put it. We can't afford it. And after six weeks you'd forget all about it. It would be just like the trumpet."

I'd forgotten about the trumpet. True, I'd gotten her to buy me a trumpet a couple of years back and after a while had given it up. But trumpets were a whole separate category. It wasn't like I wanted her to buy me *another* trumpet. I'd discovered nothing cool about the trumpet. The only place I could play a trumpet was in the school orchestra, and that bunch of dorks had nothing in common with the power and majesty of a rock'n'roll band. And besides, I played trumpet in front of the mirror once and didn't like what I saw. Trumpets also made weird noises and were hard to control. But she had me on the defensive. I back filled as fast as possible. I admitted the trumpet was a mistake. I'd been led astray by seeing Louis Armstrong on TV. It wasn't my fault if he could play the trumpet and I couldn't.

Cornered, I came out fighting, throwing questions left and right. Was my entire musical career to come to a halt just because I couldn't play the trumpet? Was my only option to follow one success after another in a long string before arriving at the instrument I was meant to play? How steep a mountain did I have to climb to prove my good intentions? Drums were it, I told her. There wouldn't be any slacking off on the drums. I'd play them constantly until I was good as good could be. I would be a model of concentrated discipline. You'd be able to set your clock by my practices—just let me have the drum set. I worked all my best arguments but didn't quite win her over. It was only by getting down on my knees and pleading that she even agreed to "think" about it.

My mother, when she thought about things, would not keep me informed of her progress and, in fact, refused to bring the subject up at all until she had made up her mind. This was very difficult for me. For all I could tell, she'd forgotten the issue and was expecting me to forget it as well. What I wanted were regular signs and indications, like a furrowed brow or long periods of solitude, to reassure me that she was working her way toward a decision. Each and every day she did not mention my future drum set was a day fifty hours long. I was growing faint with inactivity but could do nothing about it.

Finally, one night at dinner, after a deep depression had washed over me twice that day, she said, "I've decided. You can have the drums. But only if you pay for them yourself. This will mean getting a job. Do you understand what that means . . . a job?"

I think I ricocheted twice before sticking to the ceiling. I was overcome with joy. My life had acquired a focus. I'd suddenly become a rock'n'roll drummer. The drum set was as good as in the house already. A couple of details still to be mopped up, like signing papers and getting a job, but the set was mine.

The next day after school I was down at the music store again—as I had been every day for months—but now no longer the humble questioner of clerks. My sails were full. I'd come to lay claim on my future drum set, to give notice it shouldn't be sold to anyone else. I'd known which set was mine for several weeks already. Through a process of elimination called "fourteen-year-old logic" I refined my choices and options. There were five sets in the store but two of them I knew were too big and expensive for me, and I'd never sell my mother on either one of them. Another set was for beginners and was smaller and cheaply made. The chrome plating was no good and the drum color was some sort of black with a gold stripe. Very indistinct. I had no intention of buying a beginner's set because I had no intention of being a beginner for very long. The remaining two were both four-piece sets: a Ludwig white pearl and a red sparkle Rogers. At first I could have gone either way but after I'd thought about it, it seemed to me the white pearl was somewhat conservative and not quite rock'n'roll enough for my blood. It was certainly pretty and under the right light you could see small rainbows in the finish. But ultimately I preferred sparkles, red sparkles especially, like red stars twinkling on and off around me as I played. I understood all too well that the selection of a drum set would say a lot about my personality and fix my identity in the public mind.

But complications kept flowing in my direction. Nothing was simple. The music store wouldn't reserve a set without a down payment. Promises didn't count. Finding a job turned out to be a major endeavor. My resume was too simple to be impressive. I had no contacts to call. The job market seemed full to bursting with applicants at my level. After an enormous amount of bother the best job I could come up with was as a janitor in an elementary school after hours. I had ten rooms to clean, five afternoons a week, two hours a day, and for this I received $75 a month. It was a blow to my pride but "Struggle" had become my middle name.

Once I secured the job I expected events to accelerate quickly but the next hitch developed. I was informed by the loan officer at the bank that they had a policy of requiring their own down payment on such dubious items as musical instruments, and that a double down payment at my low wage would require an additional four months of working. Going to that janitor job every day and then coming home and not finding my drum set was very hard on me. I could only pray it wouldn't be sold to some stranger walking in off the street.

Then to keep things complicated, the old man at the elementary school, the head janitor who knew I was only doing this for a drum set, developed a negative attitude towards me and became demanding and insistent and somewhat shrill about everything being perfectly done, forcing me to work late and without extra pay. He seemed to want everything surgically clean, literally glistening, and would follow me from room to room, fault-finding and bitter in his old age. The whole thing became so burdensome I almost gave it up. But at night in bed the vision returned and I saw myself on stage, radiating red light, and this was what kept me strong.

When the day finally arrived my mother and I signed the necessary papers at the bank and then walked over to the music store. It was clearly hard for her as she had not yet shaken the belief that she was acquiring more junk for the attic, bright and shiny junk, red expensive junk, but junk nevertheless. For my part, I would have signed papers all day. A twenty-four-month payment plan was no stretch for me. I did make concessions, though. I didn't buy everything I wanted. I didn't get all the cymbals I thought necessary but only enough to get started: a ride cymbal and a crash, and cymbals for the hi-hat. Everything else would be added later. But I had my own drum set. I took it home to the garage fully expecting to be playing long solos by nightfall.

The Science of Drumming

To stand at the very beginning of an endlessly long road requires fortitude. It requires conviction, a steely will, but mostly it requires a certain purity of naiveté. At that early point in my musical career I was still counting on a surge of natural talent to come along and carry me up to speed, make my learning curve real short. Rock'n'roll had taken over my life and I couldn't wait to bust out and do amazing things on the drums.

It took me at least three hours to get my stuff set up that very first time. Everything was folded and compact and hard to recognize. The salesman had taken the drums down for me at the store and I'd paid insufficient attention to how he did it. Along with four drums I had a mass of hardware spread out on the floor of the garage to figure out and unscrew and connect. There was no assembly manual to guide me. Professional drum sets do not come with instructions. One moment I'd be sitting like a Zen student contemplating the enigma of a tripod stand, the next I'd be arguing with my bass drum pedal trying to get it to work in a backward position. I pushed and pulled on telescopic rods and managed to lose one inside the other. I twisted and turned every possible wing nut and lug at least twice. Piece by piece my drum set rose from the dust, tiny battles fought all along the line.

Finally—after four months and three hours of waiting—I was pretty much surging and ready to go. My water had come to a boil, and even begun evaporating. I pulled the drums and cymbals together into a rough-looking unit, picked up my sticks, took a deep breath—and then launched myself off into space.

| | |

There is a hole in my memory as to what followed, but I'm sure it's fair to say that all rocket disasters look somewhat alike. Two or three minutes of the worst kind of racket, and then a long silence before the birds will start singing again. Even the insects seem stunned.

Of all the twisted and ungraspable difficulties I'd ever encountered in my fourteen years, this was the worst. My drums were totally uncooperative. For an hour or more, I banged around in a chaotic fashion, working my way into a deep-heaving exhaustion, making more noise than an earthquake on a bad day, only to realize that I hadn't progressed an inch yet. I hammered and thumped for all I was worth, and it seemed only to get worse, not better.

It was as if I were swimming in a vast ocean of potential drum knowledge, and yet couldn't manage to swallow a single drop. I could not even execute a roll, something I thought was pretty automatic. The seemingly wild playing I had admired in others, playing I thought was created out of the spark of the moment, turned out to be not so wild after all. My sparks alone couldn't do the job. The idea slowly began to break over me that the most abandoned, free-wheeling, devil-may-care whacker of drums was actually working from a deep reservoir of knowledge.

I decided to give up free expression for a while and concentrate on something more specific. I played one of the simplest beats I could imagine, a boom-whack proposition with a couple of random thumps on the bass drum and a smack on the snare drum, back and forth—kind of a funky floating thing I'd heard the day before on the radio—but I couldn't put any regularity to it. It was a beat without any discernible tempo. What I listened for and tried to achieve, of course, was that flow in my beat that I heard on the records, that perfect steadiness, that sound of inevitability. What I aimed at was that large-scale, epic feel that came from playing the notes big, because that's how I heard it in my head. All the best drummers got that sound. But my beat didn't sound big at all. Instead it was just loud. When I tried to add the cymbal to the beat, keeping time with all those blurring notes that were too fast to be counted, my arm seized up and wouldn't go. I tried to play only half the beat, leaving the cymbal part out of it for a while, and work on my predictability, but the beat never settled down. It sounded like junk. Deeply discouraged, I finally gave up and went to bed.

The next morning my arms were so sore I could hardly lift them. I dragged myself around all day, refusing to talk. I should have been wild with enthusiasm but that was impossible now. I felt like a fraud. I regretted telling my friends that I was getting a drum set because I had to field questions about it all day. Later that afternoon when old Mr. Havlick, my supervising janitor—who I hardly knew—asked me how the drumming was coming, I gave him a look intended to dry up all his interest in my personal affairs. I walked home that evening kicking dirt. Nothing was going as I'd expected. I was half ready to accept my mother's judgment that I would work for two years paying off the red junk in the attic. That last payment began to loom up like a distant mountaintop poking over the horizon. I would be sixteen and unable to buy a car because of those drums. I even thought for a while that I might rent my drums out to other boys who hadn't yet acquired a hardened sense of reality. By the time I got home I did not go out to the garage. Instead, I spent my time in my room where I concentrated on breathing deep and not looking at anything. Contemplating my innermost self.

A Ten-Foot Rope

It was my mother who rescued me. Two nights later, over dinner, she asked how the playing was coming. I said it wasn't. She said it had sounded pretty good to her inside the house, said she'd heard everything and that it sounded fine. I was dubious and knew I was being mothered. "Well," she asked, "Have you thought about taking lessons?"

I hadn't, of course. Nothing that simple and obvious would've occurred to me. She said she thought lessons might be a good idea and even offered to pay for them if I would find a teacher. I began to brighten up immediately. It was a wonderful idea. What an insight. Instead of me rediscovering everything that had already been played on the drums—which I somehow thought I was required to do—I could have someone show me.

I asked at the music store and was referred to a well-known drummer in town. His name was Rod Roadruck and I'd heard him play at the Teen Club once. He was older and very talented. Probably, to my knowledge, the best drummer around. What had impressed me most when I heard him were his fills. His fills were longer than most drummers' and they always had several parts to them with two or three little tricks built in here and there. I wasn't sure he'd agree to work with a novice like me but I made the call anyway. When I met him he looked every inch the musician. He had a beard and long hair and wore a necklace. He also used words like "hip" and "cool," which impressed me enormously. The lesson was in my garage.

What I remember most after the introduction and polite chit-chat was him taking my sticks and sitting down where I had sat only a moment before and converting those previously uncooperative drums into a musical instrument. They changed before my very eyes from a collected mass of hardware to a coherent whole. With the same attitude with which a person might kick the tire of a car, Rod took the sticks and ran a little test pattern over my drums to see how they sounded, playing fifteen of the most complicated licks I'd ever heard up close: fills opening and closing with shifting accents from one hand to the other, moving all over the set with ease and generating a huge surge of energy in me.

To test my bass drum, he whipped off half a dozen intricate beats, each one of them crooked as a snake and sounding like a steam engine—changing from Latin rhythms to rock to jazz in a fluid and casual way before nodding his head that the bass drum was satisfactory.

"Your bass drum pedal needs adjusting though," he said. I nodded and tried to sound experienced, "Uh . . . yeah, I thought so too." He bent over and looked at the pedal more closely. "Ordinarily," he began, and there was a long pause while the blood ran to his head, "it would be the tension control. But your pedal seems to be all out of whack. Batter height is wrong; swing is wrong; tension is way too high; the beater isn't even centered. Have you got a little brother or someone who's been messing with it?" I stumbled around a moment and there was an awkward pause.

Rod decided that the first order of business would be to tune my drums, but when he asked for my drum key I looked around and couldn't find it. I could tell Rod was becoming impatient.

"You need to get a drum key. Buy a couple; they're cheap." Then he pulled one of out his own pocket. I immediately understood that the mark of a true drummer is to always have a drum key permanently on his person. I decided to always carry one in my pocket, if only to be able to pull it out in the off-handed way he just did. Henceforth, whenever I paid for something, there it would be. "What's that?" people would ask and I'd say "drum key" just like it was one of the family jewels I had to carry around.

Rod started with the snare drum, first loosening all the lugs and then tightening them back down in a criss-crossing manner, jumping back and forth across the head to adjust opposite sides. "You need to have even tension," he said. After he finished with the top head, he turned the snare drum over and started on the bottom head. It took him ten minutes of performing surgery on that bottom head to get it right. Then he started on the snares. The snares are those curly wires stretched across the bottom head that create the snarey sound. Rod was very unhappy with my snares. Seemed he'd never come across snares so poorly adjusted. He eventually had to take them completely off and then put them back on to get them right. Once he'd finished with the drum he played a press roll with a little roller coaster in it to test the dynamics. It sounded like a different drum, a professional drum, a drum with music in it. Then he went to the tom toms, finding many problems along the way. The bass drum itself didn't require much work, but then I hadn't messed with it much. The bass drum pedal taxed him to his limit but eventually he was able to balance swing and tension and all those other things into a harmonious whole. He tested it again with some odd time signature beat and I could tell the pedal had become extremely fast and punchy.

Up until this point I thought the lesson was going very well. I felt I'd learned a lot already. Listening to him play was a revelation to me. Simply standing so close to a live drummer was a thrill. Everything I asked him to play he played. I wanted to see a press roll done again and he executed one that sounded like pouring sand. I wanted to hear different beats so he played twenty or thirty. I even asked him to play a solo and he spun one out just like he'd thought of it that moment. Along the way he would give names to beats he played like "Rumba" or "Down Home" or "Funky Butt" and say that this one was a variation of that, and with learning one beat I could change it slightly and know three more. He ran through a whole catalog of drum knowledge as he played and I watched closely and attempted to photograph it all into my memory. It seemed to me that if I could just watch him for six months I'd become fabulous. Already I felt skill was seeping into my hands. I couldn't wait for him to leave so I could try some of this stuff.

"Now," he said, wiping the sweat off his face, "it's your turn."

"Me?" I protested that I had nothing to show yet, that I would need some practice alone before attempting anything publicly. I tried to remind him I was a raw recruit. He didn't seem to hear. Instead, he got up and told me to sit on the stool.

"The first thing is how you hold your sticks. Show me how you grip the sticks." He handed them to me and they lay in my hands like two dead fish. "You seem to use a matched grip. You have a choice here. You can hold them both the same way, which is how most rock drummers do it, or you can hold the left stick like this," and he moved the butt of the stick from the heel of his hand to the joint between thumb and forefinger. "There are advantages to both. This is more of a jazz grip. You have added control this way but you lose power. Which way do you want to go?"

I thought about it a moment and then asked, "Which is easier?"

He shook his head like a fly had just buzzed through. "Easy has nothing to do with it. It's a matter of playing style. A matched grip is more for power playing—if you want to kick two and four, then you hold the stick like a club—the jazz grip gives you more bounce and finesse. You can always switch back and forth. I do. It depends on the song. If you want to play mostly rock'n'roll let's go with the matched grip for now."

"Yeah . . . rock'n'roll," I said, but it sounded weak.

"Fine. Now, tighten up your grip a little bit but not too much. Don't choke the stick. Play some and let me watch you." I started flailing away, nailing everything in sight. He stopped me almost at once. "Fine, good. I just wanted to see how you hold the sticks."

"Now, I'm going to show you one thing today I want you to practice. Don't worry about playing fancy solos or songs, just practice this one thing until you've got it right. It's a beat, and one you can play, so don't worry about it. Get up and I'll show you." We traded places and then he began playing the world's simplest beat, one so unimpressive I didn't see any reason to learn it. "Practice this beat and the rest will come later. It's very simple. The bass drum plays a straight line: one, two, three, four. Just start the bass drum going, nothing hard. Boom, boom, boom, boom. Then on top of that you put the accents on the snare drum. The accents are on two and four. So: boom, pop, boom pop . . . like that. Got it? Your left foot plays along with your left hand: close the hi-hat at the same time you play the snare. Your right hand keeps time on the cymbal. You're playing eighth notes. Do you know what that means?" I started to guess but he cut me off. "It means there's eight of them to a measure. Just count to eight. Do you know what a measure is, one bar?" He was testing to see how deep my knowledge of music was. I could've saved him the trouble. I was wondering why he only counted to eight and not ten. "Doesn't matter. Lots of drummers don't read music. The cymbal is twice as fast as the bass drum and the bass drum is twice as fast as the snare drum." He did it again and made it look idiot simple.

So I tried it and my humiliation was complete. No amount of bluff or positive thinking could get me through that beat. I could not get the different limbs of my body to cooperate. "Slow down and just play the parts," he'd say, talking over my shoulder. "Start with the cymbal, get that going, then add the bass drum." I started it fifty times and eventually I had a primitive version under way. Then he told me to add the snare drum. I told him the snare drum wouldn't fit. I had too much going with the right hand and right foot to think about adding the left hand too, but he insisted. He had me break it down again, playing slowly, until finally I had both hands and both feet going all at once. But it was rough, very rough. My left foot insisted on jumping off the hi-hat pedal every other beat and getting tangled up in the stand. Not every snare note coincided with the bass drum. At my best, I could hold the whole contraption together a few seconds before I'd wake up to how complicated it was, and then one part or another of my body would fail me. Each time he had me start again and each time I began with the right hand on the cymbal, then added the right foot on the bass drum, tentatively bringing in the left hand on the snare drum and left foot before it would all crumble again and stop. This beat was complex beyond belief, like trying to juggle balls and tap dance and sing hallelujah all at once. We stayed with this routine until I was too tired to lift my arms anymore.

"You'll get it," he said. "You just have to practice every day and eventually it will come. Believe me."

Slippery Sticks

I began a long private agony. No one is as lonely as the young drummer after his first lesson. Left with an impossible standard to meet, I knew I would fail. When Rod picked up a stick, that stick became inspired. When I picked up the same stick it lost all balance, became as big as a log, and refused to read my mind. My sticks also had an annoying habit of flying out of my hands when I least expected it. In that sense, I was a dangerous drummer to be around. If I'd been in a band during those early days, every musician within twenty feet would've been wounded. Any guitar player foolish enough to turn his back on me would pay dearly. As it was, I only abused the walls of the garage. Occasionally, I'd sling a stick so hard it would actually puncture the drywall. I would require insurance before joining any bands. My little brother, who at first liked to watch me practice, experienced a couple of near misses and then refused to come in the garage.

Those were desperate times. I was surrounded by incompetence: my own. I struggled on every front. I managed over the next five days to drive all the music out of my drums, returning them to their previous uncooperative state. When Rod left that first afternoon there was a charm radiating from the set. There were possibilities I could explore. When he played, my drums had become warm and expressive. But after just a few days I pounded all that away. Instead of an instrument of meaning my drums returned to their primitive state of chaos. They were hard and cold to the touch.

I worked on my one beat. I worked that one beat for twenty solid hours over the next week and found I had no aptitude for it. Simple beats are, in a sense, the hardest to play. They require precision and finesse. You can't bluff your way through a simple beat. Every note counts in a simple beat. The body must move in a fluid fashion, firing off those single notes in an emphatic way. I played like a drunk octopus. Half the time I couldn't even find the snare drum, and it was between my legs. If I paid attention to the right hand on the cymbal, my left hand would become forgetful and go into a coma. If I concentrated on the bass drum, my cymbal would jump off the beat. For hours at a time, different problems rotated among my four limbs. But I stuck with it. That is all I can say in my favor. I played that boom, pop, boom, pop proposition over and over every night until I was called in to bed. My mother stood up well to all this. I could see the years passing over her face, the jerky look in her eye, the fatigue that showed in the dark circles she'd developed, wrinkles getting deeper by the minute. I'm not sure I could've listened to that idiot repetition without murdering the cause of it.

Saturday came again, the day of my second lesson. Rod showed up on time but he seemed early to me. I'd practiced all morning trying to nail down that beat, to get it in some sort of decent shape to show him. I was tired and irritable when he walked in the door.

"Hi, sport. Sounds good."

I looked at him with a deep suspicion.

"Play it for me again and let's see what you've got."

I fired it up one more time. That beat had become the single theme in my life. I was obsessed with getting it right but it wouldn't get right. I started the right hand on the cymbal, laying down the count, added the bass drum and everything was going fine, but as soon as I stuck in the left hand and left foot things got wobbly and uncertain. I lost the tempo first, then my left foot jumped off the hi-hat, then the bass drum sped up while the snare slowed down. It all hung together for maybe an instant before collapsing like a house of cards.

"Good!" he said. "That's much better than last week. You keep practicing that beat and I guarantee it will come easy as breathing in no time."

He sounded sarcastic to me and this was unnecessary. I did not find it motivating. It may be that these things were easy for him, but then he obviously had a natural gift of large proportions. I now knew I had no such large gift. In fact, I suspected I might have a musical impairment. If I'd really learned anything in the past week it was that my drumming abilities were modest and that it would take six months to learn each single thing I needed to know. In five years I might be eligible to play my first song.

"Now today I'm going to show you two more things. I'm going to show you another beat you can practice, and I'll show you a fill."

Things became vague and I felt weak again. I knew I couldn't keep up with such a high-speed teacher for long. We traded places and Rod sat down at the drums. "Okay, here's your beat." And before he even stopped talking the beat was flowing out of his hands and feet, natural as water from a hose. "What you want to do," he said over the playing, "is add an extra note on the snare drum . . . like this." And with one note he transformed that groveling humiliation of a beat I couldn't yet play into a rhythm with snap and swing to it: boom, pop pop, boom, pop; boom, pop pop, boom, pop.

He played it over and over while I watched him. It looked simple enough but for the life of me I couldn't figure out exactly where he was placing that extra snare note. It didn't seem to fall on top of any other note in the beat but instead was dropped into one of the open spaces. Finally I asked him and he said, "It's only a problem if you think about it. It's like dribbling a basketball: if you think about each single bounce, you can't do it. And if you try to run and dribble and think about every single step and bounce and push, you'd fall on your face. You just have to learn to 'do it.'"

This was a new confusion. One I was not supposed to think about. The science of drumming was deeper than anything I'd encountered before.

Then while playing the beat over and over, he inserted a fill. It was a simple fill, even I could tell that, but he didn't stop the beat to play it. Instead, he played the fill on *top* of the beat, like slapping a sticker on a moving train. I lost all hope. My humility spread out and acquired a new dimension. "How in the world am I supposed to do that?" I wondered.

"You will," he said. "Trust me; you will. It's just a matter of practice."

And he was right. He wasn't right for several weeks, but eventually his prophecy came true. I went through eighteen stages of depression and sweated buckets and came close to quitting almost daily but finally the remarkable happened. I did learn the beat, both beats in fact, and the fill. And he was also right about not thinking too much about it all. I discovered—in an early and inarticulate way—that the playing of an instrument cannot be deliberate. That to think too much about what you're doing is to handicap yourself and sound musically wooden. The muscles must learn on their own, the body develops its own coordination, while your attention goes entirely to the overall effect you're producing. I eventually began changing from an unenlightened larval drummer to the beginnings of a butterfly. Not a whole butterfly yet but one with a single wing and the ability to slowly twirl his stick.

Growing That Second Wing

That was the extent of my formal musical education: two lessons. Rod unexpectedly went on a six-week tour with his band. He gave me the name of another teacher I could call until he returned but I never called. Instead, I followed the great American tradition of self education. I moved an old record player out to the garage and found myself a pair of headphones and began playing along with songs. I found songs that were simple enough I could fake them, songs with a single straight beat and no fancy breaks or fills. This taught me tempo. No matter how I flubbed the beat, the song went on without me. Eventually, I learned those songs and staged remarkable and exciting concerts in my garage, playing with the likes of Aretha Franklin and the Beatles. It's the simplest thing in the world to close your eyes and then populate the surrounding walls with bleachers and screaming fans. Day after day I moved to larger venues until finally I played only before crowds that stretched beyond the horizon. I could see it all in great detail, pick out particular faces in the crowd. I'd wave at my friends from high up on the drum podium. My concentration was so absolute I could pass hours in this condition. I say 'could' because inevitably my mother would sneak into the garage and come up behind me and tap on my shoulder, shattering a perfect moment and causing me to almost jump out of my skin. As a general rule of thumb, it's not a good idea to sneak up behind drummers.

In retrospect, I think more drummers could benefit from this learning approach. There are different schools of percussion in the world and a practiced ear can tell them apart. There are those people who care only about the drums, and who (it seems) only begrudgingly play with other musicians. When you hear them you can tell they are only listening to themselves and not to the rest of the band. These drummers love to play solos and complicated fills, regardless of how it may fit into the song around them.

And then there are the more musical drummers. These individuals are plugged into the music first and foremost. They tend to play simpler rhythms, they let the song decide what fills are appropriate, they will almost disappear at times and let another instrument take over. When those drummers learn a song, the first question they ask is not "what's the neatest thing I can put in here?" but rather "what will make the song sound best?" A radically different proposition. Some bands are tight, cohesive units and others are loose collections of talent. Some musicians over-play constantly and others are more precise in their expressions. In bands where each musician listens only to himself, huge battles are fought for dominance. The overall effect becomes confused. Great fills may be played, great rhythms and melodies may occupy the song, but the overall effect is not greatness. I did not understand this at the time; it was only dumb luck and the absence of a teacher that led me to play with records and think musically instead of working on long solos. Ignorance can be a great teacher, but I did not know that either.

But then, what I didn't know at the time was encyclopedic. A person could bring up almost any subject and there would be something fresh about it as far as I was concerned. At the time I was an apprentice drummer I entered into a state of perpetual wonder at the music I heard. Perhaps the finest thing about learning an instrument is that it focuses your attention on the particulars in a song. As an aficionado of rock'n'roll I found much that was thrilling in the records I heard, but as a larval drummer I discovered a whole new level of engagement with the music. Instead of hearing only the overall sound of a song, my attention gathered mostly around what the drummer was doing. The consequence of this was that I ceased to be a passive listener and became a partisan.

Everything in the song affected the drum part and everything the drummer did affected the rest. In the tension between melody and rhythm upon which every song is built, my sympathies were fully in one camp. This made the stretching riffs of the guitar and organ all the sweeter because I felt the conflict between beat and melody as something personal. I would even be pulled off the beat by a particularly good guitar riff and then snap back the instant the riff ended, feeling I'd betrayed my side and vowing not to let it happen again. At my moments of purest engagement, I crawled so deep inside a tune it became like four walls around me. To the nonmusician this may seem merely the natural dynamics of music, but to the fourteen-year-old drummer sitting in that room, there was a great tug of war going on. At the surface this war is reflected on the musician's face in the tics and jerks you see while he listens to a record play.

In the late 1960s I had ugly musicians I looked up to. B.B. King or Joe Cocker battling with tunes reminded me of ancient gladiators suffering the blows of swords. B.B. King in particular looked like his appendix was being yanked out without anesthesia; as a consequence, every note he played was evocative and personal. It looked like he was fighting for his life up there.

Such behavior on my part when listening to records did not pass unnoticed around our house. I quickly learned that if I were to enjoy my agony in peace I had to listen to music alone in my room. Every little thing I learned on the drums increased my pain and pleasure when listening to a song. Eventually, I learned to accentuate the conflict between rhythm and melody when I played, sharpening the tension and acquiring some small degree of musicianship for myself. I was beginning to sprout my second wing.

The First Song

My own assessment of my playing was all I had; there was no public opinion because I practiced alone. No one had heard me play. No one, that is, but my mother and brother listening through the walls, the six or eight families living nearby, and anyone who happened to be walking down the street or driving by with his window down, but I tried to ignore this small crowd. I allowed no one to come into the garage while I practiced. I began latching the door and I put curtains over the windows. I also played with the lights out, hoping this would help my concentration. As much as possible, I preferred keeping my mistakes a secret. If I'd had my druthers, I would have rehearsed on a remote mountain top somewhere in Peru. Like all young drummers, I was sensitive to criticism. I was reluctant to expose myself to the slings and arrows I knew were waiting for me as soon as I began playing with other musicians. You could say my early musical education occurred at a private school, with me as both teacher and student. This lasted about four months.

My first actual song, played live with another actual musician, happened by accident in my garage. A guitar player named Bruce called me on the phone one Saturday morning and talked me into letting him come over and "jam." I resisted the idea vigorously at first but Bruce used the argument that I had to play with someone sooner or later, and that playing with him the first time would be better than playing with a whole band. And besides, *he* wanted to play. Bruce was one of those cocky fourteen-year-olds you couldn't say no to. Wiry-haired, bright-eyed, like a squirrel running up your leg, he was going to come over regardless of what I said. Eventually I caved in. Playing along with the records had become easier for me lately and I had some reason to think I might not sound too awful. I knew three or four beats and some general-purpose fills. So I said yes and hung up the phone and immediately regretted it. I experienced my first case of stage fright while standing in my bedroom.

Ten minutes later Bruce was walking into my garage carrying his entire rig under his arm. He was the proud owner of a Sears Silvertone guitar with the amplifier and speaker built into the carrying case. A very convenient arrangement for transporting purposes but nearly worthless for the sound it put out. He was set up in thirty seconds flat—the time it took to find a wall socket.

I was having big trouble even adjusting to his presence in the garage. What little I thought I knew about playing had flown out the window. I tried to stall for time and perhaps let myself get accustomed to his presence, hoping this would allow a return of all my drum knowledge, but he was ready to go. I tried to engage him in conversation but he kept hitting chords and saying, "Do you know this? What about this?"

Bruce ran through parts of several songs and called out the name of each, but I failed to recognize any of them from the way they were played. To me it just sounded like random strumming with no melody at all. Like listening to the fourth flute part of a symphony and having to provide the rest in your own mind. I was failing badly already.

We went through his whole list of songs before picking one at random to try. I can no longer remember the name of that song, and feel fortunate. It might've been by Creedence. Bruce counted it off and we came in together and immediately it was like getting lost in a sand storm. His amp put out nothing but distortion and fuzz. I listened as closely as I could to his chords and strained to watch his hands but this explained nothing to me. I concentrated on keeping the beat as straight as I could, hoping he would find it soon—all while Bruce stared like he was waiting for me to notice something incredibly obvious. The song finally stopped on its own, somewhere in what I supposed to be the second verse. It sounded so different from the record that my first thought was that Bruce must be just a horrible guitar player. Maybe one of the very worst.

I tried not to say anything. I was the beginner here and was in no position to criticize. We looked at each other for a minute. It was a very pregnant pause. Finally, I asked, as casually as possible, "Are you sure you're in tune or whatever?"

"Oh, I wouldn't worry about me being in tune."

"Well, what about the key? Don't you have to be in a certain key?" I was groping for an explanation.

"We're in E, just like the record."

I could stand it no longer. "So what's wrong with the song?!"

Bruce got a shit-eating grin on his face and said, "It's not me."

This put me into a spin. I didn't know what, if anything, I was screwing up—I'd already listened to the record ninety times and didn't have any problems playing along. Maybe there was some mystery to playing live that I had been unaware of. Maybe playing with records was a huge mistake. I didn't know, but Bruce seemed so cock sure the fault was mine I could only agree to feel guilty and try harder.

I played the beat for him and asked, "Isn't this right?"

"I don't know. It sounds right, but I'm not a drummer. Let's try the song again."

We started it up a second time. I brought to bear every particle of concentration I had. Bruce began his strumming and I listened to that flat, featureless wall of sound for what I figured was four beats and then jumped in.

If the Tower of Babel is ever turned into a movie, we had the theme song. Bruce was bobbing his head frantically up and down where he thought the beat should be, and I'd watch him and try to get in sync, but every time I went there he'd move it again. Then Bruce turned up his volume, thinking perhaps this would help, but the effect was like shouting at me in Chinese with extra reverb. We plowed along, grimly determined to make the song happen, thinking it would gel eventually, that we'd fall in together, that gravitation or some other force of nature would come to our rescue. It was hopeless, but he refused to stop.

After ten minutes of this racket, we heard a loud hammering on the garage door and saw it jerk up and down several times against its lock. We both froze in our tracks. Then there were steps around the corner of the house and the side door opened. It was my neighbor Mr. Hanson, red faced and breathing hard. I thought perhaps he'd had an accident and come for help.

"Shut up!" he yelled, and slammed the door.

So went my first song. Canceled by public demand. I retreated back into my shell for several months to come, playing lightly, removing my headphones every few minutes to check for complaints. It would be more than six months before I knew that what Bruce had done had been a cruel hoax, him coming into my garage pretending to be a guitar player.

Garage Bands

Possessing a garage was as important as owning a drum set for entry into those early bands. Places to practice were rare beyond description. Some bands had to jump from location to location, one step ahead of the police. I cannot say that any of my near neighbors actually approved of our practices. When we flipped on the amps, windows slammed shut for two hundred yards in every direction. Early on we generated the predictable complaints. The people right next door called a few times to ask my mother if we couldn't turn down "just a little bit" so they could hear their TV. The folks behind us took to standing on their back porch all afternoon, staring hard in my direction, as though the social pressure alone might crush me and my ambitions. My musical seed was growing in hostile and unwelcoming ground.

My mother too had early complaints but quickly resolved them by being gone from the house running errands during practice time. I knew my hold on the garage was tenuous. I lived in fear of being put in handcuffs and fined large amounts of money. I always reminded the musicians before we started to keep their volume moderate, but inevitably, some spark would start a fire and we'd be wailing away in there and get loud. This would usually flush out my across-the-street neighbor, Mr. Hanson.

A war soon developed between Hanson and me. He had the sort of dominant personality that certainly made him an important person over at his house, but to me he was just abrasive and ill-mannered. The man did not have a diplomatic bone in his body. Instead of attempting some kind of dialogue that might lead to compromise and understanding, he only became more and more abrasive, as if each time he had to get out of his chair and walk across the street cost him another year off his life. I'd never met such a tense person. He became a plague on our practices. I call this the "Hanson Phenomena." Most every garage band has experienced it. I'm sure that if you asked Led Zeppelin or the Allman Brothers or the Beatles, they'd all have their own stories to tell about neighbors early in their career.

Hanson was a guy with a crew cut who made things out of bricks. His weekends were devoted to getting up at five o'clock in the morning, driving nails around his house and testing out his power saw, constructing things like a love seat, a wishing well, or a bird bath.

One would think that any person slapping bricks into place and sweating under the hot sun would hardly notice a little music from across the street. His truck's muffler was louder than we were. But Hanson was very sensitive about rock'n'roll (I believe privately he was a polka man) and would sooner or later, if we played above a whisper, come storming into the garage with veins standing out on his neck and a wild gaze in his eye, looking like he was just shot out of a cannon, cussing at everybody and making demands. It became so much of a routine that we began scheduling Saturday practices "from two o'clock until Hanson comes over."

Two additional facts about Hanson will illustrate the extent of my courage in having a band practice across the street from his house. One, he was locally famous for his skill as a rattlesnake catcher. This hobby probably doesn't exist outside of Oklahoma or Texas. Every year there was a rattlesnake festival in Waurika, and Hanson always entered the catching contest. He won more than once for biggest snake, and each year he was the man to beat for sheer poundage. Apparently, he was a snake-catching fiend, using his bare hands to grab them behind the head. Any man who can walk out into a field and come back with a burlap sack full of snakes, using nothing more than his personality to catch them, has to be listened to when he kicks in your door.

The other important fact about Hanson was that he apparently had a minuscule brain. I suspect it was about softball size and supported by a network of cobwebs in the center of his skull. Consequently, he saw everything as a moral battle. Every autumn when the time came to rake leaves, Hanson would carry a baseball bat out to his yard and begin whacking home runs on the trunks of his trees, trying to get the last hanging leaves to shake loose, cussing about the whole thing. He destroyed more than one bat in the process and knocked a lot of bark off the trees. Looking back on it now, it's astonishing I didn't die with his hands around my throat.

Sometime during the sixth month of our war, a lucky disaster occurred which shifted attention away from me and gave Hanson other things to think about. He had bought a guard dog for his wife as a Christmas present. The wife, in turn, had bought him a pistol. I'm sure they were both thrilled with their gifts. Christmas Eve night Hanson was drunk and sitting in his armchair and trying to figure out his new automatic pistol. He had a little pamphlet that gave step-by-step instructions explaining how to throw the safety on, then throw the release up, pull the clip out, throw the safety off, and then cock it by pulling the top part back. Then you do a dry fire just to be sure. Apparently Hanson had done this fifteen times and got so comfortable doing it that he was able to think more between steps, and probably even paused once or twice to take a sip, and I'm sure no one was more surprised than Hanson himself when the living room filled with a sound bigger than the whole house and smoke was everywhere and his wife started screaming and trying to jump up. Then all you could hear was the dog barking like crazy while Hanson tried to calm his wife and explain it was only a flesh wound in her leg.

This episode took all the starch out of his position as neighborhood complainer. After the subsequent publicity, Hanson kept his head tucked in his shell and peace returned to our end of the street.

| | |

Meanwhile, I was in probably five or six bands. Practice bands. Informal Saturday afternoon bands where we attempted one song or another, usually missing some vital part like a bass or a singer when someone couldn't come. And when we did have a singer, his voice was usually "going through the change" and half the time would jump off the register, sounding like a loud bark in the middle of a song and surprising you at odd moments. I suppose those little practice bands could be compared to a baby whale flapping in the water: not very productive but full of energy and good will. There was something organic about how we transformed ourselves from one ensemble to another, members floating in and out, band names changing like the flags on a ship, getting odd combinations of members coming up time and again. Some people you play with in three or four bands, others you play with only once. There's no pattern to any of this. It's like watching a heap of fungus turn into a mushroom. It was just mixing available musicians together to keep something going. Over the next year I might have been in six bands and not one of them played a gig. They were practice bands only. A place where sounding raw and ignorant was tolerated because it was epidemic.

One of the unfortunate reoccurrences in this sequence of bands was Bruce. The infamous, pushy, pimpled Bruce, who had turned fifteen a little quicker than everyone else and felt himself entitled to be leader. My first lessons in band politics came from Bruce and his conniving ways. He was always forming coalitions, which left you either on his side or against him. Just getting along with Bruce took most of the band's energy.

Nothing is as unstable as a band. People must get along to play music. The slightest unresolved argument can wreck months of work. A band is a collection of volunteers and represents democracy in its purest form. This freedom to play is what makes the songs sound so lively. Bruce, as I already knew, had a dictatorial, Republican personality. As long as everyone let him run things, he was happy. To question his superiority in any area was to risk him yelling loudly, and then getting even more pissed off. I would have been content to let him make the decisions but for the decisions he made.

Worst of all, he considered himself obligated to comment on everything I played. Nothing makes a person more shy and timid than a running commentary on his every movement. That very first band practiced maybe five times. We worked up half a dozen songs, they sounded mostly okay, but Bruce kept everyone agitated and off center. Trying to get along with him, I discovered, was somehow unmusical. Which is only to say that in bands where you have a dictator, people become wooden and cautious. They stop thinking for themselves and begin spending most of their time checking to see what the dictator thinks. The dictator, of course, thinks different things on different days and so keeps everyone confused. The only thing constant about dictators is the importance of their current opinion.

About this same time I also came to realize, in some murky and inarticulate fashion, what it was about bands—beyond playing and showing off and getting girls—that made them so important to me. I looked forward to those Saturdays even if I didn't look forward to seeing some of the musicians. It was important just to play in a band, to make sound with other people. I began to discover that tribal joy of breathing with others and seeing the results magnified. The act of playing music in a rock'n'roll band was, at bottom, a tom-tom thumping therapy for us boys. Like Indians around a fire, our heartbeats got in sync. Nailing a note with one or two other musicians is to share exactly the same emotion at exactly the same instant. We weren't that precise very often, but it's what we strived for and found occasionally. And each time we did, it sharpened our herd instinct for playing.

Even in bands where everyone hates each other, a person can play music because the emotion is already there, it's prescribed for him. All he has to do is lend himself to it, let it carry him, and the worst enemies in the world can start acting like chuckling fools. This is another reason why bands are so confusing.

After the group with Bruce broke up, we found ourselves

reforming about two weeks later without him. At the time it seemed an accident. We were young, kind-hearted boys and had broken up in good faith. Then Butch, the bass player, stopped me in the hall at school and asked about getting together that coming Saturday for a little playing and I said sure, no problem. He mentioned that Chico, our old rhythm guitar player, would like to come too and that Bobby, the terrific lead player, wasn't in a band and might be interested. It was all quite innocent. My main thought was that by playing with Bobby my stock would go up with the other musicians around school. It was only after this new band had practiced two weekends in a row and everyone was enthusiastic about how things sounded—how much better in fact it sounded than the last band—that I realized nothing had changed but the lead player. At about the same time I made this discovery I noticed that Bruce was shooting me ugly looks in the hallway when we passed and had figured things out much quicker than I had. I felt sorry for Bruce. He was a despot in exile, looking like a bottled spider whenever I saw him. I took alternate routes to class when possible.

Bands are like meandering streams that go where they can go and are always changing direction when they run up against an impediment, like Bruce.

That band held together for a while and then split up because Bobby got a better offer somewhere else. Butch and I stuck together but Chico quit the business when he got in trouble with his grades and his parents made him sell his guitar. Another band formed because Bruce put it together, and then another without him. Mostly without him. None of these bands played anywhere; we didn't have a PA and we never had enough songs for a full night's playing.

My Budding Reputation

I don't guess anyone is born a perfect and solid human being. We each change and grow and remain in flux, but the fool is forever declaring himself a finished product at each step along the way. Because I played with just about every guitarist in school, I became rather well known and acquired something of a reputation. The truth of the matter was that I worked with some good guitarists, and working with good musicians makes you sound good. It was a reflected glory, nothing more. But anytime my name was mentioned, it would be followed by my resume: "Oh yeah, isn't he the drummer who played with Eugene, and before him Bobby? He must be good." This sort of reputation building really took off when I sat in and played finally with the notable Randy.

At every school there is at least one guitar god. At our school, it was Randy. He was considered a prodigy because he'd begun playing piano when he was four and had switched to guitar when he was ten. There was an animal intelligence in his eyes; his instincts seemed closer to the surface. It was said that Randy could play anything he could hold in his hand, even drums. He stood alone, seemed to exist within a halo of light, and was frequently struck by inspiration. He was not someone you could casually approach and slap on the back. His standards were high, and he associated only with "his" bass player, a guy named Neil, and with Bobby, who was considered terrific but not quite as good as Randy himself.

It was only a jam session, or what passed for a jam session in those days. I was in high school by this time. Someone, I forget who, arranged for several musicians to come over to his house one Sunday and play. I think his folks were out of town for the weekend. There were six or eight guitarists and a couple of bass players and another drummer. I was probably asked only as a relief player, someone to keep the rhythm section fresh while the guitarists worked out. There weren't all that many drummers around, and for all I know some of them might have been sick or otherwise engaged that day. But that jam session solidified my reputation. Tom, the drummer whose set we used, was clearly the superior musician. He was Randy's personal drummer, someone who had already played three years and knew all the songs. His bag of tricks was much deeper than mine and had several extra pockets. I was content to just sit and watch him. Some drummers become inspired when there's another drummer around to appreciate them. I was just the opposite and became intimidated if anyone knew too much about what I was doing. You can bluff guitar players into thinking you're good if you don't make mistakes, but another drummer will see through that bluff to what your real abilities are. Tom was playing in top form. He was hot and Randy was hot, too. They played many synchronized riffs together and showed evidence of mental telepathy. I was not eager to sit in.

It was my first time to see Randy up close and he was impressive. He clearly knew more than the other guitarists. He played longer than I thought was tasty but everyone there admired him and no one challenged his playing time. Three, four or five guitar players would be plugged in at once. They took turns at lead and then backed off and played rhythm while someone else took a turn: the basic format of a jam session. After a while, one would get tired and be replaced by another guitar player. But Randy was plugged in the whole afternoon. No one seemed eager for me to get up and play and I didn't volunteer. Tom was so impressive I became less and less interested in getting up and showing my paltry few beats.

After two hours of solid and strenuous drumming, Tom started to show wear. I noticed that instead of pushing the beat and driving the others, Tom was merely holding the fort. He hadn't screwed up or anything, but had come close to it a couple of times and had backed off the fancy stuff, keeping only the necessary time. I knew he would expire soon if he didn't take a break, and he knew it too.

After the song ended he held the sticks out to me and said, "Your turn" and got up. A couple of the guitar players switched as well while I got settled in. His drum set was arranged entirely differently from my own. While mine was adjusted for convenience and the length of my arms, Tom's, it seemed to me, was set up more for show. His cymbals were eight feet in the air, his toms were ten inches above the snare, making an otherwise easy roll from one to the other more of a leap. His floor tom was over in the next neighborhood but I was able to drag it in. The snare drum was tilted in the wrong direction but I could fix that. His stool was so high I could barely reach the pedals. Tom was way over six feet tall, had bug eyes, no lips and steel cables for arms. He said to me, "Adjust anything you want," but I knew that drummers always said that and never meant it. I did move the stool down a notch but that only resulted in the cymbals being out of reach. I brought the cymbals down a foot or two but then noticed they were in too close. I tried to move them out but the tripod legs were all tangled around each other so I had to leave them alone. While I was making all these adjustments everyone else waited. Randy in particular was chomping at the bit and playing little riffs to himself. The hi-hat cymbals were too high by a foot, the bass drum pedal was tight, and his sticks were not my size. I played a little beat to get the feel of the set, and it felt all wrong. Instead of being comfortable and well placed like my drums, these made me feel like I was about to learn a new instrument.

"Let's try a slow blues," I said. I needed something easy to warm up on and a slow blues I could play in my sleep. Randy had a quick trigger finger and launched the opening riff. A standard B.B. King sort of intro; I came in at the top and the groove was there immediately. The very first thing I realized about Randy was how solid he was. A dead man could find the beat in that song. I'd never played with a guitar player so easy to read. Randy's riffs were nailed to the floor, clean inescapable guitar licks that figured out everything for me. Everyone played watching Randy. He was a five-foot-eight metronome, rocking back and forth, solid and predictable. A regular brick. Everyone sounded clean with Randy because he made it so easy. And for the first half of the song he didn't play any riffs that distorted the time at all, nothing that stretched beyond the beat, no fakes and dodges that sound so good but might be misread.

My confidence was rising with each chord change. I didn't have anything to worry about; I just had to follow Randy. I became so absorbed in what he was playing I could anticipate what he would do next. He didn't seem to be throwing in random riffs like other lead players I'd heard; all his ideas flowed one from the other. He was logical. It was a logic I'd unconsciously picked up listening to him for the past two hours and now that I was playing alongside him I knew exactly where he was going. He would start low and go high in his runs, simple little eight bar essays he would build up to a tight moment and then resolve with two or three high stretchy notes before clipping it short and starting all over again. He came at it from different directions, changing the feel, but the structure always explained itself. I was so deep in lock step with him, and his leads sounded so much like what I'd heard on records before, that I started hearing the drum fills and accents that went along with those leads on the records, and without a conscious thought in my body began putting those accents just where I knew he wanted them. This inspired Randy to no end. He was easily stimulated.

He and I moved in unison through a high reaching and sprawling lead that seemed like a song I'd known all my life. Each twist and turn came at the right moment for me; everything was transparent and natural. I was so plugged in, I wasn't even aware we were ending the song until we were holding out those last long chords and the whole thing finally started rolling and tumbling and sliding towards a halt. We hammered the very last note like a big nail and I looked up at the other players. Everyone's eyes were glowing. I thought, "My god, what happened? Was that me?" Randy was grinning too and said, "All right!"

The bass player called out a rock tune and I was glad for it. Rock'n'roll was what I practiced most and with a guitar player like Randy I would find out what I really knew. The bass player started it out with a fat, driving intro and I plowed into it alongside him. I felt strong. I felt good. I was about to do something wonderful but I didn't know yet what it would be. Randy came in like the king of rock'n'roll and behind him we went charging back up the mountain—when, suddenly, the bass drum pedal stopped working. The bass player looked at me and I looked down to find the cause. The beater wouldn't move at all. I had to stop the song, deeply disappointed. "What's the matter?" someone asked. "I don't know; no bass drum. I think it's the pedal." Tom came over to examine his pedal and I got up. The spring had broken and he didn't have another. The jam session was over. You can't play rock'n'roll without a drummer and a drummer can't play without a bass drum; it just sounds awful. The whole band depends on that one spring.

But what a stroke of luck. I'd only played one song, it had sounded wonderful, and before I could screw up anything we had to quit. I don't think I'd ever played a song without mistakes before, but the first time I did, several important witnesses were around to see it, and my reputation was made. We all slumped around for several moments, disappointed. I put on a glum face and acted peeved that I couldn't show more of my stuff. Some of the guitarists still had riffs to pump out of their system and these were played out into the empty air, but in a desultory fashion. Finally the amps were turned off and the boys regained their voices and started talking and the gloom dissipated. Everyone suddenly became interested in me. A couple of the guys said

I shouldn't have waited so long to sit in. Randy came up and told me we'd have to do this again. Even Tom, who probably hated my guts, was kind enough to say I sounded good. He didn't blame me for the pedal breaking. He said it had broken before and that the pedal was hard on springs.

At school the following Monday the word had already spread about the "hot new drummer in town." Other guitar players and drummers who were not invited to the jam had heard about it and said things like, "Man, I had no idea. I heard you blew Tom right out of the water." I let this slide. It was hardly true but I didn't dispute the statement very vigorously. I let them say whatever they wanted and acted modest. Everyone began treating me in a high fashion. I started eating at Randy's table. Girls became interested in me. Other musicians began chumming around like my long lost friends, calling out to me from way down the hall. "Yo Mike! How you been, man!?"

And I began to believe it. Every word of it. I knew in my heart of hearts I couldn't play that song again as well if I'd practiced it for a month. But for the rest of that week and probably most of the next, my feet did not touch the ground. I became a paragon of vanity and self conceit. If foolishness gave off a smell, I would have crippled every nose in town.

Learning Not to Think

Once my local celebrity was established I began practicing even more earnestly, not out of a new-found confidence or purpose, but out of the fear I would be discovered as a fraud. It is the nature of luck to be unreliable, so I knew I had a barren stretch ahead that I must get through on my own merits.

One of the basic mysteries all musicians face sooner or later is that of how to improvise or jam. I'd been struck by lightning once, and now had to figure out how to become a lightning rod so it would strike again. It seemed impossible to practice improvising, a contradiction in terms. I could store up a supply of fills and beats that I knew well enough to toss into a song at an instant's notice, but that wasn't improvising. The whole miracle of jamming was to play what you couldn't anticipate, to be carried by the song. So how do you prepare yourself to do what you can't anticipate doing? Just another example of the imponderable nature of drumming. I considered this question for a while and then called Rod for the answer. Rod had the reputation in town of being the jammingest drummer around.

"You just do it," he told me. "Same as you talk or breathe or take a dump. You ever watch people dance? Watch them. There are two kinds of dancers in the world: those who were dragged out onto the floor because someone wanted them there, and those who like to dance and don't need an invitation. Look at the ones who like it. They're hooked into the music. They let the music move them. Study those dancers. It's the same as a bird singing. You just have to like it first and then you can do it."

I assured him I liked it plenty enough already, but that didn't seem to answer the part about 'how' it was done.

"Don't think about 'how' you do it; just be in shape and play a lot and let your instincts tell you what to do. If you think about it, it won't happen."

I thanked him and hung up. It was like a game we used to play when I was a little kid. The game was to not think of a white dog. You had to stand in a corner and not think of that white dog and if you thought of one you lost and had to say so. This game was my mother's idea. The problem I always had with that white dog game was that I'd stand in the corner long enough to forget why I was there and my thoughts would drift all over the place, then I'd realize where I was and wonder why and then, inevitably, every time, remember the white dog. It never seemed to me a particularly smart game to play, if someone had a really bad memory, like my brother, he'd win every time.

Either jamming was a gift and I was just out of luck, or it was an ability I could work toward if I could only find the way. It seemed to me there might be a certain hump on the brain that handled this activity, and I had to find that hump. I spent long hours listening to records of people jamming, or what I thought was jamming, but it all sounded too perfect. I developed notions about "Inner Peace" and "States of Grace" and other nonsense from the time, but nothing answered my particular problem. I even read a book on 'creativity' but that didn't help either.

The smart thing would have been to go to every jam session I heard about and learn by watching and doing. The trouble was that I knew people would want me to play, and if I did, the public humiliation would defeat my purpose. I was delicate about these things back then. I listened to records and tried to jam at home.

At other times I turned on the radio and tried to improve the songs by adding stuff, listening closely to the drums and trying to find possibilities. And that turned out to be my problem. I wouldn't figure it out for months, but the key to jamming, for me, was to *not* listen to the drums. It was in the other instruments that I would find ideas. It took me forever to figure this out, but once I did I started stealing: from the guitar player, the bassist, even the singer. After I loosened up and abandoned my soul to perdition, jamming became easy. It's just a matter of intelligent thievery.

I discovered this one night when I was too tired to discover much of anything. Probably because I wasn't trying to understand, it snuck up on me. I'd turned on the radio and a song I particularly liked was nearing my favorite part—a lead the guitar played. I don't remember the song but I remember the lead: a grand sounding thing with huge, cathedral-sized riffs like Led Zeppelin, one of those frozen rope leads that just seem to go up and up. I wished I could play it on the guitar. That four-bar lead alone would justify the work it took to learn the guitar. As it started I followed along with it like it was my own, yanking it out of the different strings, pretending I was the guitar player and improving, fixing, elevating things all over the place. My riffs were much fatter than his and reached even higher. Improving guitar parts—because I knew nothing about it—was much easier for me than improving drum parts. As I pushed the lead to its climax, the whole band surged up behind me, and I heard the most fabulous drum fill that fit the lead perfectly, intersecting with it on the last note and creating a little chill up my back. The drum fill wasn't on the record. But it should have been.

I began to realize that jamming occurs in the heat generated *between* two instruments. But to generate that heat, you have to listen. I'd been so bogged down thinking about drums, had had so many technical problems of my own to deal with, that I'd mostly ignored listening to anyone else any more than I could help it. Trying to jump start myself, I hadn't paid attention to any of the power outlets around me. I didn't completely understand this all at once. It had to be repeated fifty times before it became obvious to me. But once the sun did come out from behind the clouds, I understood what had happened that day with Randy. I started going to every jam session I could, not to learn anything about the drums, but to listen to guitar players.

The next time I saw Rod I tried to explain this to him. "Well sure," he said. "It's just like dancing. People dance in pairs, don't they?"

Small Towns

In southern Oklahoma and northern Texas there is an active and ancient belief that dancing is the devil's work. This is Baptist and Pentecostal territory. Some people there routinely claim to see demons and angels running loose over the countryside. Sometimes God talks to them while they drive their car.

For young bands just starting to get out and perform, this created a large problem: there were not many places to play. You could work at the Teen Club but the crowd became too young after a while and they didn't serve beer, a problem for many musicians. School dances came along once or twice a year and paid well, but once or twice a year would not keep a band going. Most bands couldn't last long enough to play two school dances in a row. The solution was to play weekend dances in small towns nearby.

Too often, "small town" also meant small gene pool, as I could tell by looking in the phone book at the large number of identical names. After the dry winds of the Depression had blown through those little towns, the only people left were those who couldn't be killed off by starvation or sandstorms or even isolation, those seventy-year-old moral pillars with pinched lips and tiny eyes who could look depravity straight in the face and say, "Scat!" It was hard for bands to gain a foothold in those towns. A person may not recognize it from the air, but many of those little villages are actually fortresses.

To throw a dance was a complicated and sometimes dangerous process and required me to go into enemy territory. To the intrepid musician desperate for a gig—car gassed up and map on the seat beside him—a whole day could be spent driving through small towns and scrutinizing them for their dance potential. And be scrutinized in return.

My hair had grown down to my shoulders and sometimes I wore a ponytail. In small-town Oklahoma, during the late sixties, a ponytail was a significant indicator of character. Drive into any of those towns with a ponytail flapping in the wind and you'd better be ready to answer to "Honey" or "Sweet Meat." I'd park the car and get out and look around to see people staring at me with an angry kind of x-ray vision, a squinting, scrutinizing, incredulous, loose-jawed gaze that gave me a bad itch. I was a pioneer of sorts, taking my ponytail into those places. For many of the people I was probably their first opportunity to verify in the flesh what they'd only seen on TV during riots.

These excursions to find gigs would start early in the morning. I'd buy a box of chocolate donuts and aim the car toward a cluster of little specks on the map that might show promise, if only because they were isolated and full of starved teenagers.

Too often I'd drive into one of these little towns, pass by the water tower, look around for a hall to rent, and find nothing but churches up and down the streets. If I didn't see a local teen club or community center downtown, then I'd cruise the edges of the settlement until I located an American Legion or Moose hall. Because no one is ever actually in one of these buildings during the day, I would then have to inquire of a neighbor to find out who was in charge. There are some houses in small towns whose front doors look like they haven't been opened in years. To ring that feeble old button beside the door and wait an eternity for Grandma Moses to get to her feet and find her walker, and then open three doors as she makes her way from the far back of the house, and then wait longer while she fumbles with the lock, all while her tiny venomous dog snaps and flips and goes nuts waiting for her to turn the handle so it can attack—this, coupled with her inevitable reaction to my attractive long-haired self waiting for her on the other side of the screen, was just another reason I hated to book gigs.

If I was lucky, she would give me the name of the head Moose and where he worked. But then I'd drive around and finally locate his gas station, only to walk in and find myself surrounded by a number of stick-carving old men, each of whom had to adjust himself to my presence. One might spit in a bucket, another dig too hard into his stick and slice it apart, a third one work his nose up and down like he was testing the air. The head Moose might have a ring of warts around his neck and a renegade glass eye, but he'd look down on me from the clouds of Olympus and say, "We don't allow no dances here in Conesville."

Town size would seem a likely indicator of dance potential, but I couldn't depend on this either. Some good size towns might have other things going on that dilute your crowd, just enough social activities to turn your dance into a paltry, solemn affair, so I discovered the wisdom of investigating the local social calendar before booking a building. Few sights are more pitiful than an empty dance hall with a band wailing away trying to induce people to come in the door.

Only a practiced eye can read a town's dance potential. I learned, for instance, about those smaller villages without sufficient population to generate a city limits, that turned out to be lively party towns because of the surrounding farm community. A practiced eye can find those places. Dumb luck played a large part in it too.

Indian towns, for instance, were hard to book but great to play. Usually they would hire only Indian bands. I played a lot of Indian towns and government schools, but only in bands that were at least half Indian. Some of the best dance crowds were in those towns.

Other musicians could be helpful about a town's dance history, particularly if the musician you asked was no longer trying to book there. But no place was completely predictable. Even the best towns would turn up dead occasionally for no apparent reason. We'd get there, set up, wait for at least one person to show before beginning to play, and finally end up wondering if the town hadn't been struck by plague and we were the only ones who don't know it yet. Then there were towns we'd booked out of desperation, knowing the turnout would be modest, only to be surprised by the mobs squeezing in the door. It's a purely iffy business.

When I was lucky enough to find a town that allowed sin and corruption within its borders, I'd quickly book the hall and then begin our publicity blitz. This usually took the form of hand-lettered posters I'd make while sitting in the car. Something intriguing that would get people's interest and encourage them to come.

DANCE YOUR LEGS OFF!
From 9 until ?
Saturday June 19th
American Legion Hall
"TWISTED RAINBOW"
Oklahoma's Favorite Dance Band!
$3 at the door

The question mark was clearly a ruse to make people think the band might play all night. We had no intentions of going past one o'clock. "Oklahoma's favorite dance band" was another simple deceit. The band might've only been together six weeks and this would be our second gig, but you couldn't very well say "Amateur band hoping to try out half-rehearsed songs on gullible public." That may be the talk in the coffee shop the next day, but we'd be long gone by then.

Once the posters were ready I would approach stores on Main Street and ask if I could place one in their window. At this point I would begin to get an early sense of how the town felt about our presence. If the person smiled and said, "Oh sure," then I knew we had community support and might get a good turnout. If, on the other hand, I showed the old woman behind the counter our poster, and her face cracked in a hundred directions like a china mug, then I knew we had a potential problem. If I tried several stores and received a uniformly negative response, I would start to wonder why the old man who rented me the hall for $50 was so agreeable.

There have been reports, apocryphal, I'm sure, of lynching parties in small towns coming after rock'n'roll bands. While this has never happened to me, I have seen irate Christian parents show up at dances, entering with a Moses-like attitude—which means not paying the cover charge—glaring over the crowd until they found their own teenager, and then yanking said teenager by the neck and out the door. This was embarrassing for the kid and put a real damper on the festivities. We'd always play an up-beat song after this happened.

Every one of these halls looked exactly alike, as though every American Legion, Mason, Knights of Columbus, Rotary, Shriner, Moose and community hall in all of Oklahoma was designed by the very same person. The buildings were narrow across the shoulders but long and deep, as though created only for banquets. And always painted white. Parking was outside on the grass. Double doors in front, a small foyer with a coat rack, then double doors into the Main Hall which was a rectangular box with a wood floor and windows on both long sides. In one corner there was always a small kitchen behind a counter, in another corner folded chairs permanently stacked. At the opposite end of the room was the stage, a tiny wooden cave with cigarette burns on the floor and scrape marks along the walls and the ancient electric fan back in the corner, stages for dull Elk meetings and Boy Scout awards and testimonials to local celebrities. Stages with only one electrical outlet.

Stages where we came to play the blues—despite the fact that this music had little popularity with the dancing public. Blues, such as hard-driving slow power shuffles like "Born in Chicago," were hard for many people to dance to. You could empty a hall in thirty minutes if your tunes weren't danceable. Particularly in small all-white towns, they preferred what they heard on the radio, and this meant songs like

"Hanky Panky" and "Louie Louie." Every self-respecting musician hated these songs with a passion. If occasionally he happened to enjoy playing one of them, he kept it to himself. It was just not cool. We tried to play enough commercial tunes to satisfy the dancers without entirely compromising ourselves. A 'one in three' mix usually worked: one obscure blues tune for every two radio jingles.

In the beginning we tried to make these events duplicate dances we'd seen elsewhere. Someone's girlfriend would set up a table and sell Cokes. Someone else's girlfriend would sit at the front door with a magic marker or rubber stamp, taking the money and marking people on the back of their hand. We'd put up a banner with "Twisted Rainbow" on it. Occasionally we even had T-shirts made, but this required still another girlfriend.

Girlfriends generally were far more troublesome than helpful. Everything became more complex when girlfriends were involved. Finding a cafe to eat at was more difficult. Keeping them entertained while you took care of business was a chore. And during the breaks they wanted all your attention, while you really just wanted to count the money.

Girlfriends also required constant vigilance since the local boys would bother them to death. If a girlfriend was working the front door—the most bothersome position—her musician/boyfriend would stay distracted the entire night, standing at the ready in case she had to be rescued.

At least once every two or three gigs I got to watch this "white knight, fair damsel" drama play itself out. Typically, we would be in the middle of a song. And typically I would not be looking in the right direction when trouble began. But the guitar player/singer/boyfriend would be alert, and the very moment his girlfriend at the other end of the room began yelling and pushing to get herself free from some sex beggar, he would fly to her rescue. One night a bass player named

Ronnie almost dragged the whole stage with him. He was singing and I was looking at the back of his head, when suddenly he broke off in the middle of the chorus, "G...L...O...R...I... Hey, motherfucker!" and then leaped off the stage and into the dark. Only he was still plugged in, and hadn't bothered to remove his guitar, so when he jumped off the stage his guitar pulled his guitar cord, which pulled the amp that happened to be on wheels, which pulled the power cord behind it, which happened to be plugged into a junction box with the other power cords, which began a general movement of all amplifiers toward the edge of the stage before his amp finally tipped over and started humming to beat hell. All of a sudden I was the only one playing, and down at the end of the hall a fight had broken out with Ronnie in the middle of it, guitar still dangling around his neck and cord trailing behind him. He managed to ruin one of his hands before rescuing his attractive girlfriend.

Another thing girlfriends were worthless for was carrying equipment. A mic stand here or a tiny bag there, more in the way than helpful, always coming through the door at the same time I was. All in all, bands work best as rapid deployment units: compact, self-contained, efficient. But they rarely are. What you want is to pare things down to bare essentials. One person to take the money at the door, preferably male, who can also help you haul junk in and out.

But finally, after all the work of getting there and setting up the equipment and worrying about the attendance and being stared at for my hair, there came the moment when the hall lights went down and the stage lights came up and only three or four people in the whole room could stand inside those lights. Even in the very worst of bands, if the players are young and enthusiastic enough, the first chord of the first song transformed them from ordinary high school students with nothing to call their own into something dramatic and vivid. Nothing in our lives came close to the excitement of playing music. And playing it *loud*. On a really good night people could probably hear us in Texas.

And when, on those occasions it really did sound decent, we became tiny stars in that tiny town, jumping around in front of our tiny audience, and loving it.

Battle of the Bands

In my neck of the woods, the ultimate experience for high school rock'n'roll musicians was playing in a battle of the bands. This event was arranged by our high school and was attended by all the students who would pick a band for the year-end school dance. But being selected for the dance was only a bonus; the real thrill was being on that stage with five other bands, playing what to our minds was a "concert performance." I was in three different battles of the bands, and in my third and last appearance I played a drum solo.

Even for older, world-weary road musicians, the chance to get up on a real stage in front of a sit-down audience focused your attention like nothing else. Guitar players would change their strings, singers comb their hair, bass players would take a bath. Equipment would be fixed up and polished. And songs would be practiced half to death.

The afternoon of the battle all the musicians arrived at the auditorium and each band drew a number out of a hat that would determine the playing order. It was generally thought that either going first or last was ideal. If you didn't get the number you wanted, you would approach one of the less experienced bands and try to bargain for their slot. Once you knew when you would go on, the equipment was set up either in the front row where three bands were side by side, or behind in the second row. There was an enormous jungle of equipment, and no one sharing anything: six drum sets, six PA systems, four hundred miles of cable, a forest of mic stands—and everyone in a fiercely competitive mood. You didn't talk to the other musicians unless they were good friends. And even if they were good friends, you were cooler than usual.

We scrutinized the competition and talked within our own band about everyone else there. One of the dishonest things people were quick to spot was any band that borrowed equipment for the show. Particularly if you owned your own equipment you were quick to notice another band that had gone out and rented a high quality PA system. This was in the days before good sound systems were available at the local level. Every band suffered from muddy, indistinct vocals, so when someone showed up with a PA system that was meant to be a PA system, we thought the advantage was unfair. Naturally, every band would try to borrow it but you expected to be turned down. Loaning anything more than a mic stand was not in the spirit of the event.

It wasn't until my third battle of the bands that I came out in the winning group. We were the most senior band there, the best known. We called ourselves "The Fabulous Disasters." I played a drum solo which I'd rehearsed for months and received a thunderous ovation. It was a tight band, a sharp band. But the real reason for our winning was that our guitar player was Randy. By the age of eighteen, Randy had developed in ways no one expected. A gifted musician, he didn't just play rock'n'roll, but country and jazz and classical as well. He could play polkas, he could play TV commercials; he invented melodies as easily as a child finds dirt. He played the Star Spangled Banner on the guitar years before Jimi Hendrix. In fact, knowing Randy must have been a lot like knowing a young Hendrix, watching and wondering just how good he eventually could be.

Randy had what I call "Oklahoma git-tar savvy." It's that certain shrug of the shoulders, the confident muscular way he played his licks, even the way he held his guitar—as though it was the most natural thing a person could do. Randy could pick up a Chet Atkins tune or something by Roy Clark and sound pure country, then switch to some

Bach piece he'd toss out before jumping to a boogie shuffle. And do it all as casually as spitting on the ground. And he was in high school.

It didn't hurt our chances that most of the audience shared my opinion of Randy. It was pure luck getting him in the band. Other than in jam sessions, he and I had never played together before but had remained on speaking terms. Then suddenly his band broke up, he was out of a job, and the battle of the bands was two months away. Our regular guitar player was moping through a love crisis and starting to be late for the gigs. We offered him a good excuse to quit, and then fired him when he refused. The addition of Randy was enough to make everything twice as tight and twice as expressive. For a full month we practiced the five songs we would perform, and even had to refrain from killing them completely by taking a few days off before the show. By the night of the battle we were ripe. We were primed. We had every single molecule in those tunes worked out and glued in place. And we drew last place in the playing order. We may even have had a full moon that night. We were unbeatable.

There was only one other band that could possibly give us trouble. They were a horn band, eight piece, had been together over a year, well rehearsed, played a lot around town, called "The Cavaliers." A good band. The problem with the group, from a musical point of view, was its size. Big bands tend to be unwieldy, like an old Cadillac attempting hairpin turns, it will lurch and sway a bit more than you want. With a band that size you have to work entirely off arrangements and emphasize precision, otherwise you get a mess. The advantage is you get a big fat sound, but you're getting it from an army and any single person can miss a beat and hurt the tune. You have to be entirely tight or you sound drunk. This band was tight, but it's harder to inspire an orchestra than an ensemble, so we had an advantage. If they were only tight, and we got hot, there'd be some floors to mop afterward.

The Cavaliers drew third place in the playing order, which

meant they were the last band before intermission. The first two bands had been thrown-together operations, young bands just getting started, working more off enthusiasm than experience. They were a snack for us and we didn't take them seriously but they got the crowd warmed up. The Cavaliers moved onto the stage like one of Caesar's divisions. Three horn blowers, a stand-alone singer, and a four-piece rhythm section with piano. They played the stuff you'd expect, the same songs I'd heard them play before: Blood, Sweat & Tears, Chicago, The Buckinghams, Tower of Power.

During their show we were standing in the wings watching, not six feet from one of the horn players, noticing how they breathed, listening for little imperfections. To me they sounded like they were straining; something wasn't quite right. They were starting too cold and trying too hard. I'm sure everything sounded fine to the audience. But it wasn't fine, and the band knew this, and they let it bother them. When something goes wrong in a band that size, all they can do is marshal around the drums and play to the beat. Until the band has their groove no one can really play wide open, and they never found the groove. After their last song they received a huge round of applause but they came off the stage looking dejected. They knew the applause wasn't to be trusted. Each band had ringers in the crowd to cheer and encourage the audience. We had about fifty of them out there, as did the Cavaliers, so the applause probably sounded forced and artificial to them.

After the Cavaliers came off and people were moving equipment, Randy was grinning and whistling and wiggling around. He was a great whistler, too. If I'd thought ahead of time, I would have worked it into one of the songs, maybe "Sitting on the Dock of the Bay."

The last two bands before us were slightly better than the first two. One was a soul band, a puny sounding Indian soul band that had come with their own cheering section, but the crowd at large was only lukewarm. The remaining group, "The Young Brutes," had been around for a couple of years and had become something of an institution, but as a band they painted by the numbers.

Randy won the night with the first riff he played. It was a tune that started with the guitar, some big arching boogie riff, and from the very first note Randy was deep in the pocket. That was the thing about Randy. Any groove for him was like the Grand Canyon: big and inescapable once he was in it. It was a dramatic introduction, made doubly so because he started before the stage lights came on. There was a pause between each band's performance when people moved on and off stage and a Student Senator announced the name of the next group. We were already in place, the stage was dark, the announcer had just finished our name, and Randy launched the song before the lights could come up. It was a surprise attack on the room, like a large dog sneaking in through the back door and barking in your ear. A perfectly executed riff, four beats long, all by its naked self, before I came in with a fill and the lights came on. A roar came up from the crowd, the beat was as hard as a granite pebble, and our singer, Johnny, threw both lungs into his first note. Lord, it was fine.

The students were already applauding before we finished, and like a consummate artist Randy segued into the next tune. The other bands had dicked around between songs, letting the applause die out before starting again, but Randy would have none of that. He was smoking that night: he worked the room hard, giving them no time to relax.

Of course we'd arranged the tunes for dramatic effect so the best was saved until last. Each song had built on the one before. The boogie tune was followed by a hard driving dance song, followed by a funky hand clapper, followed by an inspirational fast blues where Randy's lead filled the room like chain lightning. We finished the show with our magnum opus: a four-part harmony, throw-everything-into-the-pot, gospel, "Joy to the World." We had even rehearsed the breath we all took before the first note, before Johnny busted out with, "Jeremiah was a bullfrog!"

I had my drum solo in that song. Maybe it was only one or two minutes long, but for me, half way through it, it seemed to stretch ahead like the plains of Kansas. I was so afraid of screwing up that I ran on automatic. I knew the thing inside and out, I'd built it around all my strengths and avoided anything I couldn't already play in my sleep, but that night, with 1500 pairs of eyes on me, I just knew I would drop a stick or fall off my stool.

I can say with certainty that not once during that solo did I experience an instant of creativity. What I hoped looked to the audience like unbridled passion and the flash of inspiration, was in truth a prolonged terror. I'd designed this solo to build to a fever pitch and all I could think of was staying in front of the curve, not letting it slacken for an instant, maintaining enough funky tension so the band could come back in at the right tempo.

I came flying out of the solo and caught Randy's eye for the cue. The band clicked off their safety, came back refreshed and surging and moved into that drawn-out gospel ending like they wanted it to go on forever—and for me it did. Pounding as hard as possible and slamming rim shots everywhere, the solo had drained me early and I was playing at the limits of my strength. It took everything I had just to maintain the pace. The band was blowing flat out and Randy was levitating half a foot off the floor. I was numb and sucking air but hung on until we finally got to the ending. People told me afterward I'd played the solo perfectly. And they said it with flushed faces and loud voices, so I believed them.

That night we won by a landslide. I built castles in the sky for weeks after that show, floating up there as I did in my own personal blimp over the town, looking down and having to use a telescope to recognize my friends. It was deplorable behavior, but highly natural for me.

|| PART TWO:

JOURNEYMAN

What Else Could I Do?

The Fabulous Disasters lasted long enough to play the year-end school dance, but then broke up when Randy wanted to try something else and moved to Austin. Then our singer Johnny packed his bags and headed to Chicago. I lay around a while, all that summer, practicing by myself in the garage, waiting for someone to call. When no one did I enrolled at the local college that fall, under duress and deeply disappointed. I'd like to say that my mother was crippled and I had to stay home and take care of her, but actually my mother was in great shape and wanted me to move out of the house.

I was privately mystified. How could someone with my qualifications not be snapped up right away? On those days when my sap was high and I was feeling particularly gifted, I'd parade into the music store and maybe talk technicalities with the clerk a while, then look over the heads of any young musicians who might happen in to ask a simple question and test everyone's patience. I had a discreet notice advertising my services tacked to the bulletin board and my one purpose in being in the store was to ask the clerk if anyone had looked at it or expressed interest. No one did, so after a while I started calling some of the old gang: Chico to play rhythm and sing, Butch on bass, and I was even at that point of squinting distantly at Bruce to come in and play lead guitar when fortunately a new guy moved into town named Clarence who was okay.

It was a decent band but my heart was not in it. I'd get these chirpy phone calls from Randy just letting me know he saw Willie Nelson the night before at a local Austin club, and jammed with him a little bit, and got to know his bass player real well and was supposed to go over to his house that weekend. Stuff like that gave me stomach pains and dizzy spells and I always cut the conversations short. My giant problem was my consistently good health, which was about to get me drafted and sent to Vietnam. This was 1971 and the local selection board had already notified me that if I wasn't in college then I would soon find myself hiking through rice paddies and slapping mosquitoes in the service of my country. Randy was lucky enough to have flat feet and one leg shorter than the other. Another musician friend of mine was blessed with poor vision. Everybody that summer came down with something and got a deferment, or went off to college in some much better place, and I was left to turn off the lights.

I had to have at least a temporary short-term plan, so I made the phone calls and put together a little group just to keep my chops up and doors open. I had to make something happen, but I was gritting my teeth while things worked out, hoping for a little last-minute magic the whole time. Chico was badly out of practice and hadn't picked up his guitar or sung in over a year. Butch the bass player hadn't worked steadily in months, Clarence the lead player had a bad tendency to rush the beat, and the only keyboard player I could find was a guy named Larry, who was Chico's friend from some karate club they were in. A patched-together band if there ever was one, born of desperation, but a case study in how such things are done.

||||

I'd come to love being a sideman. I had no responsibilities beyond getting to the gig and playing music. I didn't have to schedule practices, didn't have to round up lights, didn't have to carry extra guitar picks in my trapcase, didn't have to do anything but groove to the tunes and get paid. And the truth is that ninety-nine percent of all musicians feel the same way—with the remaining one percent demanding extra attention and acting out childhood traumas. Other than some lead singers, most musicians I'd known were modest, happy people who didn't require lots of spotlights directed at them. But here

I was, doing all those things I hated to do, being the point man for the band. Every phone call to schedule something had to be made four times, I had to be real sensitive to everyone's feelings, book the gigs, and use my car to give people rides: one demand after another if I was going to have a group to work with.

Under my amateur guidance for the next two or three months, the band began that stewing around process of learning songs and establishing roles and rules and our own unique strategies for dealing with things. We practiced three times a week in a circle, everyone's back to the wall. Our stuff stayed set up in my garage, old pop cans accumulated under my floor tom; everything became dusty and personal and terribly routine. My bandmates weren't very quick on the uptake and we had to rehearse forever. Some weeks I'd make them practice twice on Saturday, just to hurry things along, which not only made the guys in the band irritable but reduced me to the status of pariah whenever I'd walk out into the yard and spot one of my neighbors driving stakes through a little voodoo doll with long hair. I didn't care. Being popular in my neighborhood would mean buying a pickup truck and hating foreigners. I didn't grow up in a think tank.

And this little band wasn't going to win awards for musical research either. It might've been that we were all technically college students, but that didn't mean we could play a blues shuffle and make it sound right. Any illiterate Delta blues band could've walked all over us and we wouldn't even stick to their heel. I'm just glad my mother kept feeding me because on my own I would've starved. My intentions were moronically simple: keep playing at all costs and suffer as much as necessary to achieve my goals—which at this point was to levitate a four-ton chunk of lead up onto some musical plane high enough to work gigs at the local bars.

As band leader I had to help the others as much as possible. I came up with a starter list of about twenty songs every group in town played, songs the local bar crowd would expect us to know, and we spent the first two months trying to practice those. It was sick and pathetic but we drilled those songs over and over until we were at least playing on the beat and stopping at the same time. That was an accomplishment. Next, I turned my attention to our vocals. They weren't very good and as a nonsinger I didn't have much expertise to bring, but as band leader I was required to take little critical jabs at the boys whenever they'd start screeching or go totally flat. Chico, who was a fine human being in every other way, got so touchy after a while I hated to say anything to him, but I did anyway and it was for the general good. And Butch, who had been a friend for years, started calling me 'Unka Mike' behind my back, and that hurt.

And then there was Larry. I had major problems with Larry and soon regretted ever asking him into the group. While he was a decent singer and could do Kinks and Stones tunes fairly well, his keyboard playing left everything to be desired and for the most part resembled an open wound I had to continually dress and clean out. Larry could learn a riff and play it right for up to a week, then start missing it in the most flagrant way. Then he'd get it right again—then lose it again. And this was with every note he played, so the opportunities to screw up were basically endless. Larry was as perplexed by his mistakes as the rest of us were. Each time he'd push a button you could see the terror in his finger, not knowing if he was going to hear a pipe organ or a wide-awake rooster.

Musically, his contribution was noise, but in terms of band fiber Larry was good friends with Chico and quickly became friends with Butch and Clarence. I didn't see any easy way to kick him out. Larry brought the reefer to practice and this made him valuable in a limited political way, but as soon as the amps were on and we were playing, he'd skate through the breaks and blow the bridges and throw in sour notes and get me so upset I'd require more joints before calming down.

But we started to sound reasonably good and after a couple more months of this stewing around phase I determined we had to get out and play some place, any place, just to put a working edge on the band and give us focus. Bands tend to go flabby and soft-headed if they don't get out and play in front of people. They get too accustomed to making mistakes and passing it off with a joke; bad habits form quickly in songs. Besides, I needed the money. I looked high and low for a reasonably obscure stage where we could play and work out the knots without drawing too much attention to ourselves, but it was Larry who actually found the gig.

It was a benefit for the local handicapped children's society, to be held at the Knights of Columbus hall. The sponsors had looked all over town for a band cheap enough to do it. I didn't expect to see anyone there I knew. It would be mostly for kids and their parents and relatives. We would be more of an excuse than an attraction, but I realized we had to do the gig as soon as I heard about it.

Then Chico dug in his heels and looked doubtful, and Clarence wanted another couple of months in rehearsal before showing his stuff. Butch didn't seem to care but Larry got a little panicky the moment he realized we were actually going to do the job. I think Larry might've only mentioned the benefit as another joke. He didn't know how serious I was. He probably thought we were playing for fun.

The Real World

We all walked around like condemned men that first hour while setting up, everyone thinking the same thing, and dreading it. First gigs are always an anxious experience, but in a bad band doubly so. A bad band is like a teepee: the individual sticks holding things up are slender and wobbly and not worth much unless strategically arranged with other such sticks. Everyone leans on everyone else. Of course, you don't want any spastic sticks or harebrain sticks or splintery sticks; you want nice smooth, sturdy sticks. I'd looked at the band from every angle and decided the only smart thing to do would be to keep the floppy side of our teepee facing away from the road—which meant trying to get Larry to turn way down.

I anticipated one of two scenarios: either we'd get lucky and the stage and audience would perk us up and we'd avoid making too many mistakes, or things could go to hell quickly. I'd seen some cold disasters and knew what they looked like. Tunes get so stiff and frosty that the slightest trouble just spreads and multiplies and everything crumbles. I wanted to avoid that so I smiled and said encouraging band leader things to the boys while we stood around getting ready, trying to break the tension.

"Hey Chico."

"Yeah, man."

"Hope you don't fuck up."

"Thanks man, hope you don't fuck up either."

I glanced over at Larry and he looked away quickly, busying himself with unfolding his keyboards. I felt like a sadist for making him do this and didn't know how to approach him. He seemed to be quivering with tension. Even his T-shirt had a twitchy, damp look. He'd smoked four joints before coming inside, some crappy ditch weed that didn't do him any good. His jaw had a hangy, loose look, which contrasted sharply with the willies in his eyes. I found an opportunity to stand next to him while I set up his monitor and mentioned he might keep his volume as low as possible. Larry nodded right away.

It was only after we were set up and ready to go that we noticed the crowd. With about ten minutes before start time the 200 kids in the room all seemed pumped and waiting and looking at us. I began to feel an electricity in the hall, palpable anticipation. This was their big event of the year. All the kids seemed to be between six and sixteen, half of them in wheelchairs, a few of them with tanks or bags attached to the frame and tubes running around. Several of the wheelchairs had been outfitted with bows and ribbons and party balloons. There was a lot of yelling but there were other sounds as well. Yips and yaps and occasional shrieks. At times the place sounded like a country and western bar. They all looked pretty excited, assuming the arm-waving movements I saw weren't due to muscular problems.

We were up on a stage with a thirty-foot-high metal ceiling above us. The echo would be intense. I told everyone to pull their monitors in close. As the moment to start playing drew near I looked over once more to see Larry reaching critical mass. His skin was starting to bubble up with large beads of sweat. We all exchanged one last encouraging glance, Larry nodded in a hesitant fashion and Chico counted off "Johnny B. Goode"—it was one he sang—and he got it way too fast. Pumped up and calling out like a speedway announcer, Chico yelled, "Two! . . . Three! . . . Four! . . ." and bang, we're into it, just going to beat hell. From the first note the sound bounced in so many different directions and we had so much echo coming back at us it was hard to even recognize the tune as we raced through it. Everything sounded totally different from the practice room. We hit the ground running, and immediately fell into a ditch.

Enthusiasm couldn't rescue us now. Pure confusion on stage, all five of us sending out distress signals and flashing red lights. The meter was wrong, the phrasing totally screwed, Chico could hardly croak out the words at that speed, but the crowd had gone apeshit. A combination cheer/moan came up from the room during the intro, and by the first verse they were already deep into their party, migrating toward us. Because of their mobility, the Down's Syndrome kids had seized early control of the dance floor. Within ten minutes, though, the wheelchair crowd began a pincer movement around the edges and soon had cut the dancers off from the band by lining up three deep in front of the stage.

For a moment I was satisfied that the crowd at least liked us, regardless of how we sounded, but only for a moment, because the third song into the set our monitors died completely. Which meant *we* couldn't hear the vocals, which meant we went from sounding weak and trashy to sounding simply incoherent. It didn't make any difference; the crowd never stopped cheering. We were into the show and couldn't stop for repairs and ended up playing as sorry an opening set as I've heard before or since. It was a blow to our collective pride, but especially mine. We called an early break just because none of us could go on any longer. We had to regroup, we had to fix the monitors, and Larry had to get outside and refresh himself five or six more times.

This worked out fine because the organizers had lots of trophies and plaques and certificates and ribbons to hand out and it took them over an hour to get it all done. I not only twisted and turned every single knob we had and pulled on all the cords, trying to fix the monitors, I moved all the microphones around, amps were tilted new directions, monitors brought in much closer, and in between all this we managed to work our excuses into the conversation. "No wonder our harmonies sound so bad—damn monitor amp was only set on two before it went out. Who the hell did that?!" Then I'd turn it up and it would start feeding back and everyone would remember why it was set on two.

There wasn't much energy for playing the last set. Butch had a grim look in his eyes. Clarence and Chico seemed off in another world. Larry looked like he'd been electrocuted and he smelled like burnt rope. We would've packed up and left but for the 200 kids still waiting for us to start again and entertain them another hour.

We might've played ten songs that last set. We might've played six. Hard to say, as they all seemed so long. Bad songs really are more complex than well-played songs. A song properly played is simple alongside one that is totally stirred up. Everything we did had the same basic problem: no pocket, no groove, no swing, no lift, no glue—no, none, nada. Just your basic bad band playing on and on.

We would need lots of stage time, lots of playing, we needed to breathe cigarette smoke and get yelled at by drunks and there was no shortcut around it. Even before the last song was over, I knew I'd have to go back out to the little towns again and throw dances and work without even a guarantee, just scraping around for gigs until we got some stage time behind us. I knew the boys would only get good at something by continual repetition. We'd only taken the first step. That night, driving home, the glamorous world of rock'n'roll seemed to be moving even further away.

Larry Lays an Egg
& Other Dismal Adventures

Before twenty-four hours had passed I was dealing with open mutiny. Larry didn't even want to bring his stuff back over to my garage, all because I'd pushed them to do a gig before they were ready. Now *I* was responsible for them sounding bad. I argued with each of them, of course, pressing my point of view that we had to get out before an audience a whole lot *more*, not *less*, but finally caved in when I realized I wasn't getting anywhere. I ate salt and said to each one of them in turn, "You're right. Lord, what a miscalculation! We should never've played that gig. Huge mistake. I'll listen to you next time," blah, blah, whatever they wanted to hear just so they'd agree to come back and try again.

The problem is needing something, anything, too much. Once you need it that badly then you're bare-assed and blown by the wind.

Vulnerable, open to failure, you try extra hard and end up squeezing things to death. I was learning this a bit more each day.

When we finally did reassemble in my garage that next Tuesday, the boys still had an angry, wasp-like attitude, directed mostly at me. I tried to tell a couple of jokes but nobody was laughing. I could see they were going to vent their feelings a bit more so I sat there and took it, part of my band leader responsibilities. They didn't even want to turn on the amps. Pure talk. After I was raked over the coals twice, Larry broke out and confessed it was the first time he'd ever played in front of an audience, and didn't have enough time to prepare himself (because of me) and now wasn't sure he could do it again. Everyone took a turn patting Larry on the head and telling him it was okay, then we all shifted our attention to Chico and attacked his monitors as being inadequate to our needs. I guess we worked through five or six major emotions and got things mostly vented out, repaired all our hurt feelings so no one felt unduly picked on. This took about two hours and at the end of it I thought I was mostly out of the woods and we could get on with business.

Then Butch announced he had acquired a home movie of us playing at the benefit and wanted everyone to come over to his house and drink beer and watch it while his folks were gone. At that point I gave up on getting anything done. I felt adrift, helpless, in the wrong place at the wrong time. We all piled into Butch's car and I sat next to Larry in the back.

|||

I'd never seen myself play drums before. Never practiced before a mirror. Didn't even think of myself in the third person yet. And I can't say I enjoyed it when the movie started and I finally had to look. Is this what people had been seeing all those years? Is this why girls didn't pick me up? I looked like an ax murderer back there, hacking up bodies. Butch said I looked like I hadn't eaten in three days and had just caught a squirrel. Clarence said I looked pissed off. Which I was: plenty.

After we'd seen the film twice, it was Butch's idea that I start wearing a cap and sunglasses. While the film played in front of us for the third time, he offered up that advice like it was a perfectly obvious suggestion. "I think it would help the looks of the band, man. I think you're scaring people. A band needs to look like it's having a good time, man, not escaping from the law. Look atcha."

"What? You want me to wear a bag over my head, maybe?" I asked, thoroughly riled and offended.

"No man," Butch smiled. "It would probably get twisted and you couldn't see. But a cap and sunglasses would do the trick. Maybe buy another cymbal or two if you want."

If I had been less mature I would've been crushed. As it was, I secretly had to agree and feel myself sink to a new low.

I sat there ruminating on it while the rest of them rewound and played the film over and over. I couldn't understand why they kept watching it. Clarence even said he thought certain parts of it sounded good, and Butch and Chico agreed.

| | |

We hunkered down for three more months, time I could've spent making money in another band, if one had asked. In their own perverse fashion the boys coaxed themselves up to speed. I tried to lighten up and let them find their own pace, encouraging them where I could and not pressing too hard. Three practices a week, twelve straight weeks, probably thirty-six total practices, all mixed in with my own private rehearsals, which had grown to two or three hours on the off nights. The band underwent a lot of revision and reorganization, stuff that needed to be done and that I had to do. Our songlist was redrawn and relearned, with each song getting at least an hour's attention. Even the simplest tunes, like "Oh Donna," something you wouldn't think a person could spend ten minutes going over, benefits from this attention. If nothing else, we learned to relax and let the song play itself. All of us got those meters drilled into our heads. In bands with good meter, *everyone* has good meter.

We worked to expose those little buried mistakes, those tiny half-played licks that sound okay as long as they're played quietly. Larry was particularly affected here. Any song he had a major part in was excavated down to the roots, even to having him play the whole thing by himself without accompaniment, the four of us listening for imperfections.

Butch and I scheduled practices alone so we could go over rhythm tracks, working to make tunes like "Mony Mony" and "Gimme Some Lovin'" sound total and complete even before the guitar and organ came in, learning to blend our sound and become a single piece. Butch had gone on a practice binge. He spent every evening at home holding that bass guitar. He told me if he was dead tired he'd still play scales while watching TV just to exercise the fingers. He listened to tapes in class. He grew calluses and chops. Butch became a really nice bass player in short order. He almost wasn't the same person three months after that first gig. He'd walk to school so he could practice his vocals, singing along with a tape until it was memorized, fretting the air until he had it right.

This is my trained monkey theory of musicality. Every band leader knows about the principle. It doesn't take triple IQ points to play a song two hundred times and then finally know it. Running the boys through the drill, I hoped and believed, had to show results eventually. If nothing else, I was counting on each of them, out of self preservation, to bear down and practice and preserve their dignity. The next time we played would be at an actual, regulation, pay-at-the-door dance, and they had to be ready.

While I knew Chico, Clarence, Butch and I sat at home on our off nights doing the drill, I couldn't guess what Larry was doing. For three months, thirty-six consecutive rehearsals, Larry would show up saying he'd practiced the tunes, but then struggle along doing his barnyard impersonations. Not knowing the keyboard wasn't enough of an excuse after a while. Hell, I was learning the thing just being next to him. I talked about this with Butch and we decided that my teepee theory still applied. Everyone leans on everyone else.

I redesigned the songlist again, taking out those tunes Larry couldn't seem to comprehend, and substituting songs with a stronger guitar or rhythm part. Larry was a plenty good singer; he did an extra good job on Beatle tunes. He just couldn't play. And as Clarence and Chico's new best friend and singing buddy, he wasn't likely to be replaced. So Larry (unbeknownst to himself) became our utility player. Butch got him some used conga drums, a tambourine, a cow bell, got him to sing a whole lot, and basically reserved the keyboards for simple tunes with easy chord patterns Larry already knew. And the amazing thing was, it worked.

Larry sounded so good he even got a little cocky after a while, having ideas and correcting my drum parts. I'd only listen to this so long before saying, "Show me," and handing him the wood. This is how I kept him off my case. About the only problems Larry really had to worry about were four or five songs that Clarence insisted on singing that required a dominant keyboard part. That, and "In the Mood."

"In the Mood" was a curious song for us. Everything else we did was a mix of rock'n'roll greatest hits and blues shuffles, but Butch had this idea for doing a swing tune and wanted to do a slicked-up version of "In the Mood." And it sounded wonderful. Really one of the coolest tunes we did. I knew it was going to be an giant hit with the dancers. The only problem with the song was that it had an eight-bar intro, originally on clarinet, that Larry had to execute on the keyboard. It required him to not only start the tune, but play those eight bars all alone before we came in. For him, this was a little bit like swinging out over an open pit on a greasy cable. Sometimes Larry could do it flawlessly. Much of the time there were one or two honkers in there but it mostly sounded okay. It sounded close enough, often enough, that we considered it "a tune we do" and had it on the list.

We ran over the tunes, and ran over the tunes. Every Tuesday and Thursday night, and again Saturday afternoon, we'd meet with a nod and a tip of the hat, pull off the covers and turn on the amps and do the drill again. My mother started leaving Cokes for us on a tray before she left. We were even required to do a couple of band room cleanings since the pop cans stacked up so high and candy wrappers were blowing between amps.

Clarence was the last holdout for booking a new gig. He put it off a full month longer than Butch wanted. The band had been together six months, but it felt like a year. I was more than ready. Larry was patched up and made to go. Butch had rounded and polished every note he played. And Clarence was starting to play decent guitar, even if his meter remained weak. At least he *sounded* good. Clarence played by the numbers so there was a questionable amount of soul behind his notes, but the numbers he played were the right numbers. As long as he didn't get excited and start rushing, or confused and start dragging, he was a fully serviceable lead player. And an okay singer on about six songs. But he was still shy and had to be convinced we were ready before he'd agree to start booking again.

A new club opened north of town called "Uncle Sam's," and it was the hottest thing around. It became the place to be if you were a local aspiring alcoholic. A lot of them were friends of mine, which is to say, bar friends—people I only saw in bars and only talked to during breaks, people I didn't have a last name for. Uncle Sam's was also the newest meat market amongst the eighteen- to twenty-five-year-old set. The outstanding feature of the club, from a musician's point of view, was the stage and acoustics. Only three feet off the ground instead of five, plenty wide and deep, the stage had built-in lights and sound, nice carpet, and great acoustics. At least we thought so. None of us had played there. It was what Butch called a "tit gig." I agreed with him, but didn't expect him to go out there and book it.

When Butch announced at practice that we had the job in three weeks, Clarence almost had to pour his shoes out. "Good God, man! When I said to book a gig, I didn't mean in there!" Clarence wanted to cancel but Butch refused, saying if we were going to come out we might as well do it with a bang. Butch was even getting posters made to hang up downtown. Then the bar ran their usual ad in the paper. Everywhere Clarence looked he was seeing the name of the band. He practiced with a vengeance that last week. We all did.

We were booked under "Jelly Belly and the Tectonics," a name I thought appropriate. By 7:30 we were set up and ready to go. We wouldn't start until 9:00, so we milled around the club and said encouraging things to each other like, "Hope I don't fuck up. Hope you don't fuck up too." About 8:45 some friends arrived and I was able to divert myself with them. But even that made me nervous because they seemed to have large expectations for the band and I tried to put a damper on them. I suspect they were impressed by the stage and lights and the general look of the place.

We all went up on stage five minutes early. I put on my sunglasses and hat. We double-checked all the knobs, eyeballed the settings, hit each of the drums once to make sure they still worked. Then we all took a last drink of beer. At the last possible moment before starting, a friendly voice called out from the audience, "Go Larry!" Butch and I both smiled. *I* counted the tune off—it was "Born to be Wild"—and it was deliberate and even ponderous but precisely right.

I'm not sure anyone but me heard that first song. They were all so concentrated on their individual jobs, so intent on not making mistakes, the song just happened with the boys standing there. I too avoided throwing my sticks and managed to play every single note. All I know is that we finished and then there was applause.

At that moment it seemed all our tensions melted. A grin popped on everyone's faces, Butch hit a big "Boing!" and I threw in a cymbal crash. It had worked! We could actually sound minimally competent before an audience. Now it was a proven fact. If we could keep it up, maybe I'd finally be in a working band once again. The applause continued and a few people yelled. Chico had gone into a self-appreciating trance, so Butch called out the next tune, one he sang, and the set turned out to be rather successful, even by my high standards.

By the third set I realized Larry was scared shitless and getting worse. All night there had been a jabbing quality to his keyboard playing. After every other song, Butch had gone over to remind Larry to keep his volume up because the keyboards were beginning to disappear. We got through three sets like that with Larry getting just a little weaker all the time, but still keeping up. During our final break I thought about buying Larry a beer. He'd been drinking Coke all night and the caffeine was probably making him twitchy. But when I offered him a beer he said it made him woozy so I backed way off the idea. I got him to take a drink of water instead and breathe deeply for a minute.

| | |

I don't feel stage fright. I think about two percent of the population is like this. Some people say a little stage fright stimulates their performance, but my one experience with it was stultifying, not stimulating. It was my very first gig, in Carnegie, Oklahoma. The county fair. We were in a metal barn and up on a high, impromptu stage five feet in the air. With about fifteen minutes left before start time, my brain suddenly seized up and I felt an icy, windswept terror. I couldn't move—they had to carry me to the stage, actually carry me up to my drums and sit me down behind them. I could feel every eye in the room scanning me, hunting up faults and peeling away the lies. I kept telling everybody we couldn't start yet, that *I* couldn't start yet, that I wasn't able to play because my arms were frozen, but it was summer and I was ignored and they started the tune and my stage fright was gone before we were three songs into the set. I haven't felt it since. So it's not that I'm unsympathetic; I'm plenty sympathetic. When I'm around someone that scared, it starts to bring it up in me too. Normal stage fright I can ignore, but naked fear has a growing presence on stage. Everyone was just hoping Larry could hold together a few songs more and we'd be through for the night.

It wasn't to be. The club had filled up and there must have been a hundred dancers out on the floor, most of them friends of ours. The audience was applauding and yelling after the tunes and most of the band felt great. We had about thirty minutes to go. Then we came to "In the Mood." We all shook our heads and Butch asked Larry, "You want to do it man? We can skip it. Don't matter, man. . . ." And Larry, I guess thinking he had to do his part and not let us down, replied, "Sure . . ." tremble, tremble, "You bet. Let's do it."

Standing there under the blue and red lights, Larry took a giant breath and looked down at his keyboard like it was a box of snakes. He paused and took another deep breath and then reached in. The start was a little wobbly on the intro but he was getting it done, covering beat after beat, sounding just like Benny Goodman, Jr.'s clarinet. But on the fifth measure the riff changes, and when Larry went for the note he found some wild Charlie Parker variation way off the scale, and it so surprised him the next note came in wild too, and then the one after that, and before you knew it Larry was off in the weeds and thrashing around. He finally stopped playing altogether. The floor was already packed and people were swing dancing with arms in the air when the song fell apart. There was a large groan from the crowd as the four of us looked tenderly over at Larry and tried to forgive him on the spot. But Larry was already in the land of the unforgiven. Nothing we could do or say could bring him back. Larry's eyes twitched around a bit more and he tried to focus on the keyboard, squinting at it hard. A scary, primal moment on stage. Then he started on the intro again, determined to get it right. The dance floor came alive, a happy groan swelled up from deep inside the crowd, people were shuffling and swaying with total abandon. Then Larry got to the fifth measure and once again dove off into the weeds.

It looked like the jaws of hell had spread open beneath him, like a fiery whirlpool was sucking him down. Larry couldn't even look up at us. It was a gravelly situation. I felt totally sorry for him. The crowd started actively complaining; a few people close to the stage saying things we could hear. Nobody knew what to do, so I grabbed my mic and said, "Ladies and Gentlemen . . . your attention please. This has been brought to you as a public service announcement. Do *not* drink and drive."

People laughed and Butch smiled and picked up the cue and grabbed his mic, "Or play the piano!" I gave a boom/crash and Butch leaned around behind Clarence, talking to Larry. "Fuck the intro. Just start her on the verse." Larry—standing there cold sober, the spotlights shining on him, finger up his ass—nodded and I counted it off and we jumped straight into the song.

After the set was finally over I was the first one to hand him his beer. "Here, drink this. Get woozy." Larry sucked it down in three gulps and I ordered another. Stage fright is an ugly business and I could only wonder what Larry would be like down the road. Either he'd get over it eventually or he wouldn't, in which case we'd have to set up a band fund to buy him tranquilizers each night.

Howdy Doody Time

One of the hazards of being a musician back then was the flourishing drug culture and all the variety of things people would offer you. I was probably more mild and low key in my approach to drugs than many of my friends. If I saw a pill on the floor in a bar, I wouldn't pick it up and eat it. A little pot now and again was enough for me. Nothing in excess. A few beers maybe if I was thirsty. I liked to think of myself as a moderate person who'd always look for the middle way in any situation.

Clarence was the one who first turned me on to acid. It was all so innocent; he was being friendly and generous and I appreciated the offer. My curiosity had outgrown itself and I was more than willing to swallow that little piece of purple paper and chase it down with a Coke and see what might happen. We were in his room and his parents were out in the den. It was mild and pleasant and I saw a few little explosions and such, a couple of tracers, nothing really dramatic. Afterwards I was disappointed because the stories I'd heard had led me to believe I would step into some kind of cartoon world where I could talk to the dog or watch a house plant transform itself into a parrot. I'd heard these stories and had believed them until my own mild experience showed me otherwise. After trying it once I had no strong opinions on it one way or another.

I think I'll use the Mt. Everest excuse and say that I did it again "because it was there." A lot of my activities back then fell into this category. My specific reason was that I was already a fairly visual person and thought it might improve my imagination.

Clarence got in a new batch he called windowpane. It was supposed to be stronger and have a "different flavor." I thought I would experiment and see what playing music at a gig was like tripping on acid, see if it might not enrich the experience or deepen my knowledge of music, so I swallowed Clarence's little blue pill about the size of a baby aspirin and waited.

Nothing happened for the next thirty minutes, so I tore down the drums and packed up the PA while Clarence wrapped cords and filled boxes. Clarence had taken some windowpane as well so we were both watching each other to see who would click on first, who'd see the first tracer in the air.

We were about to lift a footlocker, one of us on each end, when Clarence bent over to grab under it and touched his chin to the lid for an instant. His chin somehow stuck there, like the locker was covered with amazing glue—when he lifted and stood his chin stayed on the locker, while his whole face stretched and pulled and spread upward in a long, gigantic melt. Instead of looking up to see Clarence's real face and maybe correcting the misperception, I kept looking down at the locker and the mouth moving there. I thought, "My god, this actually is an hallucination! I've seen a real one now." Then Clarence clicked on and looked at me and immediately knew I was tripping too. I don't know how we kept from dropping the locker.

That old garage room came to life and suddenly the walls blossomed with rainbow colors and the concrete floor undulated a bit and the air itself began to sound like white noise.

"Boy!" I said to Clarence. "This isn't like that other stuff at all! I feel totally snakebit."

"Yeah, man," was all Clarence could manage.

Then Chico and Butch and Larry showed up and helped us start loading equipment, Clarence and I working together off on the side and not getting much done, grinning mostly.

|||

Ten minutes later I was rolling my trapcase across the patio to the driveway where the trunk of my car stood open. I'd built up a head of speed, was really getting involved with the "art" of loading equipment, working out multitudinous schemes for improving things.

I was coming up to a break in the concrete where a patch of grass separated me from the car. I measured my steps on the fly, counted them exactly, and at just the right moment lifted the trapcase, sailing it over the grass and right towards my trunk in a perfect trajectory. Loading equipment really can be a beautiful thing if you're high enough on acid. The trapcase was at the apex of its arc through the air, I was striding and lifting at the same time, there was a massive ghost of me and my trapcase stretching back ten feet, and I was grooving on the whole thing. Then the earth corkscrewed under me and I was looking at clouds for an instant and then two trains collided in the middle of my spine. The trapcase turned loose of me and buried itself in the grass. I staggered backwards and came to rest leaning against the side of my car, looking down and gasping air, all while seeing each and every blade of grass in the yard turn a separate color. I looked up and Chico's face seemed to be floating in the air in front of me, little lights flickering around his head, looking wild and confused, yelling something. I experienced about thirty seconds of the wildest chaos imaginable, and then settled into a bushwhacked jumble of multiple impressions. It took me a minute to remember the English language sufficiently to find that one word I needed, "Back! It's my back!"

Chico opened the car door and got me seated with my feet still on the ground, dark explosions of various magnitudes going off in the air around me.

I hadn't been acquainted with serious physical pain before, didn't know what it looked like. I met up with Mr. Pain in those next two minutes, saw his ugly face, talked to him, and realized the world was a much more evil place than I'd thought. Not the proper material for an acid trip.

I was getting deeply bummed. Clarence came up and told everyone I was tripping and they all murmured a moment and then Chico asked me how I was doing. I evaporated and rematerialized a couple of times before answering, "Oh . . . man . . ." I moaned. "What am I going to do?"

"Don't worry about it," Larry said, just about the most fatuous advice imaginable coming from him. Hell, how could I not worry? I had a gig to play, was hallucinating out of my mind, and could barely sit up. Lifting my arms was almost impossible. And I needed the money.

I sat there melting and assuming various mathematical shapes for the next ten minutes while this giant scream inside my body washed every thought out of my head. My back felt like it had broken into several large pieces and every single nerve in my body was ringing like a telephone exchange. When the boys gathered around me once again it was Butch who'd figured things out. I tried to focus on him while he talked.

"I'll drive your car. You ride in the passenger seat. We got plenty of time to set up and see what happens next. One thing at a time. Let's get to the gig for now."

I agreed. There wasn't anything else to do. I didn't want to go lay on my bed in my room and be all alone feeling like this. Maybe the acid would wear off, maybe my back would get better, maybe we'd run over a bag of cash on the way to the gig. I got in the passenger seat and Butch backed us out of the driveway.

There are moments on acid when you can fall into a bottomless despair, a misery so sudden and complete that life begins to look like a joke and you're the all-time biggest fool to ever draw breath for not seeing it sooner. "The sun's going to burn out," I realized. "None of this means anything. I've been kidding myself." This is what's known in academic circles as the 'cosmic howl.' A large portion of those twenty miles were covered with me in the passenger seat feeling totally sorry for myself, and at the same time thinking I was maybe growing a third eye and acquiring wisdom. Then, when I did start looking out the window near the end of the trip, all I could see was the road switching back and forth like a video game with continuous hairpin turns. We might have been driving 35 MPH. A four-hour trip that took most of thirty minutes.

I didn't even try to get out of the car. Everyone gathered around my window and Butch provided the penetrating vision. "We'll unload this car first, then you guys set stuff up while we go find a chiropractor."

"Chiropractor?" I asked. Horses started stampeding all around me and I was swimming in dust. "I've never been to a chiropractor before, and I don't feel like experimenting anymore right now."

"You'll love it," Butch said, and climbed back in behind the wheel. "We passed a chiropractor driving into town, that's when I got the idea. Didn't you hear me mention it?" He looked over at me a minute, feeling sympathetic, broadcasting his feelings like radar. "It won't hurt. Trust me." I wasn't in a trusting mood but my choices were limited. I wiped my face for the hundredth time and said, "Sure." We drove off to have my bones popped back into place, me feeling more weak and pulpy by the moment.

Butch reassured me the whole way that painless healing was the wave of the future and that I wouldn't even notice it when my spine was realigned. A hard thing to imagine since every breath was killing me already. Rigor mortis had begun to set in and my mobility was declining quickly. I walked into the doctor's office like Frankenstein after a bad scrap, eyes glowing, leaning on Butch the whole way and dripping sweat like we'd just come through a lawn sprinkler. "Nothing to worry about," Butch kept saying.

The doctor was one of those small-town cheerful types you hate to see in a moment of crisis. When he heard I was a broken drummer in need of a patch job, he positively started shining. "Oh sure. I work on drummers all the time." I didn't see how this was possible but was glad to hear it. "I can't cure you completely, you'll still have to heal for a few days, but I can relieve the pressure. Get up here on the table and I'll examine you." Which he did, poking his fingers into every single sensitive spot he could find and causing the whole room to throb. "Yeah, I see the problem. She's right here." Another jab and poke which caused the stars to come out there in his office and one of his chairs to melt. "Yeah, boy . . . that little baby is sure twisted. Got her jammed good. You must have been walking when you lifted."

He laid me out on the rack, a motor-driven device that tilted every direction thinkable and had certain clamps and couplings. The doctor positioned me on the table precisely so I couldn't get away from him if I tried. He felt around a little bit more, got his knuckles positioned square center over the vortex of pain, stiffened his arms, then told me to take a deep breath and let it out slow.

He paused long enough to allow me to center all my mental awareness and imagination on that one spot where he had his palm resting. If anything, my sensitivity increased tenfold in those last five seconds. I finished letting out the air and he waited until I was almost breathless. Then he popped me. The sound that comes from bones is unique and easily identified, whether they're dried out or still covered with meat. I'd never heard my own bones before. But the more impressive thing was that my body, that totally cohesive, nineteen-year-old entity called Me Myself, became for an instant a thing apart when the whole edifice jerked and grunted and emitted muted thunks from deep inside.

When I heard that collection of fractures and explosions in my own carcass, all of the visual synapses in my brain fired at once. Then nothing. I was prepared to scream loud enough to bring the police, but nothing happened. My vision cleared temporarily as I searched for the pain and all I could find was a huge echo where it had been. Then suddenly I relaxed so deeply I damn near dripped off the table. From somewhere, far down that body of mine, a little squeaker of a fart sounded, not connected to me at all.

I lay there, my cheek pressed against the Naugahyde, feeling myself begin to glow and relax and spread out all over the room and up the walls and out the window until I was floating with the birds and exploring the clouds outside. I think I smiled. Butch's face leaned down and into view. "Well?" And he smiled too.

I think I promised that doctor to name a baby after him, but I'm not sure. I do know that when I lay down on that table I had the Devil laughing into my face, and when I got up I was thinking, "Hey, I could probably jump fences now." I even gave a little shimmy to test the structure. "Don't tempt the gods," the doctor said. "No violent movement if you can help it, keep your back straight, don't lift anything, and you ought to make it fine." I thanked him six or eight more times and then we left. I was still stiff, the more I moved the more I was reminded, but I was playable.

When we got back to the club, Chico and Clarence and Larry had unloaded all the equipment and had the drums out of their cases. From my chair next to the table with my iced tea on it, I gave Butch instructions on setting them up.

After such high drama, the gig itself wasn't that special. The acid was mostly worn off by the time we started and I didn't find myself playing any more creatively than usual, if that much. I mostly concentrated on keeping my spine straight. After that I bought a back rest for my stool and laid off acid completely.

Me and Mary Lou

People started to drift in and out of the band. Larry didn't last another three gigs. Playing in front of people just took too much out of him. We went without a keyboard player for a while and Clarence had to pick up the slack, playing all the lead parts by himself now.

And Clarence didn't like it, didn't like being stretched out so much, didn't like working so hard, so his vote started to look tentative as well. Along about the eighth month Clarence started doing a whole lot of LSD—maybe to compensate for his weak lead playing, I don't know—three or four times a week, maybe more, and this made him unreliable in the extreme. When he'd finally get to practice late (if he showed at all) I could always tell if he was hallucinating. Anyone could. People on acid have this busted-out look, every pore is dilated, the iris in the eyes is a thin string around the pupil, they're flushed and dumbstruck. He'd walk in the side door of the garage and look up at me sitting there like I was a twenty-foot-high billboard written in old Greek. I'd squiggle my fingers at him and wave my hand to check for tracers. As soon as I'd see those busted eyes of his, I knew he'd be stalling out in his leads as he stopped to sniff the flowers and lounge amongst the grass and rub dew all over himself and leave the rest of us to move on in real time with the actual song. I also knew he'd screw around with his sound and get too much feedback—which was the one thing I suspect could still rouse Hanson across the street to action.

It was a tangled situation, made worse by the fact that the war in Asia was heating up and my student deferment was getting shaky. I hadn't really thought much about minimum grade requirements and class attendance until I got a letter from the dean announcing I'd be put on probation the following semester "if you choose to reenroll," and mentioning only casually at the end that "probation may affect your status with the selective service board as well." So I was scrambling on all fronts.

Then Chico quit because he got the same letter from the dean I did and the band went through a couple of revolutions before we got Johnny, who had just returned from Chicago and had lots of stories to tell. Johnny had a better blues voice than Chico so the band changed its sound once more and became mostly a blues band with lots of guitar leads and less and less radio rock'n'roll. We started calling Johnny 'Jelly Belly.' He was a decent front man, and we began to build up a little following.

I might have been making $25 a night at those little gigs we booked in towns nearby. Driving and hauling my stuff up and down staircases in the dark, picking up my trapcase ten times a night with my bad back, slinging around that bass drum in its case, pulling stuff in and out of the car, plus hauling the lights and setting them up, and practice, practice, practice. I stayed worn-out and peevish and seemingly lost in bad luck, waiting for it to break, waiting for anything.

| | |

I overheard a comment in the music store that settled me down quite a bit. A couple of guitar players were talking about a drummer they worked with and one of them said, "Yeah, he plays alright but he don't sing, and I can't be doing it all night. You need that extra voice, y'know?"

It was an ordinary comment I'd heard many times before. Singers seem to rarely like singing. Most everyone I knew who sang didn't want to. If most singers had their druthers they'd do five songs a night and quit. They sing because they have to and continually moan about it and their tender voices.

Up until this point I had no interest in singing at all. Singing for a drummer is much more difficult than it is for guitar players and keyboardists, anyone who plays *with* the melody. Standing there listening, though, the thought occurred to me that these two guys were in a band that worked every weekend, had a good regional reputation, traveled a little bit up to Oklahoma City and down to Dallas, and was making steady money. It was a band I'd like to be in. If I was already a practiced singer I could amble over there and slap one of them on the back and mention some opera I'd just learned. "Yeah, I was singing 'La Pavaratchi' last night while working out on the drums. Nothing like a good workout to stay in shape. Boy, do I love singing."

The problem was I truly didn't like singing. At birthday parties, when the time comes to do the song, I'm the guy who makes even the little baby sound like he's talented. I used to feel badly about not being able to sing. When I was seven my mother stuck me in choir for the summer just to have a place to leave me for a few hours. The choir director ended up moving me from the front row where all the little kids stood, to the back row with a bunch of men who smelled like cigar and sang bass. After two months I ended up playing tambourine and turning pages for the pianist. About the only positive singing experience of my whole young life was in assembly at school doing "God Bless America," where there were 800 other voices to drown me out.

During my early garage band days, when I was so eager to please it was pitiful, I'd agree to sing a little backup, but even in that raw environment my voice stood out and attracted attention and sooner or later no one would loan me a mic anymore. Not only did I not mind,

I was usually happy about not singing. Singing is naked in ways drum playing is not. If you don't know something on the drums, you can sometimes fake it as long as you stick to the groove. Your true voice is not fakable, and what fakability is possible requires skill.

Some people want to bare their soul over a PA but I've never shared this enthusiasm. Playing drums was much more comfortable because it wasn't me that people heard but the drums. The ideas were mine and the feel was mine, but those were musical ideas and musical feelings, not my innermost secret personality. When a person sings in a bare-assed, amplified, solo voice, it's all there and it's all exposed. I cringe at bad singing in ways I don't cringe at bad guitar playing, and it's because it's so personal and naked it makes me feel itchy.

Singing is also harder for drummers because so much of the time the melody and rhythm are at odds with each other. In the world of rock'n'roll drumming most everything starts on one and ends on four and repeats itself a whole lot, moving in a straight line. Things are either on a downbeat or an upbeat and regardless of how complicated it might get there's a linearity to it. Everything a drummer does has to make sense. Simple, square, even-numbered sense. Not that singing doesn't have to make sense too, but the parameters are considerably wider apart. A different kind of sense. Straight lines don't have much to do with it. In most tunes the melody sprawls all over the place. Melodies start early and stay late. And they pause in unusual places for a drummer. Songs are usually built on the tension *between* rhythm and melody, accentuating their differences—to execute both simultaneously requires a divided brain and two independent thought patterns running alongside each other at the same speed. All of which seemed like too much for me. I like doing one thing at a time.

The other thing I didn't like was the presence of this ball mic right in front of my face every time I'd move. When I remembered it was there I could tilt my head and dodge around it when reaching for a fill; when I forgot about it (maybe half the time) I'd bump my face on the thing, knocking it six inches away and requiring one hand to pull it back in. I'd never felt so hemmed-in in my life. Had to sit up straight all the time.

But I bought the microphone and boom stand and started joining in on the backup parts, not singing real loud but getting used to it. My excuse to the band was that without Larry singing we needed the voice. Old dogs and new tricks became my theme for the next several weeks. Admittedly, things might have been much easier if I'd *wanted* to sing, but I didn't. It was a career move. First, I had to get used to my voice over the PA, and this took some time. My voice pretty much drives me to distraction. It's kind of bassy and all the syllables are rounded off and it sounds very Oklahoma. It was *not* how I heard it in my head. Just as my image of myself playing was shattered by Butch's home movie, so was the very sound of myself thinking given a new slant by all this talking and singing I had to do into the PA. Half of which Butch would record and play back so we could analyze it for multiple imperfections.

I didn't like any of it. And I particularly didn't like having that mic so close picking up everything I said or any noises I might make and bouncing them off the walls. I would occasionally express myself during tense moments in the song but this was never meant for public broadcast. I also apparently had an unfortunate tendency to make grunting noises and occasional growling sounds while playing fast rolling fills. It was not something I'd ever noticed before because I couldn't hear it with the drums playing. In the past I'd come home from some gigs with a sore throat, but always passed it off to all the cigarette smoke in the air.

No one noticed my grunting at first. But Johnny had all this new expensive PA equipment, and there was a rumble somewhere he couldn't locate. He called the music store and complained to them, even hauling the amps down there for a diagnostic check. He and Butch pulled out schematics and made sure everything was plugged in correctly. They talked about ohms and impedance and all kinds of complicated stuff. Johnny was getting near the end of his rope and had taken to standing with his ear right next to the speakers, listening all the time for that rumble, making small adjustments, looking for the pattern and not finding it. Finally, in the middle of my big drum break in "Hippy Hippy Shake" one afternoon he started glaring at me and yelled, "I know what it is!" We all stopped the song and Butch asked him what he was talking about. He pointed to me and said, "Play the drum break again. Punch it up." So I started the beat and Johnny and Butch and Clarence were over there with their ears to the speaker. Everyone got a sour look on his face. "Yeah, you're right," Butch said. "He's making noise."

They bought me one of those foam balls that go over the end of the mic, guessing that would cut down on ambient grunting. Everyone also decided I would have to pull the mic in and out for the backup parts from now on. It was all hugely unpleasant and I had to will myself forward.

Randy called and told me he was making a demo tape but didn't like his drummer and sure wished I was down there in Austin. I told him he was a fine human being for saying so but that I was stuck in hell and sinking fast.

| | |

I looked around for a tune to sing and had great trouble finding one simple enough for me. I kept thinking there had to be one out there I could handle and not be too embarrassed. It had to be a recognizable hit and it had to be danceable. Every song I listened to had one drawback or another. Some of the singers held their notes too long, others jumped around on the scale and used too much variety, still others didn't have sufficient backup vocals. Then every time I found a song I liked and wanted to try, I'd discover the drum part was in some way a complicated counterpoint to the vocals and I'd split myself in half trying to play and sing it at the same time.

I finally narrowed my few choices down to two: a very simple Ricky Nelson tune called "Mary Lou" and a Bobby Lewis song called "Tossin' and Turnin'." The Bobby Lewis tune I actually kind of liked and so preferred it above Mary Lou, but the very reason I liked it kept me from singing the song. There were breaks where the words were: "Jumped out of bed," dah dah dah dah, "Turned on the light," dah dah dah dah, "Stumbling all around it was the middle of the night." I had no problem with the words, and I had no problem with the sixteenth notes in between, but to do it right included doing a little bit of overlap in a couple of places. This overlap had to be a hundred percent perfect to carry the groove. I practiced for a week but it refused to fall into place.

So I fell back on Mary Lou. No drum breaks to worry about with Mary Lou. Straightforward, old-timey Texas shuffle, words laying right on the beat, nice middle-range notes, nothing too flashy. I didn't expect it to be a big hit. I privately hoped that people would use the song as an excuse to go to the bar or rest room and I would be ignored while I practiced in public.

I was told everyone's voice sounds odd to them at first, but that you get used to it. This didn't seem to be happening for me. My singing voice was low and rumbly and my Oklahoma accent made it sound like I was singing into a sock. That foam ball didn't help either. Mary Lou sounded like "Maury Moo." It wasn't a voice trained to hold a note true for very long. In fact, my voice seemed to skip around quite a bit, sort of glancing the right note but then falling off the beam and getting back on. If I'd learned to ride a bicycle like this, I would've ended up in a body cast.

The band spent two whole practices on me and Mary Lou and I experienced major difficulties getting a decent sound. Singing backup is a difficult enough business; singing lead really takes up all your attention. Little things—like the band playing faster during the hard parts—began to bother me. I had trouble keeping the right distance from the microphone and so was overbearing in places. My breath failed me in other parts. The beat was a little jumpy. Some of my melodies resembled search and rescue missions. The words never would stick in my mind, so I had to keep looking down at the cheat sheet on my rack tom. I was nervous about everything. The second time we did the song at practice, my little fan caught the edge of the paper and blew it to the floor—which suddenly expanded the song's narrative to include pregnant elephants and hot fudge and other incongruous items. "Well, hello Maury Moo . . . I didn't know you were Zulu." Stuff like that. But worst of all, I had three top-notch singers listening closely to every note I sang.

The Tectonics had a gig booked at a large local dance hall called "The Mad Dog Saloon." It was a big gig for us, one we'd looked forward to, and it would be my coming out as a singer. Extra equipment was rented, the drums were all miked up, four-color posters were made and ads run. And the turnout was decent, probably 300 people.

We started with our regular opening tune, "Born to Be Wild," which Butch sang, then went to "Born in Chicago," which was Johnny's tune, then "Don't Be Cruel," Butch again, and then "Runaway" to get Clarence in the picture. Butch had done something new with the lights which I found entertaining for a while. Under my two new shiny crash cymbals, one on the left and one on the right, Butch had installed high-wattage yellow lights on the floor that shone straight up on the underside of the cymbals, which mirrored the light back to the floor. When he first turned them on they created a halo around my drums. But the best thing was when I hit one of the cymbals it would throw a beam of extra-intense light out over the audience. I thought this was kinda fun for a while—when I popped the cymbal I could see the whole beam cut across the smoky room and then fall back to the floor by my drum set. We were on a high stage and I was up on a podium so I had considerable range. From where I was sitting I could pretty much tell what direction the beam would go in, but to people moving around and shuffling on the dance floor it seemed to come as a surprise each time I flashed them because the ones looking right at me would squint up and glance away. One guy with thick glasses was standing in exactly the right spot and I zapped him like a ray gun.

We were mobbed during the first break. Clarence was sober and having an exceptional night, Butch was solid and working the pocket, and Johnny managed to shake up a storm and even jumped down with the crowd once and danced around. Other than some unnecessary but flashy cymbal work, I sounded pretty decent too.

People were coming up, wanting to talk, and we handed out a lot of cards. Butch in particular looked a little overwhelmed as he began discussing wedding dates a year in advance. He must've scribbled down five phone numbers in fifteen minutes. Walking back to the stage he said, "Man, we got these people bullshitted good. They think we're great."

The second set started on a sure foot. Confidence was high. We got past our pretty opening numbers and started pumping the people a little. Butch did "Pretty Woman" and packed the floor all the way back to the bar. Clarence did "Gimme Some Lovin'" and got a rousing cheer afterwards. My fan was on high and I looked like I was doing a rain dance back there. Johnny did one of his B.B. King tunes, "The Thrill is Gone," and a girl on the floor started waving her tits at him. Beams of light were shooting all over the room. The crowd was in our pocket. Another break and more slaps on the back. Maybe one of the best gigs we'd had. Butch had already gone back and talked to the manager and it looked like we'd be rebooked the following month.

We started the third set. Then came "Mary Lou." Then I seemed to pass through a black hole in time—everything just stopped for a minute and reversed gravity and only started up again slowly.

It's astonishing the power a vocalist has to affect people's moods and alter their spirits. The vocal arts have a much stronger impact than I'd ever realized before. To sing a song and have an entire room undergo a transformation right before your eyes is a most singular event, like standing in front of a stampede and bringing it to a complete halt.

I don't know what happened. Some how, some way, I got real tense when Clarence called out "Mary Lou." I'd been hearing the song in my head the last ten minutes. I already had the tempo in mind, had my cheat sheet positioned and taped securely on my tom, the mic was pulled in and properly placed. I did everything but hum and find my pitch before counting it off, afraid the mic would pick it up. That's how much of a rookie I was. Then we started and it was like I had a throat spasm. I pitched myself an octave too high on the very first note and couldn't come down.

Clarence, Johnny and Butch all seemed to flinch at once. Johnny, who was standing right in front of me, shrank six inches and hunched up. I couldn't see his face. Clarence, over on the right, went into a high grade panic and just froze. I kept singing but turned to Butch and gave him my 'ship in distress' signal. My voice was way too high and squeaky and there didn't seem to be a thing I could do to find the right key. I sounded like I was being attacked by a pair of pliers.

Butch immediately went fishing up and down the scale looking for a key that might fit my voice but Clarence waved him off. The audience seemed to congeal before me. Dancers became paralyzed and clumsy, faces rigid. A certain wide-eyed unfocused look swept the room like a fog. Suddenly, everyone was just going through the motions, pretending to dance, pretending to smile, pretending to be there.

I wanted to stop after the first verse but Clarence read my mind and kept his back turned to me so we'd have to finish the song. It was his philosophy that people would believe anything if you just packaged it right, so he was hellbent on pretending this tune was an ordinary event.

As the song slowly progressed and we moved into the second verse, my voice started to give out—being unaccustomed to singing at that high a pitch. And as the singing deteriorated, so did the music. Clarence got sloppy, Butch broke loose, I didn't do so good myself. The song sounded like one of those long screechy train wrecks. By the last chorus, everyone was just waiting for it to finally grind to a halt. If there was any entertainment value at all in the song, it was in the smile of relief that came over the room when we finished. We quickly launched "Midnight Hour" and Johnny got to sing again.

I wasn't worth spit the rest of the night. I was mortified, graveled, sunk down to the molten core of the earth. I'd made the whole band look like a collection of idiots displayed under high wattage lights.

During the next break there was a lot of laughing and my ribs were poked from every direction. People I hadn't seen in years came up to me. Then everyone wanted to tell a story about the time he heard whatshisname sound even worse. Butch seemed genuinely amused but Johnny's laughter was a little forced at times. I knew the night was passing into local lore even as I lived it.

After we were packed up, Johnny and Butch went back to the club's office to book another job. When they returned they both were smiling and Johnny said, "Yeah, we got another date, but only on the condition we don't do Mary Lou." This set them off again and they were still chuckling during the meal a half hour later, sporadically choking on their potatoes and just shaking their head. I didn't sing any more after that and nobody brought it up.

Dancing with the Giant

Then I got a break. Musicians I knew were getting drafted into the army left and right and every evening on the news there was film of bombs that had exploded in Vietnam the day before. It was a bad time to be nineteen. It seemed to me those bombs were falling here at home, too; half the musicians I knew were turning into little smoking craters as they were picked off one after another. I struggled to keep a 2.0 GPA and my student deferment intact.

But for every one saved there was one lost and the drummer for a very good band called "Snapshot" got his ass drafted and suddenly there was an open position. I knew all about the band. A friend of mine named DJ played keyboards with them. Luckily, they weren't looking for a singing drummer; the band already had three front men, all of them good lead singers, and with a fourth even had three-part backup. They could do Beach Boys and complicated Beatles, and they were good players. Snapshot was really probably one of the two or three sharpest rock'n'roll bands on my side of the state.

After the audition and the first few gigs, the guy I hooked up with was Curly, the bass player. A fine, fine bass player. Certainly the best bass player I'd ever worked with. Nothing is more important to a drummer than playing with a good bass player, and Curly had all the virtues. As soon as I heard him play I wanted to work with him. He had a large Ampeg with two speaker boxes, one on each side of me, burying me in bass sound. Just the most comfortable place a drummer can ever be. I could not only hear him extremely well, but I could *feel* him too. Playing with Curly was like lounging on a large pillow. Meter was perfectly solid, punch was always there, chops all night, and he was a good lead singer too.

I gave the Tectonics two weeks' notice and had them move out of my garage. Nobody took it too badly. They got another drummer, not a particularly good one but okay, and started practicing over at Johnny's.

Snapshot worked all over southern Oklahoma and northern Texas and had a strong reputation. The band had been going over three years when I joined them. The lead front guy, the one who stood at the edge of the stage and hogged all the attention, was Steve. He didn't play anything but tambourine and sang lead on about half the tunes. Danced a lot. At first he seemed okay. At first. Steve was a good-looking guy, totally fascinated with himself, and expected no less from others. In every band there's always one, and Steve was our particular ego problem. I should've been looking for him.

Bobby was the lead guitar player, the same Bobby I'd played with five years earlier. He'd grown up skinny and focused and seemed to live for that guitar. Bobby had perfected a blistering sound that gave a sharp edge and a crispness to all the songs, very clean on the attack. And then DJ and his multiple keyboards stacked on two sides and three high, another adventuresome soloist who complimented Bobby perfectly and who looked a lot like him, only with longer hair. And then Curly and I back on rhythm. How could something this good happen to me?

I smiled a whole lot those first few weeks, offering to help out wherever I could, carrying other people's stuff for them. They had scads of lights and a huge sound system, all of which we carried around in a panel truck Bobby's father owned. I went on a major practice binge and tried to learn all fifty of their songs in one week. I didn't go to class at all.

I also bought equipment, on credit. Two extra cymbals I wanted anyway, and five microphones for my drums I needed even to be heard. Snapshot was rather loud. It was the one thing they told me up front: I had to have mics because the whole band was run through the PA system which gave them a lot of control and a homogenized sound. This was still a rather advanced technique for the time. Most bands didn't own fifteen microphones and a mixing board and loop their guitar amps back through the system. A lot of bands didn't even have PA monitors. At least not in Oklahoma in 1971. In this band I had two large floor monitors, one on each side. Everyone did. Snapshot sounded great, in large part because they always had a great mix. The band had a sound guy named Arthur, first sound guy I ever met, half Apache with long hair and a big nose, who had been with them two years and was a full paid member of the band. Arthur was a complete flake in eighty different ways but he did know how to mix sound. During the gig he was always welded to the mixing board, wearing headphones, fiddling all the time. And from what I heard of the drums back through the monitors, he had a plenty sweet ear.

| | |

The band was rife with politics. From the first practice to the first gig to every time two or more of us were together, there was politics. Somebody always complaining about something, and implicating somebody else, most usually Steve. I quickly learned that a certain inbreeding occurs in successful bands that is different from every other band. In a successful band, everyone *needs* it, no one wants to lose this thing called Snapshot. Snapshot was bigger than any of us, even Steve, and everyone knew this. On the other hand, being trapped in a band with an idiot is no fun either and Steve was the idiot who kept everyone stirred up.

But I was the new guy and laid low. I didn't comment on Steve one way or the other. I studied my parts, wore the appropriate bellbottoms and such to the gigs, smiled a lot and tried to stay out of the way, dealing mostly with Curly whenever possible.

This political bullshit was the background noise between the notes, behind the notes, surrounding the notes we played. It was what we in the band heard, and had to ignore, the whole time we rehearsed and played and got better, working some really nice gigs along the way. One of the things I purely loved about the band was the size crowds we played for. These boys had worked themselves to the top of the regional food chain and we played some huge dances. One place in Wichita Falls *seated* 2200, and easily packed another 500 inside standing. There is a qualitative difference in playing drums for a crowd of 50 or 75 dancers in some ordinary bar, and playing for 700 or 800 dancers, all moving in sync with each note I played.

This was a thrill I got used to quickly. I had four major drum breaks during the course of the night's show, scattered amongst fifty songs, and if the dancers numbered over 600 I witnessed an amplification of my playing that went way beyond the mics and the sound system. It was something much more than just me playing a beat and them dancing—it was instinctual and primitive and, to me, totally unexpected. Like tossing a rock into the sea, and having it tossed back.

I discovered crowds that size have an animal presence. I could feel it look at me, feel the eyes on my skin. My every movement acquired 360 degrees of meaning, seen in ways I couldn't even imagine. A very large crowd, with hundreds of points of view, paying exclusive attention to me, was like stepping into a magnetic zone where all the little hairs would levitate off my arms. To play some tricky beat and hear it thunder out over this pulsating beast throbbing up and down, and to fancy it up and see the throbbing mob surge and change step along with me, was both awesome and scary. Scary because every now and then during such moments of dancing frenzy I'd realize there was nothing holding the whole room up but a synapse firing in the back of my head, and if the pilot light were to go out all of a sudden I'd drift on the beat and the groove would be lost and a creeping chaos come over a large number of people. That is truly scary and is the one thing no drummer should ever think about during those moments while dancing with the giant. Self-awareness is death to a drummer. Everything's an act of faith but my faith was still growing, one piece at a time.

| | |

It was August and we were playing outdoors at some daylong festival in the country. There were three other bands before us but I didn't get to hear them because we were so busy setting up. Everything about Snapshot was a big production and we'd rented extra equipment for the show, all of which took hours to assemble and test.

Woodstock had happened the year before and the film had reached Oklahoma. Naturally, someone came up with the idea of renting a farm pasture and getting a few bands and selling tickets and T-shirts. Paying out as little as possible and seeing what they could make. The headliner was somebody like B.J. Thomas. We were the fourth band of the day and were scheduled to start at six and play until eight.

Then the schedule got thrown back an hour and a half because—as part of the gala event—four hang gliders jumped off a bluff at the back of the audience and were supposed to soar over the heads of people and land in tandem on one of the two stages. Three of the four hang gliders did land on the stage, but one guy somehow caught a bad wind, veered way off to the side and collided with the power line, snapping it like a string and leaving both stages completely dark. And then he landed in the crowd. The promoter told us there were about 4000 people there and I supposed that poor old hang glider dragging his broken kite probably had to walk past most of them. I'm surprised he got out alive.

When the juice was finally back on and the band before us started again, rain clouds began moving in. This made the crowd delirious, as if the rain were a scheduled event. For the band, though, it posed problems. Particularly if you were putting your lips on a microphone. Water and electricity being old enemies, we were hesitant about playing during a rainstorm even though there was a canopy overhead.

And besides, in Oklahoma they don't have these little drizzles where lightning might flash once a week. Your ordinary Oklahoma thunderstorm is typically measured by how many barns are blown over. Silos snap like twigs and tornadoes are not unknown. When somebody in Oklahoma gets excited about the weather you can expect that the National Guard have already been notified.

We were hoping it might be a quick little thunder burst that would pass quickly. Maybe a one- or two-barner, something light and easily ignored. No one could tell when it would arrive, but as we got ready to start, the clouds kept rolling closer and the sun finally set.

We were set up on a stage about eight feet high under a thin blue plastic canopy. Occasional wind gusts would lift the edges. The air smelled like rain and marijuana and beer. None of us wanted to think about how bad this little gig could get if the weather turned real ugly. In front of the stage it was already so crowded people were shoulder to shoulder and couldn't move. Two cattle gates, chained together, ten feet in front of the bandstand, held the mob back far enough so we could breathe, and so no one could grab your ankle and break your neck. It was a dangerously tight-packed mass of humanity, mostly male, mostly drunk. Three or four fights broke out even as we watched, like bubbles popping on a vat of boiling oil, still few and far between. From the stage, looking over all the heads, I could see the beer stands on the far side of the crowd and the trucks behind them rolling new kegs of beer out to the troops. I wasn't sure what to expect, but I was probably the only one. Steve, Curly and the bunch had all made up their minds this was already the gig from hell and wanted it over with quickly.

The closer it got to nine-thirty the stronger the wind began blowing. Big drops the size of hen's eggs started crashing into the canopy surface up above, creating ripples in every direction. Steve's hair was mussed and his mood fairly foul. The promoter brought a lot of folded plastic tarps up on stage and stacked them around in case they were needed. I went ahead and covered my drums. People in the crowd started yelling at us to start playing but we just stood there, talking to the promoter, looking at the clouds and waiting to see what might happen.

Then it looked like it wasn't going to rain and the storm clouds might blow over, so the promoter told us to go ahead and start. I pulled the tarps off my drums and halfway through our first song the storm broke. It hit like one of those tidal waves that wipe out Tokyo occasionally. Bang, and we were wet. Then there was that frozen moment when no one breathed, followed by Steve, Curly, Bobby and DJ—as one—making a wild dive for their power switches. I just sat there dripping a minute, then used my towel to push the snare mic away to a safe distance, careful not to touch any of the lights on the floor around me, hanging on to my optimism. Only then did we drag the tarps back out and cover the wet instruments.

We had to wait for the worst of the storm to blow over before we could start drying stuff off and turn the power back on. Meanwhile the crowd stood before us out in the open, pelted 9000 times a minute, looking real glum. Steve used this time to somehow blame Curly for booking a gig when it was going to rain, saying he should've known better. Curly didn't respond. We all stood there looking out onto the same giant mess in front of us and felt despair. Four thousand totally drenched, half-naked drunks being hammered by giant rain drops, murmuring occasionally and growling. Lightning started flashing overhead and the wind picked up again. During the heaviest part of the rain it became fairly quiet. Stewing in bad feelings, not talking to each other, we just wanted to finish this thing and go home.

Then the rain finally broke and the crowd started yelling again and we began drying things off. As part of the cheapness of the event, each band had to bring their own PA and Steve told everyone he believed his speakers had been ruined. We talked about whether or not to risk electrocution. It hasn't happened to me, but I've seen what happens when someone puts their lips to 600 watts of charged microphone: small blue lightning bolts shoot from mic to tongue. This is the one thing all singers hate the worst. Regardless of how bravo they are in other areas, checking their mic for a ground after it's been wet turned even Steve into a mincing fool as he tried to touch it and not touch it at the same time, hopping from foot to foot, hoping and praying he wouldn't die from a heart seizure in front of a big crowd. Even after they decided the ground was okay, Curly went out to the truck and got rubber floor mats to stand on.

This gig already had more hassles to it than any five we'd played so far. We had a real bad mood going. Steve was grumbling out loud about whether we'd be able to get the truck out of this mud afterward. I could have packed up and left right then. My attitude was equal parts "I don't give a damn," "Fuck 'em," and "It makes no difference anyway."

But a certain depth of desperation and pissed offness leads to feeling liberated. I don't think it mattered to any of us that we sounded good. Not at first. I think actually we were playing with a little vengeance. We were pissed off enough to treat the gig as the piece of shit it had turned out to be, and not feel guilty in the least. It was a no-fault situation. Screw up all you want; it would make no difference here.

But it was more than that. After the storm blew through and left behind a light steady sprinkling, the wind stopped and a fog descended over everything, creating a swampy tropical ambiance, good for voodoo. Insects swirled in the halos given off by our colored lights. On stage it was like we had a smoke machine going. All quite eerie. I was sitting inside a yellow glow populated with flying gnats. The mood of the crowd had changed as well. After all 4000 of them took a half dozen steps in each direction, the field was turned into ankle-deep mud. Once we started playing again and people tried to dance, the mud started splashing around and getting on people's faces. More beer trucks pulled up on the horizon and the crowd seemed to lose a bit more of its collective mind, dancing in place and hooting and hollering and waving their cups in the air with renewed energy. The light rain kept falling.

On about the fifth or sixth song Steve reverted to his preteen self and got down on his knees and started dancing, waving his arms left and right. Probably out of a purely bad mood, he was growling into the microphone and twisting his body every which way and singing the hottest lead I'd heard from him. The whole band was surging and suddenly everybody was taking chances. I tricked up my beats something awful, slowing down tunes like "Born in Chicago," letting all the nastiness I felt merge with Steve's and turning that song into an exorcism of sorts, unaware of the effect we were having on a half-pissed, delirious crowd.

It was along in here that two young ladies looking very much like college students on a lark came out from behind the bandstand dressed in the extra-small variety of bikini and started doing a provocative dance for all the young males on the other side of the cattle gates, three feet away. Curly smiled and called "Pretty Woman" and I started it off.

After a couple of verses, the mud churned up under them and the two girls seemed to drop into almost a Pentecostal trance. This was jungle dancing, crazy dancing, go-nuts-in-the-mud dancing. Being wet and filthy and a few feet away from fifty hands reaching out toward them, the two girls became unbuckled; each seemed to turn a personal corner.

We segued into "Land of 1000 Dances." One of the girls reached behind and undid her top, starting a slow striptease that ended with her twirling it overhead. The other girl followed suit and by the time we got to my big drum break there was a wall of red male faces straining in a serious way over the cattle gates, reaching as far as their bones would allow, clawing at the air and screeching obscenities. The chains were all stretched tight. It was then the girls started dancing up to the fluttering hands and then backing away, almost getting touched but not quite.

We segued straight into "Mony Mony" and the next time I looked over one of the girls was waving her panties, naked as a robin. I could hear the crowd even over the music. It was a low, animal sound that seemed to last a long time. Girl two took off her bottoms and we bridged into the chorus.

They started dancing right up into the fingertips, heads thrown back, hair dripping, the beat pounding, holding themselves there for eternal instants while the local males nearly killed each other for a place at the front line.

The last thing I remember before going into the drum solo was looking through the gnats and glancing at the chains holding the gates together, then over to the girl's naked butt and the mud flecks all over it. Then it was as if I fell backwards ten centuries and everything got deeply primal. This complicated, thundering beat I was playing transformed into something more terrifically simple than I'd ever felt before. All the left hand, right hand maneuvers disappeared even though the sticks were still fanning both sides of my face. Regardless of how I tricked it up, it became like a pulse again, a simple heartbeat at that perfect tempo where it played itself. I relaxed and let it happen. I found myself riding on that outside rim of the beat to where it seemed to breathe, and I pushed it, aggravated it, like picking at a sore.

I made no decisions at all and yet each decision was perfect. Even my body was invisible to me, weightless and effortless. All I really felt were the sticks and pedals—each with the perfect heft and balance—my heads a perfect bounce. It just felt *good*. It even felt inescapable. Fuckup-proof, like whacking a hammer on the floor. I looked at the two dancers and they'd both gone into a spasm.

I'd never seen anything like this before. Or *felt* anything like it. The crowd was roaring at me and the two girls were caught up in wild, jerking, obscene movements coming off every part of their bodies. Both of them looked badly in heat and near the point of foaming, dancing buck-naked in the rain with mud squirting out from under their feet, mud they'd scoop up in their hands and rub over themselves, letting the rain wash it away.

Then girl number two got up a little too close to the cattle gates and someone caught her by the wrist and she was lost in a wild fluttering of hands. Just like a little fish being swallowed by a large sea plant, she only had time for a last bright look in her eye, and then gulp, she was gone. After a moment she reemerged being passed overhead from one side of the crowd to the other, rolling and reaching and not able to grab hold of anything, suspended on an endless supply of ever-changing, groping hands. A beautiful girl really, she had kind of a lost look in her eyes, but impossible to read. Drunk as she was, it might've been her version of hog heaven. Or hog hell. I couldn't tell. They didn't set her down until we stopped the song; only then did I recognize the connection between the music we'd been making and the scene we'd been witnessing. They set her down in the middle of the crowd and she didn't make it out for several more minutes.

"Boy, these rednecks know how to party, don't they?" Steve's eyes were lit up. It had been our best night since I'd joined up.

In the Belly of the Beat

In the weeks that followed I discovered something was happening to my drumming. It *seemed* to have slowed down without changing tempo at all. But I couldn't be sure. Was I just hearing it this way, or was it really happening? And what was the difference? I felt like a fly discovering my first window pane; I was utterly perplexed.

After the mud festival gig I thought about it for days—and I mean *really* thought about it. There's nothing like a legitimate experience to perk me right up. They're so few and far between I can measure my life by them. Yet I could feel the sea change. I could feel it when I was driving the car and tapping along with tunes, and I could feel it at home when I practiced, but I had no easy way of explaining this difference to myself. I could only describe it as the "Ted Williams Effect." Williams said that while he was standing at bat waiting for the ball to reach him, his focus was so clear that the ball seemed to slow down and that even the individual stitchings became visible. I think the first time I heard this story I assumed Williams was drunk and just talking. Baseball tends to turn people into poets and Ted was taking his turn. Later I discovered everyone believed him, that Ted Williams was a model of rectitude and if he said so-and-so it was true. That only left me to assume that he was some kind of wizard who could see things others couldn't, and that this gift must've been with him since the cradle when he first saw his mother's porous face move in slow motion above him. So fancy my surprise when I realized the same sort of thing was happening to me, at age twenty. All the stitchings came out in the tunes—or at least a lot of them did. Instead of rushing to do things, I was waiting for them to come to me, watching and waiting, studying the seams.

I think my concept of tempo changed. I mean, I wouldn't have thought it could—tempo being something that's just there, like a metronome—but I suddenly started thinking of tempo in a new and different way, not in terms of how 'fast' but how 'slow' it was. I'd had this thought in mind for several days when one afternoon I was driving my car out on the interstate and it hit me that there were at least two different ways you could drive 60 MPH: you could drive 60 in a rusted out, flapping-in-the-wind, straining piece of rattletrap junk that will barely do it; or you could drive 60 in a Cadillac that's capable of doing 120. Sixty MPH is radically different in each situation. Both speedometers are accurate but describe different realities. It came to me then that for every moment of my young playing life, at some basic reptile level, I'd always been straining. My basic approach to life up to this point had been a rush-to-meet-it proposition, a white knuckle experience. Tense, anxious, always wanting to get it right. But now, at some level I didn't even know existed, I started to relax.

This was one of those world-altering notions that—once it's made—begins to find evidence everywhere. I became more patient at stoplights. In checkout lines I found interesting faces to study instead of frying the clerk over a low flame. Even little children started to be amusing. Suddenly I felt like I'd moved out to the center of the river and caught the main current. I wasn't paddling as hard and began to breathe more deeply. I'd discovered the back side of the backbeat.

Naturally, I pulled out some tapes and listened to different drummers from all different periods. And lo and behold, what did I find? I found young drummers going like a buzz saw and straining every muscle to drive the song, and I heard older drummers from every time slot floating back deep in the pocket, almost being pulled along by the tune. Punchy as hell, particularly the blues drummers, but more casual about it somehow. Instead of acting, they were reacting. The older they were, the more relaxed their playing.

I don't know how this could've escaped me up until now. Rock'n'roll had matured and it took my personally struggling to find a groove to bring this fact home. I'd been at odds with myself, trying to play drums with all my old attitudes intact, my old buzz saw enthusiasm, when my instincts had started to develop in another direction and I was hearing something entirely different. From that moment on I noticed every older drummer I saw or heard and each one of them had this large, spare, utterly confident sense of time that struck me as totally mature and endlessly refined. At its very best, it seemed to me simply as a big lazy left hand. That totally independent "in the pocket" articulation that lifts the whole song. I listened to people like Little Feat's Richie Hayward and was amazed at how much punch he got out of beats that, at bottom, were so relaxed and even swinging. His backbeat can back up so much it's like a caboose being dragged on a twenty-foot chain—it seems to come that late.

That relaxed, punchy sound began to fascinate me and I worked it into every tune I could, trying to invigorate it and make it personal. I was not playing *at* it anymore. I became more impressionistic in my fills and beats, much more relaxed even in my most frenzied moments. This made me extremely steady. My sense of phrasing became more articulate. I began playing the songs *my* way, on the back side of the beat. Before, I'd let Steve or Curly or Bobby count off the tunes because they sang them; now I began counting them off so they'd feel right to *me*, grounding all of them on some kind of root beat I could feel beforehand. And there were no complaints. In fact, after a few gigs the whole band seemed to relax and lounge back in the tunes more. Steve commented on how "solid" the beat was and Curly said, "Whatever it is you're taking, keep on taking it."

The effect on our songs was to give a ricochet quality to hooks and fills, everyone sneaking up on the beat and then playing fat and slow. We sounded twice as lively and twice as professional. Our songs were littered with big clean articulate holes now, everyone phrasing exactly the same way. Even T-shirt sales took off. I take credit for all this. The band started to surge, getting better than before. We started raking in the cash. We were even getting a little more notorious. The last piece had fallen in place: me.

|||

I had to have something to believe in and at the time it was rock'n'roll. The whole country was in a spasm over Vietnam and Oklahoma in particular, especially my corner of it, was twisted in a tight knot. I saw fights in bars over the subject. "Love it or leave it," seemed to be the question everyone had to answer. Added to this, there were still many people who considered rock'n'roll music to be suspect and perhaps treasonous during times of war. As a long-haired person in a redneck town, I didn't usually talk about politics or rock'n'roll unless I knew a person well, or was pinned up against the wall, which happened more than once. One discussion in the music store between me and an older jazz drummer named Don turned into an argument where he was raking the Beatles over the coals and insisting that Ringo was an idiot, while my position was that Mr. Starr was the absolute perfect drummer for the Beatles and any sane person would marvel at his eloquent simplicity, and try to copy it. But that was the tempo of the times.

The more divisive people become over issues, the more entrenched they become, and I lived in a bunker forty feet underground—sitting down there with Curly and DJ and sometimes Bobby on those afternoons when we didn't have practice or classes, smoking joints and drinking beer and listening to records and coming up with little tunes and making big plans. Like all such dream sessions, there was a purity to our discussion. "The strength of your convictions" was a phrase we used frequently, as was "Practice makes perfect." Each of us really talking to himself. We told stories, mostly stories we'd heard from someone else, about funny things at gigs, or what someone had said, or about the prowess of Jimi Hendrix or Charlie Parker or so-in-so in Dallas. A lot of myths were ginned up at those dream sessions; we made plans for ourselves. I could see a succession of better bands in front of me, I could even see Snapshot getting a break and me on the cover of *Rolling Stone*, until I saw Steve's face in the picture and it all fell back to reality. More than anything, what we all wanted was to go on the road and live the life. No one stood higher in our localized vision than the occasional musician who came through town in a crackerjack band, touring all over the country, already having been everywhere and going round for the second time. *That* was accessible to each of us and was the immediate goal we each made our plans around. Meantime, the consensus was, we'd just make do with Snapshot until something else opened up. I think we got fairly smug there for a while. Couple of months, maybe.

The Damn Breaks

According to everyone at the time, the band broke up the night we played Max's Lounge. My view, of course, is that the band started to break up even before I got with them, but nobody knew or even suspected it at the time. I joined and there was a surge of energy for a while and then all the old problems resurfaced again and things proceeded back along the path they were following before. My view is that most bands fall apart one tiny fissure at a time and are already on the verge of crumbling when things eventually become obvious enough for your typical musician to notice there's a problem. The night that everyone would point to when Snapshot broke up was only the night they finally had a fistfight and all the complaints came out into the open.

What actually happened was that the band died on its feet but kept on walking, a not uncommon occurrence. I didn't see it because I was totally enjoying myself. I loved playing with these guys. We worked gigs all that summer and fall and pulled some huge crowds of a thousand or more. I was making over a hundred dollars a job and starting to acquire a middle-class lifestyle playing once or twice a week. Had my own apartment. We were a sharp-sounding band, but only up on a big stage with all the lights turned on. That's what it took to get focused and playing together. We always sounded lame at practice in Bobby's garage, and this gave rise to some of the arguments. At gigs we had people yelling and in a frenzy and we would always get caught up in it and enjoy the huge response to what we played, even when we made mistakes and didn't always sound that good.

The band had been hijacked. The crowd had really taken over and our reasons for playing had somehow changed. All the energy for performing was coming from them, not us. We were too inexperienced to know that we'd replaced one kind of joy for another, and thought they were the same. We didn't realize the music had died on us because there were always forty or fifty faces right up at the edge of the lights yelling at everything we did. The night this truth came home for a visit was the night we played Max's Lounge, where the crowd factor was eliminated altogether for the first time in Snapshot's history.

|||

We booked the gig because Steve heard a couple of other bands had worked there and come away smiling. Steve was fiercely competitive and probably figured we would pull a larger crowd. Max's Lounge was an interesting place in that uninteresting way bars have. It was the hub of a tiny empire Max had created for himself. In those small towns in Oklahoma and Texas off the main routes, it's not unusual to find an occasional whale in a farm pond, and that was Max with his six little businesses all clustered together and all bearing the name "Max." There was Max's Chicken and BBQ, Max's Upstairs Apartments, Max's Used Cars, and a couple of others. His main business, Max's Lounge, occupied about a quarter of a city block and had a large ballroom in back.

Nothing was out of the ordinary when we arrived at six to unload at the back door. It was a Saturday night, Halloween in fact, and Max had promised a lot of publicity. We expected a reasonable night, making maybe $500 or more. We had a $200 minimum promised us if we didn't go over well but this band hadn't seen a crowd smaller than 400 people since I'd been with them.

We were set up and ready to go by 8:30 and were lounging around resting, sitting at a table off to the side of the bandstand, and Arthur the sound guy was once again telling some weak Indian joke I'd heard before. Being half Apache, he specialized in Indian jokes and knew probably a hundred or more. Indian humor, it's always seemed to me, is understated, gentle in spirit, forgiving of human faults, and entirely inappropriate in a band like this. Nobody ever laughed at Arthur's jokes because they didn't recognize the angle, but I did enjoy his deadpan delivery and sat watching him as he tried to keep the boys lively and in a good mood before the nine o'clock show. All this was routine.

What was unusual was that we were sitting in this large ballroom all by ourselves. The place was less than empty—it was vacant, filled with echoes. There we were in the back room, stuff all set up, stage lights on, amplifiers humming, looking at all those empty tables. It could've been a Wednesday morning instead of a Saturday night. Steve was slightly freaked. He'd ratted his hair for the occasion and now he was sitting at a table in an empty room out in Bumfuck, Texas and it was fifteen minutes before the show.

There wasn't a reason in the world to start but for fear that Max would dock our pay if we didn't. It's a dilemma bands sometimes face: if no one's there, why play? But then, if you aren't playing, people won't come in the door—so you start to an empty room. Curly was just taking care of business when he herded us all up on stage at 8:55. Steve didn't want to start at all. And was mad about it.

As Curly and Bobby clicked their standby switches, that *thunk* sound bounced off the far back wall. Not one person anywhere in sight but Arthur sitting at the mix board out in the middle. He grinned and waved at us. "Good luck," he said, in a soft voice we all heard.

Then three people walked in and we had to start. One of them was Max. They took a table near the back and sat watching us. Steve had lost his last excuse and we began the show.

In distress, we did what any band would do—we faked it. We only had one way of playing those tunes and that was our all-out, grandiose, arena-size show. Our opening tune, "Memphis," had only been played to cheering crowds since I'd learned it. That crowd noise had become part of the song in my mind. When we did this, they did that. We played the tune as a boogie shuffle, a little heavy on the boogie, and the beginning was always the same: Bobby's guitar intro, my drum fill, the band comes in, and the crowd cheers, in that order. Now it was like waving at someone who wasn't waving back. All those carefully choreographed moves Steve did with his hips to chord changes and while singing, seemed suddenly rather small and weak. And yet, it seemed we couldn't *not* do the show. A very awkward situation.

There was also a problem with the PA, as is frequently the case. The acoustics in the room were odd and we couldn't find a balance. While the mains out front were plenty loud, on stage the monitors seemed hardly on at all and what we heard were our actual sounds playing instead of the amplified, processed sound. Absent the 600 watts of highly filtered, multichannel, special effects control over his voice, Steve sounded a bit like a small dog with its foot in a trap. Bobby's guitar seemed incredibly thin, as was Curly's bass. And I could hear myself grunting.

Steve was wiggling around in front of me, doing his sex fiend in heat routine and I suddenly realized how big his feet were. It was that kind of set. Six more people came in and sat down, watching silently. We took a break five minutes early and everyone got a beer, no one talking.

The second set wasn't any better. We kept expecting the back doors to bust open and busloads of people to come through. Instead, one person got up to leave, reducing our crowd total to eight. Up on stage it was tic city. All the eye-rolling, knee-bending, head-snapping gestures we each used to dramatize the groove were in this situation desperate attempts to find it. Normally, musicians encourage themselves with tics and grimaces; it's a way of catching that slow, inside part of the moment. But the voodoo wasn't working. We began noticing each other in a curious way; glances became hooded and secretive, and this resulted by the end of the second set in all the tics dying out. Even Steve stopped dancing. By the last song we were all standing there like crash-test dummies, no one looking at anyone else, wondering what had happened to the band. We sounded like a cheap imitation of ourselves. Personally, I was *glad* the place was empty.

At the break Curly said he was going up to talk with Max. Steve and I took a walk out to the street. I was going outside anyway and we just seemed to both walk through the door together. He was feeling real depressed and I tried to perk him up.

I said, "Looks like things get started pretty late around here. Maybe it's stylish to miss the first couple of sets. Some places don't get going until eleven or so."

It was 11:05 and we were standing out on a sidewalk in the middle of a downtown that was at most two blocks long, and mostly owned by Max. Nine-tenths of the buildings were dark and their upper stories abandoned. Maybe ten cars were parked up and down the street. Nothing moved. All we could hear was the wind and the silence of the prairies. Steve said, "I don't think so."

"Well, it might be a Friday night town then," I lied, just making noise. "I suppose there were all kinds of people out here last night."

"Maybe not. I think we should have done the advertising ourselves. I also think we should've run ads in the paper. I don't trust Max's advertising. I didn't see any." Steve looked up and down the street, his new Afro catching the light from the street lamps. "I don't think anybody knows we're here."

It had such a plaintive sound to it. It was a terrible thing to see Steve depressed this badly. Steve's ego, which ran like an air raid siren most of the time, suddenly threw a bearing. I'd never seen him so down in the mouth. I'd run out of things to say.

About that time, Curly and Bobby and DJ came outside and Curly said, "I don't think Max is happy."

"Join the club," I said.

Steve could only wait, dreading to be told Max was letting us go or wasn't paying or some other humiliation.

Curly said, "Max says he did the advertising and that we aren't pulling a crowd."

"Horseshit," I said, the only one with no doubts.

Steve just hung his head.

"Max says if a crowd doesn't show soon we can quit early."

I could hear Steve breathing next to me.

"Max also says we should play more country."

"Lord!" I said. "Anything else?"

"Max says if no one comes in by midnight we might have to talk about the money."

"You mean our bone is in the toaster?"

"Yeah, something like that." Curly smiled. I could always count on Curly to smile.

| | |

Finally, about 11:30, a dozen people showed up all at once. Then around midnight another ten or so straggled in, giving the place a populated look. With upwards of thirty-five people in the room, we tried to go into high gear and energize the show once again, but all the extra effort just resulted in our overplaying, rushing the tunes, burying the backbeat under a lot of nervous energy. Steve went into his act again but he was depressed and it looked very fake. We stalled altogether. The songs became jokes and we were just banging them out to be over with it.

I guess the last thirty minutes of that last set was about the biggest embarrassment I experienced that particular year, and it was because it was so unexpected for that band. Stripped of our usual audience and fan club, I think we just felt naked. Worse than naked: like a corpse hung in a store window. We were an exhibit. It seemed we all realized about the same time that this band had just played one gig too many. All the heretofore invincible attitudes shriveled up and became childish again, our powerful and impressive sound system became a mere device, the clothes simply a costume. The scattered applause after some tunes seemed like salt thrown in our eyes. It was your classic Bad Gig—but that was all it took.

After the last song was finally killed and in its coffin, Curly left the stage to go talk with Max and find out about the money. I tried to tear down my stuff and pack but was consumed with a new and perverse desire to see this humiliation through to the end. I followed Curly up to the front bar where he was already talking to Max.

"Max, I'll tell you this: it's a first time for us too."

"I thought you said you had a following." Old Max was sitting in his usual spot on a stool in the middle of the bar. His barmaid stood opposite and across from him, quiet, ready to take any orders he might have. The only sound in the room came from the TV up by the ceiling behind her and Max was gazing in that direction, not even turning on his stool to talk to Curly. It was like stepping into stagnant water.

"We do. And I announced it at every gig starting weeks ago. All I can figure was they didn't want to drive this far. Are you sure your advertising was out?"

Max turned and eyeballed Curly for a minute. To be eyeballed by Max would be an intimidating experience for a younger musician. Max's eyes were yellow and covered over with large blood vessels, his three-pound, red, porous nose hanging in between, but Curly was grinning and looking sincere. Max croaked with his rusty voice, "Hell yes," like he was talking about the solidity of the earth. "I can't stay in business handing out cash to bands that don't pull me a crowd. I got one rule: a band makes me money or they don't work here."

This was fine with me, and I didn't notice Curly protesting the notion either. The last thing on my mind was booking another gig. What I couldn't figure was, where was Max's regular crowd? Did he have a regular crowd? And if not, was it our fault if he was running a failing business?

Curly said, "That's fair. You've heard us and if you don't want to book us again, that's fine. I just want you to know we tried to do everything we said we'd do."

Max seemed bored and glanced up at the TV for an instant, scum spreading back over the pond, then asked, as abstractly as possible, "What do you want from me?"

Curly has clear blue eyes and they tend to be very level and steady when it comes time to get paid. He didn't look away from Max for one second. If Max wasn't going to pay Curly, he'd have to look at him and say it. "Well, Max, I guess I expect you to pay us the guaranteed minimum we agreed on . . . $200."

Max turned on his stool and rolled one of his yellow eyes up and down Curly a couple of times, even taking a side glance at me. I wished I was holding a bat or looked more dangerous somehow.

"Look, Max," Curly said, shaking his head and feeling worthless. "I don't like it either. I know you lost money, but we did too. If you haven't got the $200, then pay us $150 and we'll call it even."

It was like Curly had stepped on Max's tail. The old man was negotiating now, cash had been mentioned, both ears popped open and his eyes acquired focus—which was even scarier. He cleared his throat.

"A hundred dollars, take it or leave it."

| | |

Steve just about pinched a small loaf when Curly told him. It was the final blow of the evening. When the subject of eating came up he agreed to go, something he didn't usually do. There wasn't much enthusiasm for the idea but somehow everyone said yes and after tearing down and loading we ended up at a pancake restaurant about twenty miles away. Ever the optimist, I thought maybe our bad experience had brought us closer together, and that eating after the gig and talking for a change would maybe set us in balance again. I drove to the pancake house actually thinking we'd have a good time. Tell some stories and jokes. Be a band. I worked on my jocular mood.

But Steve had shifted poles again during the twenty minutes it took him to drive to the pancake house and now acted like he didn't want to be there. Bobby seemed real bored, Curly anxious, DJ just spaced and not caring. Only Arthur looked slightly alert. We all sat at a circular booth, me right next to Steve, Curly across from us and next to Bobby, DJ and Arthur squeezed in the middle. When the waitress came up Steve's hair seemed to fascinate her for the longest time, and this deepened the gloom a bit more. We were all physically tired, soaked with sweat, smelling like cigarettes, hands stiff and shoulders sore, sipping water slowly and not saying anything except for Steve grumbling about Texas rednecks. So much for band spirit.

Then Steve had to get out to wash his hands so I had to get out as well. Then another ten minutes of mostly silent waiting, and the food arrived. Steve came back and I had to get out to let him in again.

We were all starved and were shoveling food when Steve said, "You know, I just don't understand it."

He looked around like he was expecting someone to pay attention. No one stopped eating and Arthur finally asked, "What's that?"

"I just can't understand people who go to the bathroom and then don't wash their hands."

Everyone at the table, with the exception of Steve, had dirty hands.

"I saw *three* guys in there walk out and not wash. My mother *always* taught me to wash my hands after taking a piss."

I thought, Your *mother*? What's this? Curly sat his biscuit down on the edge of the plate. Bobby stopped eating and took a sip of water. Steve had made the announcement with the same sort of finality he said everything else, then looked at Arthur like he was tossing the conversational ball.

"Well," Arthur said, chewing his eggs, "my mother taught me not to piss on my hands." This set Steve off; he thought Arthur had insulted his mother. It took Curly—who was as tired and depressed as everyone else—to tell Steve to cool it. I don't think Curly had ever directly told anyone in the band to do anything before, certainly not Steve, but he told him to lay off Arthur and it was a chilly moment. From that point, breaking up was a formality just waiting to happen.

We each paid our bill with cash from Max, just about breaking even for the night, then walked, mostly together, out to the parking lot and our cars. I remember Curly trying to be casual, tossing out some remark about practice, how we should get there early and check the monitors. He tacked on some reference to the upcoming gig we had in Wichita Falls. He was just talking, putting an easy feel on things, keeping the balance until everyone was safely in their cars.

Then Steve stopped cold and was looking at the asphalt, shaking his head. With considerable repetition and in his own loopy way, Steve began telling everybody that the band had just become too much work for him to do all by himself, that he couldn't carry us any longer. I glanced over at Curly just in time to see him get real still. Steve harrumphed a couple of times and told us he had a career to think about, an "image" to consider—as if the rest of us lived in trailers and slept on cardboard. The longer we stood there, the deeper he got into his complaints and the quieter everyone became. Steve made it clear he didn't want to take us to the big time with him, especially if it meant carrying us on his back. He was sorry but that's just the way it had to be.

I expected it would be Curly who would explode first, or maybe Bobby, because the two of them really carried the band in so many ways. But it was DJ—quiet DJ, who ninety percent of the time was like a plant on a table off to the side of any conversation and who never had a thing to say—who jumped into Steve's face in the worst kind of way. DJ used the sort of language I didn't think he knew. Sailor terms and gymnastic maneuvers were scattered through his diatribe. He told Steve that *we* had been carrying *him* and that Steve didn't even know enough music to pick his own keys. DJ told Steve his nose wasn't even out of the *water* when it came to music and that if he didn't have the luck to fall in with real musicians he'd be waiting tables somewhere. Steve seemed stunned, especially hearing this from DJ.

Then Bobby jumped in and it became a duo, the two of them trading off. Bobby brought the same sort of razor-edge precision to his remarks as he brought to his guitar playing. His personality really was of a single piece. Where DJ let loose with a burst of emotion and hurtful language, Bobby brought a scalpel and talked like a lawyer, using three years of evidence as proof of what a liability Steve had really been. There didn't seem to be a lot of Steve left after a couple of minutes of this.

Then Curly stepped in with probably the kindest thing said out in that parking lot: "You bought the bullshit, didn't you? Pure and simple, you believed all the bullshit and now you've made up your mind." It had a personal sound to it. Curly and Steve went back the furthest, knew each other the longest. They had founded the group, back when it was called Wonderfoam. Curly had been putting up with Steve longer than any of us and had tremendous authority on the subject. There was no vindictiveness in his voice, he delivered it cold, like a fact they both knew, a talk they'd had before. "So . . . if . . . that's what you're going to do . . ." Curly smiled. "Then . . . *fuck* . . . *off*."

That's when Steve took a swing at Curly. No one made a move to stop it and all Curly had to do was push Steve a little bit to make him jump back and start shuffling around and acting dangerous but not doing anything, his hair bobbing quite a bit and losing its shape. Bobby turned to get in the truck, talking over his shoulder to Steve, "You can come get your stuff any time." And suddenly it seemed Steve was getting fired. That's how confused everything got, how quickly the momentum shifted. Later, ten different versions of what happened would swirl around, but the ultimate truth was the decision to break up was mutual and damn near unanimous. More like a jailbreak than anything else. One person drops his load and everyone's bag hits the floor.

I, of course, was in deep denial. I thought we could still make it go. I wasn't ready to quit. These problems weren't insurmountable to me. Look at what we had built up; we couldn't let all that go to waste. And look at the cash, I pointed out to each of them in turn, that they would miss. No one seemed to care. I was deeply torn but everyone else was relieved.

After a lot of phone calls, Curly got everyone to agree to play out the rest of the contracted gigs—contracts with Curly's signature on them. Some of the jobs paid very well and we had great crowds at all of them, causing a couple of the boys to waver, but the band still fell apart. It wasn't the same after Max's. Once Steve had broken the link, the all-for-one mythology, it didn't come back together. During the three months it took to play out the contracts, the band never really sounded lively again. Instead of playing the tunes and finding any joy in them, those songs were just a series of triggers we pushed to get a rise out of the audience. Everyone on stage knew it. Making dancers delirious becomes dreary work after a while if that's all you're doing and hate the people you're doing it with. It was a mark of Bobby's and Curly's and DJ's musicality that they didn't want to stay in a band where the tunes had dried up.

The sad part is that when a band dies, a lot of songs die with it. Particularly a band like Snapshot that had some killer tunes. The particular way they're played, the ideas in them—all are gone. The proper combination of people is everything and these particular five would never come together again.

It turned out that Max hadn't paid his bills that month so the newspaper and radio had cut him off. That's why no one knew we were there. People came up to us at the next gig and asked why we didn't play at Max's after saying we would; they hadn't seen any advertising so thought we'd canceled. The whole evening was a fluke, but that's all it took to set things in motion.

I ended up at home sitting on my hands, waiting for the phone to ring. The guys in my old band, the Tectonics, wouldn't even return my calls. Stymied once again, I was ready for anything.

Stalled and Waiting

Snapshot had taken care of whatever ego deficiencies I might've had. I felt I could hold my head up with any number of rock'n'roll drummers in the eighteen to twenty-two age group living along my stretch of the Red River. I had a small reputation from Oklahoma City to Dallas. My playing wasn't astonishing, wasn't brilliant, I didn't do anything that would require a Zen master to untangle, but I was damn good. I had those fifty songs Snapshot did nailed and numbered. I felt like I could work with most any band at that point and was practicing daily to keep my chops up in my new apartment, bothering my new neighbors, waiting, working little gigs here and there.

Then my whole life turned around. The Selective Service held a lottery and I got a permanent number, 332, making me virtually immune to the draft and Vietnam. I put on the worst drunk of my whole young life that night. I celebrated until I puked and then fell asleep in it. The very apex of joy at that time.

After this euphoria, two months passed and I was still struggling along without a regular band, feeling unappreciated and invisible, hanging out in the student union, being cynical and talking philosophy, trying to plan my next move. Drifting mostly. Now that I was available and free to leave, I couldn't figure out why I couldn't get a break, or at least hook up with some kind of decent band. I had my name out all over the place.

I just wanted to *go* somewhere, I wanted a *change*. I had no taste for being a local hero anymore. Austin and Nashville and Chicago all seemed equally possible and yet I couldn't decide, as though I was caught in the overlap of three separate fields, suspended and unable to move, waiting to finish the semester.

Things were getting ugly inside my head and I was more than a little desperate, when, one Thursday afternoon, my phone rang and a husky, cigarette-breathing, alcohol-scarred voice asked me if I'd like to go to North Dakota for a week.

"And even if you don't want to go to North Dakota . . . do you wants to work tonight?" His band had just lost their drummer to some woman headed to Houston and they needed an instant replacement.

I paused half a second, my future finally spreading itself out in front of me. "Uh, sure," I said, and started myself on a chain of events that carried me over two hundred thousand bumpy, crooked miles.

‖ PART THREE:

LIVING THE LIFE

Busting Out

I joined what my mother called "a Negro band headed for parts unknown." I think in her mind, I'd signed up with a minstrel show. The look on her face is vivid to me still. She'd been warning me about this sort of thing for years.

I loaded my drums in the car and drove down to the club early. On the marquee out by the road the sign said,

THIS WEEK
FROM CHICAGO
RECORDING ARTISTS
"SALT & PEPPER"

I wished I had ten or fifteen of my friends in the car as I drove past that sign. Especially the blues players. I'd heard earlier that this band was in town and I'd actually planned to go hear them later that week. An authentic band from Chicago was a rarity. Chicago—to a blues player like myself—was like Mecca on Lake Michigan. And now, it had come to me. I drove around to the back and unloaded my stuff.

The club inside was dark as sin and I had to find the switch for the stagelights. It was a dismal place and one of the few in town I'd never worked. Only the bar area was lit, showing me three men leaning over their drinks and a bartender watching TV. Everyone ignored me. The band's equipment seemed a bit old and worn out—not quite the concert appearance I was used to—but worn out in a good sense, quality equipment that showed lots of road miles. There was a big wood Hammond B-3 organ with scrapes all over the legs and foot pedals and a dirty blanket thrown over the top. There was a wooden Leslie tone cabinet that looked like it had been dropped off a truck and dragged ten minutes. Their PA was a respectable but small club unit made by Custom and covered in "roll and tuck" upholstery, very popular a few years before. There was an old beat-up Fender 'Twin Reverb' guitar amp with stains on the grill cloth. An empty guitar stand, a wood bench behind the organ, two overfull ashtrays, a few empty glasses with cigarette butts in them, and three rickety-looking monitor speaker boxes down on the filthy red carpet. Not what I expected.

Saddest of all was the open empty spot where the drums had been. A musician can't look at an empty spot on stage and not sense the drama behind it. I mean, I was glad the guy was gone, but looking at that hole on stage was a bit like looking at Little Big Horn and knowing Custer had died there acting like a fool. Good riddance, maybe, but still sad.

I found out later his name was "Shuffling" Parnell and he had an old habit of running off with new women. Parnell had done this several times before but this time, he never came back.

I unfolded and unpacked and twisted and turned all the ninety different things a drummer has to go through to set up and finally had that hole filled. My drums looked good. It was no slouch of a set. The red sparkle had been a good choice. I'd added doodads and gimcracks here and there and everything had a nice complicated look to it.

| | |

The place was filling up about twenty minutes before start time when two guys walked in the door, one of them carrying a guitar case. I'd already gone out front to the lobby and looked at the band's poster. Besides the old drummer, it showed two younger guys, smiling, healthy looking, eager to please. The two men walking in the door both looked like gangsters, and I suspected the guitar case might have a submachine gun in it. They both wore skinny ties and black suits and pointy shoes, the very sort of smoky bar creatures I'd really not met until now. Very Chicago, I thought. We're surely going to play some blues tonight. The one with the guitar went straight to the bar while the other came up on stage.

"'M's Dennis . . . and leader. That over'm there's Vince."

I could barely understand him. It was the first time I ever heard a true, deep South Side accent. He sounded like Muddy Waters drunk. Turned out he sang exactly like he talked. It was a voice I'd been listening to for years, but had never had a conversation with.

"'Ad you here," he said, pulling the blanket off the organ, exposing two rows of keys and about eighty switches and knobs. He sat down behind it. I watched him as he went through his little ritual: he kicked off his shoes, fired up the Leslie tone cabinet (getting the horn in the top rotating by giving it a little push with his finger), started adjusting the settings on the organ, playing little riffs with his hands and touching the bass pedals with his socks, running through what seemed like a very old warm-up drill. He looked just like Count Basie. Same kind of round face and wide open eyes. I asked, "So where's the rest of the band?"

Dennis didn't even look up. What he said, translated, was, "We'll play all kinds of tunes . . . requests and such. You keep it simple and watch me for the breaks." He started fiddling again with his organ, ignoring me.

Not knowing what else to do, I sat down behind my drums and began to wait. I sat there tinkering around probably ten minutes before Vince, the guitar player, finally came up on stage. "Hey," he said, vaguely in my direction, not really looking at me, and then plugged in and started tuning. "Hey," I said. Vince stood there exhaling smoke through his nose and staring down at his guitar, squinting, twisting tuners and looking tired, like something off a tourist poster for Chicago.

Their two craggy faces under blue light with cigarette smoke curling around like vines, showed years and miles like an old tree shows bark. Everything about the band, from the speaker boxes to the eyes of Vince and Dennis, looked exhausted and old and somehow dusty. They were both in their mid forties, ancient to me. Working pros in the deepest sense of the term. This band was pared to essentials and built for travel. A real honest-to-God blues band.

Dennis turned up the stagelights to their brightest and immediately started smiling. There were probably twenty-five or thirty people sitting around us at tables. He turned back to me like I was his oldest friend and asked, in a different and serious voice, "We'll start with something quiet. You know 'Misty?' We'll do it in five."

Misty? I thought. I'm going on the road with a band that plays Misty? I was ready to play some big-time screaming blues, and they wanted to start with Misty. "Sure," I said. What I remembered of the song was that it was a simple slow ballad so I started counting slow, slowing myself down, getting prepared, wanting to make a good first impression.

Vince was finally ready to go, but not until he'd tuned every single string to his total satisfaction. He didn't look toward me at all and only vaguely in the direction of Dennis, almost as if he were standing up there all alone.

Dennis nodded and counted off the tune at twice the speed I expected and the two of them dropped into a shuffling, time-shifting jazzy thing that seemed to move in two directions at once while turning slow spirals. For me it was like walking into a discussion on particle physics. Where was the beat? I looked all over the place and found about nine possibilities. In the blink of an eye I started turning back into a tender larval drummer once again with no experience at all. Not just wet behind the ears, but steaming in the sun. Amateur night in the rhythm section. I was nervous enough without having to start off with a jazz tune I didn't know. Vince listened for about two seconds and then turned and stood looking in the other direction away from me, but Dennis started snapping his fingers down behind the organ, giving me the feel while he talked over the microphone.

"Hello, ladies and gentlemens. We're 'Salt & Pepper' from Chicago, Illinois." Down behind the organ he snapped harder, getting pissed off, but still smiling and talking. "We do re-quests. We'll do your favorites. We'll do any song written on the back of a twenty-dollar bill." Then he punched the air and glanced back at me, looking ugly. Only too late did I realize it was a joke and that there was supposed to be a rim shot or something. The tune was shifting underneath me like soft sand and I couldn't even get a clear idea where I was, much less listen to jokes and twirl my sticks. This was starting to feel a bit too much like vaudeville. "But right now we'd like to start with an old favorite . . . called 'Misty.' "

Dennis turned back to me and was almost chopping the air trying to coax me into the groove. I was playing some simple little beat, appropriate enough for a folk song perhaps, but woefully inadequate for the odd-time complex thing building around me. The song was actually in 5/2 but I couldn't figure this out. I tried various possibilities and got pretty close to the beat a couple of times near the end of the song, but only in time to play the last few chords and put an end on it.

Dennis and Vince probably exchanged a quick telepathic message and then Dennis called out a Jackie Wilson tune. I did much better with that because the beat was straighter and closer to what I knew. It took most of thirty minutes to get over the jitters enough to figure out the band sound and get my volume level right, something I should have done immediately. They sounded fat for a three piece: Dennis shuffling bass with his feet while playing double chords up above, and Vince's guitar modulating all over the place, filling in the holes and inserting spidery riffs. They both had wonderful voices and really sounded like a much larger band.

At first it seemed they did nothing that was on the radio, noth-ing I'd heard before. There was no set list I could look at. Every song came from a dusty archive in Dennis' head. And every tune had been highly personalized over the years so that it no longer resembled the original. Even their blues tunes had mutated so much the song titles didn't much apply. They had more little hooks and bumps and odd little 'dropped in the hole' accents than I'd ever heard a band play before. Over the course of the next few nights I began to recognize tiny pieces of songs from the Temptations and Platters and James Brown, but mostly I was swimming in the dark. They did lots of med-leys. I would've loved to just sit down and hear these guys with their *old* drummer.

Even the few blues tunes we played were less than inspired. I used my fanciest licks, played my most profound thoughts, dumped all my blues knowledge out on the table, and still felt like a pipsqueak.

They had to be desperate to take me. It was only months later—when I truly knew the material—that I realized how awful I'd made them sound that first night. They had years of detail work built up in those tunes, each one like a little doll house full of doodads, and I was a big slobbering dog with a strong tail. But, then, I was the only white drummer available who could go on the road, and they'd always had a white drummer. It was necessary for the name 'Salt & Pepper.'

I got through the next two nights mostly by fakery and playing soft through the parts I didn't know—which was most of them. I sus-pect Dennis was looking for another drummer right up until the last minute before we left town and was none too happy one o'clock Sunday morning when we finally tore down and loaded the van. Neither one of them had said half a dozen words to me.

Through subtle signals and various small gestures they made it clear that in this band I was just hired help and was expected to keep my mouth shut. Nobody asked my opinion on tunes, as I was accustomed. My views on loading equipment were ignored. If I thought a song sounded particularly good, and said so, I couldn't even get a grunt in return. I was a spare tire, stuck on only because I could hold air. But I *was* going on the road at last.

The Back of the Van

The van was an old blue Ford that leaned to one side. It looked like it had been used to run ammunition through Beirut for several years before being sold to some jungle outfit in Brazil and then finding its way up to Chicago where Dennis bought it cheap. Even in the dark it looked like a wreck.

It was 2:30 in the morning when we finally hit open country. Everyone was tired and quiet. The van made a variety of noises, but all of them repetitious. I soon fell asleep in the back and didn't wake up until we were passing over the Kansas border four hours later. The van had started bumping and jerking and acting like it had swallowed a rock. Everyone woke up, including Dennis, who was driving. After a few seconds the trouble passed and the van smoothed out again. Vince yawned and smacked his lips a couple of times and then lit a cigarette, greeting the new day.

"This rattletrap motherfuck van just gonna blow up, motherfucker. We's gonna hit a chug hole or something and there ain't going to be nothing but a cloud of rusty dust hanging in the air, and my ass'll be gone. Yours too if you don't get shit fixed." Vince turned around and looked over his shoulder at me. "Yours too, motherfuck. You feel safe in this piece of shit?" He turned back around, took a hit off his cigarette, and then spoke in tiny puffs of smoke, "Goddamn . . . worthless . . . tin can . . . trusting my life . . . rusted up junk you calls a bus . . . shit." Vince took another hit off his cigarette and glanced out the window as Dennis returned fire, "We're running now, ain't we? Is you feet warm enough, or should I turn up the heat for you?"

The whole thing had the feel of a gypsy caravan. The sun came up and the two in front quieted down and it seemed the country had never looked so pretty. The sun was extra bright in Kansas and the road was particularly smooth. The wheat in the fields reflected the sunshine and even the interior of the van was lit up. I propped myself next to the rear window and watched the road fall away, thinking about Robert Johnson and standing at the crossroads.

It occurred to me suddenly that no one knew me any more. Not the two in front, and certainly no one I was likely to meet in North Dakota. It seemed very liberating to me that my whole past life was now hundreds of miles away, that I could be anyone, call myself anything, and no one would know the difference. I could even take on a nickname. Maybe "Too Big" or "Pistol Pete," something like that, and invent a story for myself. I worked through a couple of scenarios before I dozed off again and soon was dreaming of cool stages and blues fans snapping cameras at me and tearing my clothes.

The second time I woke up that morning was less romantic. I had to take a leak *real* bad. I crawled over the equipment to the front of the van and in polite and reasonable terms asked Dennis if he'd pull over for a minute. Instead of stopping, Dennis sped up.

"Hey, Dennis," I said. "Got to pee back here. Pull over . . . please." Vince laughed and looked back out the window. Dennis got the van up to 60. "Hey!" I said. "Code red! We got to pull over! I think I'm starting to drip!"

Dennis shook his head and said, "You understand 'minimul speed?' I can't be driving a hundred mile an hour all day just to catch up cause you wants to be comfortable. Cross you leg."

I went into a mild panic and even threatened to piss out the window, but it had no effect on Dennis. I argued until I started to feel senile and then gave up. There was only a quarter of a tank of gas left and I would have to endure. I crawled back to my perch near the rear window and contemplated the miracle of Dennis' bladder. Apparently, years of conditioning had adjusted his and Vince's body functions to the duration of a tank of gas. The same sort of adaptation the camel probably went through eons ago. Living in the van had given them special abilities I did not yet have.

If there wasn't a stop sign or a light Dennis would zip through those little towns ten minutes apart, driving past fifteen gas stations. He was truly relentless. Dennis waited until we were running on vapor and then found a one-pump country store and pulled in for an Indy-style pit stop. I was out the back door like an escaped convict. I didn't even look for the restroom, heading instead for open ground.

Vince had a big grin for me when I returned, smiling with all eight or nine teeth in his head. He had these funny walleyes, the right eye slightly high and to the outside. It was hard to tell what he was looking at, but he was facing me so I listened. "Say man," he said. "Something you learn quick about Dennis. . . . Motherfuck don't have brain one. If I was you? I'd keep a empty Pepsi bottle back there. Just don't be spilling none on my amp."

I took his advice and bought the Pepsi and some chocolate donuts while Vince loaded up on cigarettes and Dennis bought a half quart cup of coffee. It was only nine in the morning but felt like high noon already. We'd been on the road six-and-a-half hours and—according to Dennis—had twenty-two more still to go.

As the morning unfolded I discovered the two in front weren't much as traveling companions. They never said a word. I wanted to find out about places they'd played and people they knew, wanted to hear some musician talk. Riding in a van is normally like being in a submarine; it's hard not to talk to people. Half a dozen times I tried to strike up conversations but couldn't seem to get anyone's full attention.

Each time I crawled to the front and said something, it was like they'd forgotten I was there and I was only interrupting their rest by speaking up, as though they each one had gone into a cocoon.

Hours clicked by and the sun had started falling. I realized things were not going to be as adventuresome as I'd expected that first day out. My neck was sore from my head bobbing up and down. My eyes were bleary and my back had cramped up. We passed through a lot of very small towns, towns with overly long street lights, local traffic that moved like tired glaciers down the road, empty store fronts, and people who started to wave and then dropped their hand. Nowhere did we stop long enough for a particularized impression. We blurred through Dodge City; I didn't see a thing. Same with Garden City and Oakley and McCook and North Platte. We drove through two complete rainstorms, one with daytime lightning. We visited several gas stations and ate out of grocery stores. The van filled up with pop cans and twinkie wrappers and cigarette smoke. Everyone smelled like old socks and my Pepsi bottle remained mostly full.

In the back, on top of the equipment, I had a little nest made out of coats and luggage and I sat there—despite my head-to-toe pain—hugely satisfied with myself, unwilling to change places with anybody. It was the idea that carried me. Most often it's the idea behind anything that creates the moment. Without an idea you just got a van and equipment and a couple of weird guys in front and a job you're driving to. This was different. After a gig we wouldn't go home but drive to some place else, and then some place else. An endless string of some place elses. Places I'd never heard of, one after another. The crucial thing about going on the road is that you go and *stay* on the road. It has to be open ended or you're missing the flavor.

After about eighteen hours I started noticing the bruises developing all over my body from various speaker cabinets and drum cases poking me, and found myself counting the nicks on my head from mic stands and duffel bags occasionally dropping down. The back of the van was like a frozen sea of sharp, pinching edges. I rearranged my nest ten times but it made no difference. The pinching became my main distraction later in the day. Two speaker boxes side by side, close enough in height to make a shelf, loosely packed and jiggling, moving just enough for me to settle into the crevasse, then the load would shift and I'd get a little bite. I would have to buy a blanket, or a mattress, make some kind of arrangement, if I was to survive months of this. There were only two seats in the van and Dennis and Vince would give up neither one.

Darkness fell and we were still going. Some time after eight that evening—after twenty-one continuous hours—we finally pulled in to a tiny town in Nebraska and stopped, stumbling out of the van like aliens from another world. I was numb from the waist down. I had to stand a few minutes leaning against the van, waiting for my blood to recirculate. We had our one and only sit-down, proper meal of the day. And it was in a cafe full of flies and rednecks.

I discovered greasy food tastes better if you're having an adventure. I ordered the meat loaf special with mashed potatoes, gravy over everything. Even our tired old waitress in a saggy T-shirt with soup stains across the front seemed somewhat exotic, if only because she was the first person I'd met from Nebraska. Vince and Dennis concentrated on choking down their meal and didn't look around as much as I did. Everyone looked at us but I was the only one looking back. Vince wore wraparound pimp sunglasses and kept a cigarette in one hand as he shoveled food with the other. They both wore their pointy shoes and still had on their gig clothes. I could see both sides.

What rest I managed to get that second night was in a series of groggy moments when I'd pass out briefly only to be awakened by something else. Really seemed I was waking up more than I was sleeping. In addition to all the bumps and dips and curves in the road, and the speaker boxes wiggling under me, every few hours there were the gas station bells and the bars of fluorescent light passing over my eyelids and then Dennis hitting the brakes too hard each time we pulled up to the pump, causing the load to pinch underneath me again. If I absolutely *had* to get up and crawl outside I would, but if things were bearable I'd stay down and try to preserve the moment, knowing I'd be awakened again soon enough.

| | |

About an hour before sunrise it felt like we hit a large deer or a stalled truck, a jolt big enough to scoot me eight inches toward the front. When I looked up, Dennis was weaving and bobbing and trying to straighten the van out, and Vince was leaning forward like he was trying to pull his forehead out of the dashboard.

"Wha's this?" I yelled, but no one answered. The van lurched and swayed and Dennis was gripping the steering wheel like it had come alive. Telephone poles flashed by on each side and I yelled again, "What's happening?!" We were the only thing on the highway so there was nothing to hit while Dennis fought to keep us out of the ditch. Finally we slowed and straightened out and then pulled off onto the gravel shoulder and Dennis shut down the motor.

Everything became oddly quiet and forlorn, the engine creaking and popping as it started to cool. I looked out the back window. I could see maybe seventy miles and there wasn't a single light anywhere.

"Where are we?" I asked.

"North Dakota," Dennis said.

"What'd we hit?"

"Nothing," Vince said, pissed off. "Idjit here won't pay a goddamn shade tree mechanic three dollars to crawl under the bus and fix the goddamn differential. Motherfucker's seized up again."

"Again?" I asked.

"Often enough," he said as he opened the door and got out.

Dennis was already laying on his back under the van. "We can fix it. Don't worry about a thing. Somebody find the flashlight so I can see what we got. Get the toolbox too."

I wasn't exactly sure what a differential was. Or what it did. Or where I might look if I had to find one in the dark. But it sounded important so I knew we wouldn't go far without it. Trying to help out in any way I could, I got on my back and slid under the van next to Dennis. He was shining the light on a large, round thing held together with bolts and covered with mud and oil. I tried not to sound completely ignorant.

"Hmm," I said. "That differential looks pretty used up to me. We going to get a new one?"

"Nope, just put some oil in it. Gasket leaking . . . a little. It'll be okay; should'a checked it back at the station. The level got a little low."

Vince was standing alongside the van and watering the grass, listening. "Level low? Don't lie to the white boy. Differential's bone dry or I'm pissing pure whiskey. It needs to be pulled and the gasket replaced, Dennis! I'll tell you . . . mother*fucker* . . . I'm tired of this shit. You need to spend some money so we won't be out here under the stars having this discussion no more. A person gets tired, Dennis. No bullshit. Stop messing around."

Dennis jerked himself out from under the van, snapping and growling, and started on a litany of Vince's latest offenses. I was beginning to realize that the dogfight was their preferred mode of conversation, that bands really only have one way of talking, and I didn't want to listen to it that early in the morning. I walked down through the ditch and up to the fence and had my first good look at North Dakota instead. Not much to see in the dark. Just six or seven square feet around me. A lot of grass. I didn't feel like exploring much. You have to be careful alongside a road at night. If I wandered too far I might come across the bones of the last band to break down around here— maybe some old swing band—and then I'd never get back to sleep. My sense of adventure was wearing off fast. I stood there three minutes until the yelling stopped and then returned to the van.

Eventually, Dennis poured into the differential a quart of oil that he drained out of the engine and we were on our way once again. But now the van didn't run the same. Something was wrong. We couldn't get up much speed and there was a new sound underneath. A grinding sound coming from the back end, directly under me. I think we all held our breath for the next few miles, and then got used to it and relaxed once again and soon enough I passed out for the fifteenth time that night.

It was 8:00 Monday morning, the sun high in the sky, when Dennis announced, as though speaking from the grave, "We's here."

Vince roused himself only long enough to glance around and then closed his eyes again. "Williston . . . goddamn . . . North Dakota." Vince smacked his lips a few times. "End of the road. Hope they don't have no blizzards for a while."

We were twenty-nine hours out of Oklahoma. Twelve hundred and sixty-four miles. Almost in Canada. I felt like I could sleep for a week but we were starting that night at nine. After one good look at the town and its citizens, I couldn't even imagine why we were there. Dennis drove us to a motel and I got a room to myself.

How can you tell if a bandstand is level?
The drummer drools out both sides of his mouth.

Those first six days in North Dakota were about as humiliating an experience as I care to live through again. We had no practices. My only instructions from Dennis were the occasional remarks on stage, something vague like, "Let's all come in *together* on this intro," or "Watch *me* for the breaks; not that waitress over there. She don't know the breaks."

I was off balance all week. During the day I'd wander aimlessly around the little farming town, finding nothing to do and little to look at, bored out of my mind. At night I'd wear myself out paying attention to Dennis, scrutinizing him for any little tick or casual gesture that might cue me in the song. Half the time he'd forget. The songs were so familiar and predictable to him he no longer heard the surprising shifts and dramatic turn-arounds that were sending me into the ditch time after time. Each morning I'd go by their room and ask, "Hey, anybody want to go to the club and run over some tunes?" And each time I got Vince rolling his head on the pillow, looking at me like I was a nine-foot lizard speaking Swahili, and Dennis laying on the other bed, staring at the TV, rumpled and lopsided looking, wearing his undershirt and shorts, mumbling, "No man. Not today. You doing okay." His voice reeked of insincerity. I figured they'd already called the agent to find another drummer, one who could play jazz and funk and symphonies and hard-core soul and all various fusions in between, and were just waiting for my replacement to arrive.

Our motel was on a corner four or five blocks from downtown. Usually by 11:00 or 12:00 I'd amble over and inspect the stores for a while, then kill an hour or so by sitting on a bench near the courthouse, watching the locals and speculating on why they all looked alike. Then I'd walk to the drugstore and buy a paper and take it with me into the

City Cafe. I could knock out three hours at a stretch in there reading all the little ads and local items. The waitress saw a lot of me that week. Young girl, kind of horsy-looking, with thick glasses and gray eyes, eager to please. But her spring was wound too tight and it showed. It took me a couple of days to get caught up in the cafe drama, see what was happening around me. It was the old woman in the kitchen, the one whispering all the time through the little window to the girl. It was her cafe but she stayed in the kitchen cooking, running everything by remote control through the girl. Once you could read the signs, you saw the old woman had the girl stampeded in a bad way. Considerable tension in that room. I'd eat and then read the paper for a while, glancing over the top of the page to watch the vicious whispering through the window grow in volume until it usually ended with the old woman hissing and the young girl scampering away. It got so I was leaving a big tip each time and feeling part of a conspiracy.

That was the high point of my week. Uncertainty at night, intrigue during the day. Until Thursday, that is. Thursday night something remarkable did occur.

We were in the second set, Dennis calling out obscure songs with familiar names and me scanning the two of them like radar, eyes wide open and sticks in hand, when a beet farmer came up to the stage. He leaned over Dennis' organ, said something confidential, and slapped down a twenty-dollar bill, a big grin on his face.

Dennis was smiling double wide himself and saying *yes* a lot, nodding his head and looking eager. But when the farmer returned to his table Dennis got pensive and started picking at keys on his organ, not playing anything, looking for a note. After a minute of this he instinctively turned to me and asked, "Man, I can't rem—" but then realized who he was talking to and instead called over to Vince, who had been looking the other way and paying no attention.

"Hey man," Dennis said. Vince didn't move but stood as he usually did, smoking, looking out over the room, waiting. "Hey man," Dennis called again. "Hey! Asshole! You awake?" Vince slowly rotated his head toward Dennis, giving him a cold stare. Vince could work up maybe the coldest expression I'd ever seen, like a snake or statue. Looking not so much *at* you as around you. Dennis asked him, "You know 'Drop in the Old Brown Bucket?'"

Vince glanced at Dennis and then looked away, shaking his head, thinking it must have been an academic question. "Hey man," Dennis called out again, "Do you know, 'A Drop in the Old Brown Bucket?!'" Vince looked at him again, wondering just how dumb a question Dennis was capable of asking, when Dennis held up the twenty-dollar bill.

Vince was nearly as cheap as Dennis and the sight of that U.S. currency gathered his attention. "A Drop in the Old Brown Bucket?!" Vince said, like it was a question he'd woke up with that morning. "A Drop in the Old . . . Brown . . . Buc-ket."

He lowered his head and wrinkled up his face. He turned his back on the audience and stepped closer to the wall. Lost in meditation, he began picking odd notes off his guitar, strumming chords, repeating the words to himself, trying to connect the two, stepping closer to the wall. "Old Brown Bucket. . . ." Then he'd hum a bit, screw up his face, shake his head that something was wrong, then fretting somewhere else, starting over.

I had no idea what I was looking at. If this had occurred six months or a year down the road I would've been much more alert and impressed, but coming in my first week with the band I just watched in mild irritation and wondered why we were spending so much time on this tune. I didn't see any harm in not knowing a song. Obviously. Vince stood over there lost to the world, grunting and chording and shaking his head for three or four minutes (about two months in stage time) before he hit on the right combination and the whole song seemed to appear to him. Then he was playing lots of changes and grinning, turning back toward the audience and then leaning toward Dennis. "Slow shuffle in C . . . two . . . three." He began singing an old country song about hard times on the farm and "turnips just ain't enough." He only did a couple of verses and then put an ending on it. A real cornball of a song. I couldn't imagine why the farmer would pay twenty dollars to resurrect the thing.

The old man was back up at the bandstand immediately. He broke down and admitted he was playing a trick on the band. Said he hardly even remembered the song himself. He said that he'd asked every band that came into town if they knew that song but no one ever did until Vince. He said it had been twenty years since he'd last heard that song from a living person and wanted us to know he thought we were great. Vince just smiled and thanked the farmer, said we'd be glad to do any other requests he might have, and sent him back to his chair mystified at our prowess.

I was so ignorant I sat there thinking all this excitement must be the result of sitting in a tractor for months at a time. Maybe beet farmers have a thing for old Depression-era songs that they sit out in the fields singing to themselves. I was perplexed and glad finally when the old man left and we could get on with the show. I didn't know, and had never encountered, that timeless old routine called "Stump the band." It was my first experience with that form of entertainment. And this time the farmer met his match. He had encountered, and I'd just seen evidence of, something probably neither one of us fully appreciated at that moment: Vince's photographic musical memory.

Vince didn't look like the photographic memory type and I was very slow to organize the facts as they came in. It started when we came down off the stage and Dennis asked Vince, "So, where'd you hear that song?"

Vince said, "You remember the first time we worked in Miami?"

Dennis nodded, "It was about '55, '56."

"Do you remember playing the Palmtree Club?"

Dennis had to think, "Isn't that where that white girl got stabbed?"

"Yeah. You remember that guy that came into the club after the third set that first night and told us Big Harold was playing across the street? Well, during the break we went over to hear him. And when we walked in the door? He was singing that song. Remember?"

Dennis had to smile. "Hell no, asshole. You just making shit up."

Which was what I thought as well. But then Dennis kept smiling and kidding around with Vince and acting real pleased with him. I couldn't tell what was bullshit and what was fact in this band. Maybe Vince just made the song up and the farmer believed him. Maybe he really remembered it. I didn't know, but the rest of the night I played looking at the back of his head, beginning to wonder what percentage of him might be bullshit and what part real.

I hung onto the job one day at a time but no replacement showed. At the end of the week we tore down and drove to Sterling, Colorado, only about 400 miles away. I heard Dennis in his room once on the phone, yelling about something, but I didn't hear my name mentioned. I finished that week marginally better on most tunes. We all started ending at the same time and that seemed to perk Dennis up. I started remembering some of the changes quick enough to play them and that too met with instant approval. Then I bought a small tape player and started recording us at night and listening during the day, memorizing the breaks and tempos, learning what to expect before it happened. That tape recorder was what really got me up to speed. By the end of the third week we were back up in North Dakota, in Bismarck, when Dennis began changing toward me and acting like I might hang around a while.

The Hedgehog and the Fox

With my three weeks of hard work, and the absence of any replacement drummers on the horizon, I settled into a tentative permanency in the band. I was still on probation and knew that one or two genuinely bad nights would've sealed my fate and set the agent's phone to ringing again, but I was learning the tunes and beginning to relax and settle in, and starting to get the dimensions of Vince and Dennis.

It was an unusual band in many ways, different from any group I'd seen before. They weren't a soul band, although they played the funkiest soul possible and their posters advertised them as such. They weren't a rock band even though they played every great '50s rock song written and a few of their own besides. No one would think to call them a country band, but they were capable of playing an entire night's worth of sizzling country and western music if that's what the crowd wanted. And I mean *lively* and *pure* sounding country. They weren't a supper club band, they were not a jazz band, they weren't a show band. They were a general-purpose utility band that played all those things. What the old timers would call a "working band." If there was a paying gig, Dennis and Vince could do it. Just tell them at the door what mood they were in that night and they'd immediately start humming Chuck Berry songs. Or Frank Sinatra. Or James Brown songs. Buck Owens. It didn't matter. I had to play all of that, like being in five bands at once. Dennis would laugh when he said they took requests, but he was deadly serious. Vince and Dennis had played together, on and off, for thirty years, backing up big names, cutting their own tunes and having some success, working all over the country. I believe they both started playing when they were babies. Between them they had sixty years' experience in five hundred different bands, had been in every state fifteen or twenty times, and had encountered every possible situation at least twice already. Including brand-new, twenty-year-old drummers.

I asked but was never given a total number on how many drummers they'd had. Some they had trouble remembering, "Hank? Whasa name . . . Harry? Shit, I don't know. Early '60s, I think . . . he was in San Francisco with us, I know that." Others were exceptional and made a lasting impression. "Oh man . . . that Sammy motherfucker? Jesus *fire!* He could play!"

It's a funny thing, but almost every time you get in a new band you think, "this is going to be the one." I'd experienced that optimism several times before but never with the certainty I felt it now. Every band prior to this seemed like child's play, including Snapshot. It wasn't that the band was perfect (no bass player) but that I was suddenly playing with musicians who were so polished and expressive. Really as good as I'd heard. I couldn't help but get better in a band like this.

Dennis didn't have a "style" of playing, he had "styles." Depending on the song, he'd take on the personality of the singer who recorded it. Dennis was a wonderful mimic. He'd be Wilson Pickett one minute, Elvis the next. He could come off a Bo Diddley tune, and two seconds later turn into a Mel Tormé ballroom crooner with that look of lost love all *over* his face. But I think his strongest suit was gospel. Any tune that had a hand clapping, churchy feel to it was a trip home for Dennis.

It didn't hurt that he played a Hammond B-3 organ, a huge wooden piece of furniture. It could actually shake dust off the rafters. I know of no other instrument, pound for pound, harder to move around. It had two keyboards with about sixty or eighty tabs and switches around the top. On the floor were two rows of bass pedals he danced on all night. He ran the sound through a Leslie tone cabinet, another piece of furniture about the size of dresser drawers that had a spinning horn in the top. And there was a wooden bench. I used to dread, with a deep and abiding chill, coming into a town and finding that the club was on the second or even third floor. It used to take all three of us most of forty-five minutes to negotiate one flight of stairs with that organ, one step at a time. Because I was the junior member in the band and had the youngest back, I was the one always *under* the organ pushing while those two were on top dragging, Vince cussing a blue streak and Dennis dripping dangerous sweat all down his body, grunting like a hog on the freeway. I wasn't the strongest person in the world, most of my muscles being drummer muscles, and my back was a switch that could flip off at any time, but if everyone sweated enough the organ would end up on stage eventually. A second-story gig would require a nap immediately after setting up.

Dennis was a dynamic bandleader. Big friendly wide-open eyes, round face, quick to smile, great with crowds, loved to hear himself talk, nine hundred jokes for every occasion. Just a whirlwind of activity. He would pull the microphone in and out while singing, adjust tabs and switches on the organ, rock back and forth, play chords or little doodling riffs with one or both hands, feet moving constantly over the bass pedals or reaching for the volume pedal. Sometimes he even played a trumpet he kept laying on top of the organ.

And like a lot of bandleaders he had this imperial personality on stage. At first, when he'd punch the air or make grand gestures, I thought he was just showing me where to accent the songs, but even after I'd learned these accents he continued punching or waving or grabbing and I realized this was part of the show. He liked to gesture as though he were conducting. Not actual cues, necessarily—which would come *before* you had to do a thing—but more dramatic "point and fire" gestures. There were jokes I had to know the punch lines to, kicks and accents and certain little bumps he and I did together. And if I missed one—as I was in the habit of doing—then he'd shoot me an ugly look and sometimes make a fist.

There were other hand gestures that I had to know. Thumbs up meant we were headed for the ending, "V" for victory meant a double ending, making circles with his forefinger meant repeat the turn-around, and twenty other little signals.

Dynamics in that band were something fierce. In some tunes he gave me the palm up or palm down gesture so continually I'd forget which direction I was heading. He wanted to raise and lower my volume just like I was a big radio with a knob on the front. I didn't mind the hand signals, and in fact appreciated them when they were helpful. But after a while, I started to feel like a puppet on strings; the more he'd jerk me around the more tangled I'd get.

Every time I didn't jump like Pinocchio, Dennis would start simmering and steaming and looking all hunched up. Then he started throwing quarters at me during songs. We were in Missoula, halfway through our "Blizzard Tour," working some roadhouse, in the middle of a song that had this giant, one-note accent I was supposed to really hammer. Dennis had given me the strong arm, clenched fist signal which meant "come alive and kill something," and I knew where the accent was supposed to be because I'd already missed it twice that week. But, once again, I didn't get positioned right and my cymbal crash sounded weak and my right foot slipped some off the bass drum pedal so there wasn't much of a punch there. I'd no sooner missed the accent than Dennis grabbed in his pants pocket and slung a quarter backwards over his shoulder and straight at my head. I had to dodge it to keep from being blinded. And this was still in the middle of a song. I was a little shaken and played with a tentative beat for the next few bars. As soon as the last note was played, Dennis spun around on his bench and yelled, "Hit louder, motherfucker! What I have to do? *Pay* you to hit the damn thing?!"

Vince was grinning and looking away. Half the room was gazing and smiling. I felt like a total fool. I couldn't think of anything to say. "Oh . . . you want it louder?" I said. Vince snorted and Dennis got big eyes and came close to getting off that bench.

I tried to keep these moments to a minimum and not push Dennis past his breaking point. Still, some nights there might be two dollars in quarters laying on the carpet behind the drums.

| | |

Vince, on the other hand, turned out to be easy to get along with. Once he was up and dressed and out of his room, he was actually kind of friendly. He was a real late riser and usually wouldn't see sunshine until three or four in the afternoon, but in the early evening he'd want a regular meal instead of eating out of cans heated over a hot plate, which was Dennis' main form of sustenance. Vince and I would find a cafe. I think he liked going with me because he got better service. Having a white boy along had several advantages, especially if you were a rough-looking, black, South Side Chicago musician with crooked eyes buying food in Montana. If his meal wasn't cooked the way he liked—and it usually wasn't—we'd switch plates and I'd call the waitress over to complain. That way when she'd ask him, "Your food okay?" he could always nod and say, "Oh, everything's fine here. Thank you," and give her a sinister smile. That way, he said, he didn't have to worry about glass or hair in his food for "being uppity." Vince didn't mix politics with his food. He wanted everything tasty and clean. We'd sit there and I'd steal bites off my plate sitting in front of him until the waitress returned and was gone again and we could switch plates once more. It was a damn nuisance for me but he seemed to prefer it. And in return he'd tell me stories.

You only had to ask Vince a single question to set him off down one trail or another. Even the most casual remark seemed to remind him of something else. Like, "Hey, Vince. Did you hear that hammering across the street this morning?"

He'd get a bright look on his face, chewing his food, just like he loved the sound of hammering. "I knew this sorry sombitch in Chicago? Name Leo? He used to come around and see my sisters. Only nigger I ever knew had lots of tattoos. *That* tell you something about him right there. He handled petty-ante shit, like car stereos, fancy chrome wheels, back when I knew him, till he got married to a girl named Louise. Next thing I heard the fool had him a job in construction, handling dynamite." Vince cocked one eye straight at me, full of significance. "He had to be out there first thing every morning, prepare shit and lay it out . . . stuff like that; make they coffee and sort the dynamite sticks they going to blow up that day." Vince reached for the ketchup and drowned his french fries, chewing a little bit longer. "One morning, Leo shows up and it cold as a bitch, everything frozen and iced over, and he discovers he done left the dynamite outside all night. So Leo, being a natural genius . . . " and off Vince would go in some unconnected direction while I ate my meal and listened with close attention.

I was young and Vince had me in his sights. He hadn't known anyone dull. He knew only fascinating people who, if I let him talk long enough, would usually turn up dead, each murdered in grisly fashion. Or blown up. Even the blandest person he met he dressed in bright colors. He'd get to know barmaids—sad looking old women— who later, he would claim, had told him their life stories, and then he'd spin out some wildcat tale that was just too amazing not to be believed, causing me to squirt milk through my nose half the time. I realized that's what made him a blues personality. Singing the blues is about turning pain into poetry. His stories were usually set in bars and prisons and dark alleys and were always about the worst types of sin and suffering he'd seen, but once he opened his mouth everything took on a brighter light and became attractive to me. For a while, I actually envied him some of the misery he'd gone through.

Whereas Dennis mimicked many styles, Vince had one big style. Vince's voice did not sound like anyone's but his own, a smoky, gravelly, urgent voice. He didn't try to imitate others, and didn't care to. He would sing their songs but he always made those songs his own. It was personal. Listening to Vince stuck with you. One of the great questions in my mind early on was why he wasn't famous. Like many special musicians, he radiated a sense that he had more destiny in him than most people, more purpose, as though he was made and designed for this one thing.

The view from the audience was of a multitalented organ player who was most of the show, and his number two guy, who was no slouch either. But the view from behind the drums was exactly the opposite: Dennis was just fill between those moments when Vince stepped up to the mic and laid the room bare. You'd see the waiters stop moving and the smiles disappear off people's faces as they listened. Something legitimate was happening and people could sense that.

Vince's specialty was the blues. Nothing he played really brought him out of himself like the blues. He could lift entire rooms, regardless of their size. I came to discover that Vince had had more bad luck than anyone I've ever known, but when bad luck occurs to a gifted person, watch out.

Dennis "Bird" Parker

There's nothing that says a really good musician has to be smart. I think that was my biggest discovery going to Joplin that next month. It came to me the first time I got to watch Dennis up close driving the van. You listen to him at the gig and the guy is like a little god sitting behind that organ, but put him out on the open road and require him to find some distant spot, and his stage persona comes completely unwound.

Dennis couldn't read a map—a major handicap for the leader of a traveling band. I uncovered this fact somewhere in Arkansas. The roads are more crooked in Arkansas and wrong turns easier to make than in Kansas or Nebraska. A lot of people probably get lost in Arkansas all the time. Dennis had gotten us lost a few times already but I was always in the back feeling too numb or stupid to care. It was in Arkansas, on our way to Joplin, Missouri, in the middle of the afternoon, spring of '72, that Vince turned around and said he would like to take a nap and would I mind switching places with him.

Well, what he actually said was, "Up here, motherfuck. I'm going to lay down for a while." He crawled out of his seat and into the back and we squeezed past each other and I got in front. In the seat. In the upholstered seat. With room beneath me to stretch my legs. Blood started rushing through my body again and I felt a small surge of energy up my spine as it straightened out. Suddenly I was out of cargo and sitting in first class.

Lounging there next to Dennis was a little strange, and watching him get lost much more informative and entertaining from this vantage point. I was so used to looking at the back of his head, both playing and traveling, that looking him in the eye was still a little disconcerting. He had this "boss look" all over him and I felt I was crowding him just being in the front. As a general rule Dennis didn't talk to me much more than he had to, and he mostly ignored me now. I was feeling perky and looking around, noticing the difference when the road comes at you instead of always falling away, like you're going somewhere instead of always leaving. I started to mention this to Dennis but stopped when he began to look irritated and turned up the radio. I didn't mind. It was set to a Kansas City blues station that fit right in with the ambiance of the van. Everything around me felt right.

Dennis held us steady at 55 MPH and I probably sat with my jaw stuck out and my arm resting on the door, surveying the scene for the next hour or so, until an innocent-looking sign came over the hill, announcing, "Junction 59/270 and 71, four miles ahead."

The effect on Dennis was immediate. He clearly hadn't expected it. He lifted his foot slightly and the van slowed some, he squinted down the road further than before, preparing himself—I guess—to make an executive decision about which way to turn next. Sitting so close to him I noticed he was one of those people you could actually see think, just like his head was a flashing sign or something. His face showed every thought and feeling the instant it passed—which was not comforting to me because what I saw developing was a badly consti- pated look that only spread and grew more intense until it settled in his eyes and they glazed over. Dennis hung for a minute like that and then slowly begin to rouse himself, pulling the map up over the steering wheel and trying to read it while still driving.

I saw him do this maybe five times in the first four hours I was sitting beside him, and each time was the same. First, he'd be struck dumb, then he'd pull the map up and spread it over the steering wheel, then lower his head closer to the paper and start tracing with his fin- ger, glancing up once or twice but then becoming absorbed in his map and tracking out possibilities, completely losing consciousness of the road ahead.

And in that van the driver had to stay on top of things. That blue Ford could get independent in the blink of an eye. The very instant Dennis loosened his grip on the wheel and let his mind go, that van would head immediately for the ditch as if looking for it, or into opposing traffic—wherever the danger was greatest. I think the poor thing had a death wish and just wanted to lay down in some farm pond and die since it'd been kept running so unnaturally long.

Dennis would be tracing those little lines on the map, the van would slowly begin to drift left or right, his foot would come up off the gas pedal, and then the whole van would drop off the edge of the asphalt while I yelled. This would cause Dennis to finally look up, his expression flashing to one of lead-pipe simplicity. He'd twist the wheel, throw a little gravel, and get us back up to speed, then hit the brakes when he realized once again he didn't know where he was going. Then we'd pull off the road.

The first three or four times this happened I offered to read the map for him but he treated this suggestion like a wild piece of folly and said he would read the map himself, "So's I know where I'm going. Instead of guessing along with you."

When he pulled over, Dennis gave his full and undivided attention to the map, running both fingers over it now, trying to figure out where we were and asking me the name of the last town. Two minutes later Vince would rise up in back and throw in his two cents. "Hey man, why we parking out here? Is this Joplin?" He'd look out the window. "Don't look like Joplin. Look like nowhere, nowhere. Just keep moving, man. All you gots to do is follow the numbers. It's better to keep moving, man. What number we on?" Vince called roads "numbers."

Dennis wouldn't answer and there would follow a long moment when nothing was said. The radio blaring and the smell of cow coming in the window. Then Vince would lay down again and remain still for maybe two minutes before flipping over to his other side, rustling for a minute, settling into the cracks between the equipment. Then he'd jerk a foot or twitch and rub his face, rustle a little more, rubbing his toes or scratching himself, rustle some more, unable to sleep. Dennis pitting his cleverness against the map the whole time, and me sitting there trying to be cool, reminding myself I was lost with a couple of top-notch musicians.

After several more minutes of considerable hesitation Dennis would inevitably declare our position to be "heres," and then put the van in gear and coach it back up to speed, the level of vibration and noise rising with the speedometer until it all blended into a large, all-purpose hum just before punching through the sound barrier at 48 MPH, where the front tires did a little dance. Everything sounded different up front. There were little clicks and pings in the engine, as well as running noises like tires and gears and wheels. The wind made more noise around the van, probably because there were more uneven surfaces on it than your average rolled-up ball of tinfoil. Listening to it did not calm me down. We'd whistle down the road, the radio with a cracked speaker turned up loud to be heard, and Dennis would nod like he'd figured everything out—until we reached the next intersection and the numbers didn't look quite right again and we'd go through the whole procedure once more. Once or twice Dennis actually walked into a gas station and had the attendant trace it for him, but it did no good. Dennis couldn't read a map.

We wandered lost for a while, until late that afternoon when we came across a sign pointing us to "Joplin, 360 miles." The sun set and everyone was quiet. Occasionally I'd see Vince's zippo lighter sparking back there but the van noise and radio blocked out any sound. Dennis had returned to his statue state, that coma he went into where he wouldn't move one muscle for hours, just holding the van steady. I was probably running some story in my head, killing time, wondering what Joplin would be like, when Vince in the back leaned up and asked, "Hey man, you like tea? Grass? I'm going to smoke me some. If you want a taste, you know. . . ."

Dennis perked up just enough to put some living eyes in that statue body of his and I took a second to consider the offer. Then I said yes and crawled in the back.

Vince was sitting in my old nest next to the back window, with luggage and coats piled around him. I settled on top of some monitors and lay down. There was no light back there but the occasional headlights of cars behind us. Out of his pocket Vince pulled a wrinkled, skinny, rolled-up sandwich bag with some papers inside.

"Where'd you get that?" Dennis called from the front.

Vince winked at me and smiled. "Oh . . . found it in *your* suitcase."

"The hell," and Dennis fell silent again, probably sitting up there grinding his teeth.

Vince lowered his voice, looking at me. "This here's some Acapulco Gold, man. Some of the best shit I've smoked in a long time. Been saving it . . . till I knew if you was cool . . . you know? But I can see you're cool now. You'd probably like to get a toke off this? Huh? I'll roll us up a fat one."

What he rolled was thinner than a toothpick, but it was a pleasure to see him roll it. You can tell if a person's already rolled ten thousand joints in his life, and Vince had that look, that process, that fluid ability to blindly unfold and lick and spread and close and roll and lick again all in one stylized gesture, talking the entire time.

"Oh, yeah, man. This shit gonna knock you for a loop. Some of the best weed *I've* smoked in a while. Probably kill you. I'll just let you have a little bit, so's you don't *pass out.* Couple tokes of this, man, you'll forget how to jerk off."

I smiled and told him to get fucked.

"Gots to be careful when you gets a drummer high. Mother go crazy pounding on shit, playing paradiddles on they legs, turning back into they monkey self. I knew one sombitch . . . that Sammy I was telling you about? Shit. You didn't want to get Sammy high. Motherfuck go banging on everything! Playing his solos, running shit out."

The whole time Vince was talking he was rolling and licking, mostly licking, spinning that joint, eyeballing me, gauging his effect. He gave it one last end-to-end soaking, and then held it up for my inspection. It was perfectly shaped, if somewhat damp.

"If you drop dead I'm going to pawn your drum kit."

"Just light the thing, will you?" I said. He was testing my patience with all his rigmarole.

Vince flicked out his zippo again and drew fire onto the very tip of the joint, barely touching it, a controlled small burn, embers only, no fire. He took several short hits and then pulled the whole thing into his lungs, puffing himself up for a minute while he held it. Once he handed it to me, I saw how really soggy this thing was and blew on it to maybe dry it out some.

"Hey, man?" he says in a wheezy voice, "You ever done this before? The blowing part comes *later*. You not going to get high like that."

"I'm trying to dry this thing out so it'll burn. Joint's wet as a dishrag."

"Supposed to be, motherfuck. Otherwise she'd burn too quick and you'd have runners this way and that. You just smoke the joint and leave the technical shit to me."

It wasn't the tastiest marijuana and it was dusty and dry, wrapped like an enchilada inside that wet paper. I showed off the prowess of youth and took one long, uninterrupted, heavy deep pull that burned half an inch off the length.

"Jesus fire, sombitch!" Vince was reaching for it like he was going to pluck it out of my mouth. "Why don't you just *eat* it and be done with it. Think *I* could have some? Any left?"

I started laughing and suddenly plugged into Vince in a big way. All his mumbling and shifty looks came together for me as one huge act, one giant personality, like having Richard Pryor sitting across from you. He'd cuss different red streaks, one subject after another, just reacting to himself, bitching mostly. He'd start riffing off Dennis in a low voice, looking back over his shoulder, talking about

Dennis' love life and calling him "peabrain" and telling me how one time this girl had to use a fire extinguisher to keep him off her. "Didn't take more than a squirt or two and that fire was *out*, man!" Then he'd spin off toward musicians he'd heard, painting pictures with his hands, looking as earnest and serious as possible, complaining up a storm, all while cracking me in pieces. It was beautiful.

Then, as always happens to me in such moments, I saw myself sitting there, a young, tender-looking white boy, listening with both ears, having a significant experience. And Vince sitting across from me, his back straight, waving a cigarette with one hand and doing punctuation with the other, the occasional light through the back window showing half his face, his one wild eye and broken teeth, spinning tales. This surely is pure magic, I thought.

Either that or good marijuana. Can't say now. But we covered the next hundred miles in a flash, Vince talking the whole time.

Then he started getting sleepy and I started getting sleepy and the spaces between words got longer and finally he said to me, "Think I'm going to lay my head down here a moment, see if I can't catch some rest, man." I crawled back up to my seat. We were about 150 miles from Joplin when I too fell asleep—peaceful sleep, real sleep, thoughtless sleep.

| | |

After twenty minutes I was empty and happy and deeply unplugged, when there was a loud pop and the van shook and Dennis started weaving back and forth over the wrong lane. My first thought was the damn differential had gone out again, but everything sounded different. Once Dennis regained control he threw on the brakes and came to a complete halt on the road with an excited look on his face. "Pheasant!"

I had no idea what he was talking about. At first I thought he had said "pleasant." He put the van into reverse and started backing down the road, weaving in a dramatic fashion because he wasn't any good at backing up. Once he'd gone a couple of hundred yards he stopped again, reached under the seat for his gloves, then took off running back down the road.

I was fighting off grogginess like a bad fog. Waking up so fast, my orientation was off 560 degrees. I leaned out the window and watched Dennis running like a maniac toward the darkness, waving his gloves.

Vince was awake by now and asked me, "What the fuck is going on, man?" I told him I hadn't a clue and leaned back out the window to watch Dennis some more. In the middle of the road was a bird flapping around and trying to get up. Dennis stood over it putting on his gloves. Then he bent down and began wrestling with the thing, trying to get a good grip on it. The whole business was half obscured by the dark and still looked mostly like a dream to me. I could barely see Dennis at all but the bird had white feathers and moved a lot. Finally Dennis came back to the van holding this desperate, crazy and dying thing by the neck.

Once it was inside the van, the bird's wings filled up the entire front seat. Dennis could barely close the door without crunching something. The bird was experiencing massive death throes that seemed to come and go in shudders while my heartbeat moved up to 200 strokes per minute.

Dennis clamped it down in his lap and seemed to be choking the neck. Vince, sitting straight up now, wanted to know, "What you doing with that bird, man?"

Dennis was struggling to get a grip, "I'm going to eat him."

"Eat him!?" Vince said.

"Yeah, man, this is pheasant. It's good eating."

Dennis finally got both hands over the bird's wings and had a secure grip on its neck. With one large twist, he wrenched the head off. "Oh man!" Vince said. "Don't be doing that around here!"

I think I fell back against the door. Dennis took the head and laid it on the motor cover between us. Then he reached behind the seat and grabbed a paper bag he kept empty oil cans in and shoved the still-flapping bird into that. He jammed the bag back behind the seat and put the van in gear and started off again, building up speed.

The bird jumped around in the bag, banging cans for several minutes, before calming down and dying. Vince was lying down in back again but he looked stiff. I was watching the bird head next to me, its eyes wide open and vibrating on the motor cover. Vince called out, "I'm in a good mood now."

I kept looking at the head. After a couple of miles I asked Dennis, "Do you want this bird head?"

"No man, can't eat no head."

"Sure you don't want to put it on your key ring or something?"

"No, man."

"Then I'm throwing it out." I hunted around and found a roll of toilet paper, pulled off about six feet, wrapped the bird's head up and tossed it out the window.

Dennis was quiet for a minute and then said, "Saw a deer back up the road but I didn't stop because it looked gamey."

I turned around, "Hey, Vince, did you hear that? Dead deer back up the road but Dennis says it looked gamey."

"Man, please." And Vince put his hand over his face.

That night at the club, Dennis was bragging and told me Charlie "Bird" Parker got his name the same way, only it was a chicken he went back and got. "I wouldn't stop for no chicken, man."

Slapping the Monkey

Both Vince and Dennis thought of themselves as nookie machines. To hear either one of them tell it, his conquests were a thing of legend. Vince claimed to have scattered children behind him like seeds in the wind, like little flowers that sprouted up on the prairie. He said half of one small town in Florida looked exactly like him, both boys and girls. Said he lived there almost two months and that's all the time it took. "Nine years later, man, I swung through just to say hi? See what's happening, and, Whoa! Must'a been twenty kids calling me Poppa. I *had* to believe them. Shit. They all looked like little pictures. They had they selves a little band going too, man."

Once, after a few too many drinks, Vince told me he was so familiar with the geography of American pussy he could tell in a darkened room where a woman had been born and raised, whether she was farm stock or city bred, half Choctaw or Chinese, whatever. In the very beginning I think I probably believed him, my gullibility being mixed up with my very real admiration for his playing and singing. Vince enjoyed describing pretzel-like maneuvers to me with the skill of a poet, stretching every story into some little pornographic epic, using all the hand gestures he could. I think he did it to keep me hot and bothered. It was one of his main, ongoing subjects, something he'd always bring up. We'd be walking down some sidewalk in the middle of the afternoon talking about the weather or the van or Dennis or whatever when a good-looking female would pass by and Vince would launch himself. "Oooh, oooh . . . reminds me of Bertice down in Baton Rouge. Yeah man, she was guuu-ooood," making it sound as nasty as possible. Vince'd look at the ground, shaking his head like he still couldn't believe it, grinning like a demon, even stumbling a little bit as he walked, dragging his feet like he was overwhelmed by the memory. "Bitch could take out her front teeth, man! Oh, Lord! Used to suck my *toes*, man! Wish I was back in Baton Rouge right now, tell you that."

I'd laugh and blush and glance around me and sometimes catch the shocked face of some local citizen who happened to overhear. Vince would keep smiling and fall into a strut as he moved down the street, happy with himself. When it didn't involve food or money, agitating white people was one of his main amusements.

It seemed to me that Vince must've known all the tricks of love and could charm women like birds out of a tree. To hear him tell it, it was all in the "moves." I even watched him at night as he made the rounds during our breaks, studying his technique, feeling I had a lot to learn yet.

Whenever Dennis would hear Vince bragging about his exploits, he would sooner or later have to chime in about his own long history of conquest. Dennis was never so graphic but he made clear how the women of the world felt about him, how the women of the world loved him and doted on him, how they approached him and worked him and how they held him in awe. When it came to the female point of view, basically, he was irresistible. "Can't keep they hands off me, man." He told me this point-blank, in a businesslike tone. Like it was impossible to dispute. "Really?" I said, with a little too much surprise in my voice. Then he'd run through what he called the "facts."

Dennis made it sound like he'd never met a woman who didn't bother him first thing about going to bed with her, and as a consequence he was always being distracted and never had a moment to himself. He mentioned a personal fan club back in Chicago and several other cities where he kept lesser harems. Given the fact that I hadn't seen him go to bed with anyone but himself, or even try to, it always seemed the emptiest kind of bragging to me. The most I ever saw Dennis do in a social way was sit at the bar a lot during breaks and hold court while paying himself compliments.

On those rare occasions when I'd sit with him, he'd say things like, "Hey, man. I think that good-looking lady over there's looking at me." I'd look over and nod at it being half true. Some woman *was* looking, but probably not for the reasons he thought. Dennis liked to wear these bright red or green suits with large lapels and huge buttons that he thought real attractive. Truth of the matter was that both Vince and Dennis looked as tough as junkyard dogs, and the women they hit on looked about the same. And the women I was encouraged by Vince to hit on, all looked exactly the same.

The only women I was ever interested in were at the fancier places we played, and fancy being a relative term. These women had the virtues of standing up right, being well dressed, clean, no obvious distractions, able to carry on a conversation. But I had no luck with these women. Where I was the luckiest it didn't feel like luck at all. We'd work some dive in Colorado or Missouri and every snaggle-toothed, alcoholic, female farm hand in the county would be making eyes at me and patting the seat beside her. Vince would whisper in my ear, "Hey, man, I think that little blond over there is interested in your ass. She a *fine* piece, man. I'd jump on that." And I'd glance over to find some stringy-haired thing in a worn-out jumpsuit and discount tennis shoes looking at me like I was a big bag of potato chips she wanted to eat. I guess everyone has their own expectations about sex, and one of mine was that I felt some small measure of interest going in. Maybe someone else in my place would've gone into a rutting frenzy, but it didn't happen to me. I just didn't feel like it.

Twenty percent of the places we played were out and out dives where fungus probably grew under the tables. Another twenty percent were sleazy ballrooms past their prime, where the shadows seemed to swallow up people. Another twenty percent might be rude, frontier saloons where the gals could all ride and rope and kick a little steer butt when necessary. Not my type at all. And the remaining forty percent were posh clubs in hotels or on top of banks, where my luck was always the worst. So I actually found those first few months on the road a dry and frustrating experience.

Vince made it seem easy. He'd be standing at the bar and take a hit off his cigarette, appearing casual, cross one foot over the other, Mr. Cool looking around, and then just start talking. If the woman standing next to him didn't walk away or a boyfriend didn't show up, he'd have her laughing in five minutes. Ten minutes after that he'd be whispering her secrets and having to put his arm around her so no one else could hear. And along in here she'd start backing away or waving to a friend across the room. Vince didn't care. If he had time left in the break, he'd move on to the next likely prospect, acting like the previous woman was his sister and it was just business.

Sex really was the number one subject in that band. We'd all be sitting in the booth during break and some woman would walk by, which would start Vince thumping the underside of the table, his leg going into spasm. "Oh, man, hold me back!" and he'd grab hold of Dennis or me. This was routine for him. Part of his act. Vince was always exploding in one direction or another. Laughing like a wild man. Same way he played. But I could never get over his lack of taste in women. If she was female and humanoid, she had his attention.

All this sexual frenzy in the band occurred only at the sleazier clubs. In the free-for-all of a gin joint crowd, there is always a lot of grabbing and rubbing going on and people can get away with things; but in other places, like the Oilman's Club in Dallas or the Marriett in Kansas City, women don't get a full body massage out on the dance floor. If anything, people acted like they were still in school.

We played the Oilman's Club three times a year. And they loved us. But out of all the country clubs and private clubs we played, that was the worst when it came to having a high-nosed demeanor. All the waiters looked like military cadets, bowing and scraping this way and that; the club manager had little rat eyes that shot around in his head. The patrons seemed not to see us at all. It was very unpleasant. The way they requested songs wasn't very polite either. We played mood music with a vengeance.

There were occasional college coed types I'd see in the nicer places but I found it was almost impossible to strike up a conversation while they were looking over my head. Being hot and sweaty from the bandstand probably didn't help either. Dilated eyes and heavy breathing is not what some women want to see when they turn around. I'd always introduce myself as a musician and point toward the bandstand. It didn't seem to help. It probably didn't help much either that the two characters I hung around with both acted sex starved and desperate, forever on the lookout for beaver shots.

I persevered on my quest for random and impromptu sex and believed if I could only perfect my method, or at least discover it, then could I fully taste life on the road as I expected it to taste. But, on the other hand, the women I could most easily have scored with all seemed *too* easy. They made themselves too available, and seemed too much of a psychological mess to even be with for one night. There wasn't enough alcohol in America to get me in bed with most of those women; I could never get numb enough to not notice who I was with. I'd watch and consider and what I saw were confused, desperate creatures who were stumbling around, looking for any kind of human contact, and I did not find this sexy in the least. The whole thing just made me depressed. I started calling old girlfriends on the phone and running up my hotel bill, complaining about my sorry state.

LIFE IN DOUBLE TIME ||

A Low-Toned Joint

It's the nature of road work for a band to be thrown into contrasting situations. It was not unusual to drive directly from the Oilman's Club in Dallas to a soul joint like the Coco Mellow in Hugo, Oklahoma. While the only black people allowed in the Oilman's Club had to carry a tray over their shoulder, in the Coco Mellow the only white people to be found inside the club were either following a death wish or working in the band.

I was usually treated like a prince. With only two exceptions, it was a great week for me. At the Coco Mellow we were a soul band. We played no mood music, just bump and grind dance tunes from James Brown, Ray Charles, Sam and Dave, and all the groups like the Platters and Drifters and Temptations. It really sounded wonderful and perfectly authentic. It *was* authentic. Vince and Dennis both had million-dollar voices and their harmonies were locked together down to the smallest breath. They also knew many of the people we were playing, had shared bills with them. We were much better as a live down-home dance band than as a music box setting in the corner. The population there knew how to respect a drummer and would offer me drinks and a seat at their table. That first week at the Coco Mellow was the week I began to realize that white audiences were starting to put me on edge and black audiences somehow calmed me down. I certainly played better.

The Coco Mellow had a resident midget. His name was Leroy and he was the spark plug in that place. Three foot eight and happy as hell, Leroy was a big-time talker and had once appeared in a movie. You wouldn't need to know Leroy longer than fifteen minutes before he'd mention that movie. It was called "Bingo Long and his Traveling All Stars" and was about an all-black softball team. Leroy played the catcher. He told me that black midgets are very rare and that the movie people had to look all over the country before they found him. He had a picture of himself with Richard Pryor and James Earl Jones. According to Leroy, he and Pryor became major friends during the movie.

Leroy was about thirty-five but, like Vince, he had old eyes. And like Vince he was a fountain of energy. Leroy would rotate around and sit with everyone, and everyone bought him a drink to hear him talk. He'd sit with the older ladies bunched at one table and get them laughing, then he'd go tease some young girls with fairy tales about the sexual powers of midgets. Once they were giggling he'd drag one out onto the floor and then dance up a storm, getting other people going as well.

Everything about Leroy was oversized. He was always the center of attention. I suppose if a person wanted to commit suicide, one way to do it would be to go into the Coco Mellow Club and then pick a fight with Leroy. That unlucky individual would be dead in under three seconds—evaporating under all those hands coming out of the crowd. To say that Leroy was popular is to say little or nothing at all. In the Coco Mellow, he was "it."

I became great friends with Leroy. Leroy told me that other drummers were nothing compared to me and that he'd almost stopped dancing waiting for me to come along. I thanked him for the lie and bought him a drink. You could meet the entire room sitting with Leroy. The place wasn't that big and held maybe three hundred people jammed tight, which was most of the time. I think the band probably sounded best in the Coco Mellow. I know Vince and Dennis worked twice as hard there. While neither one would break a sweat in some places, there I'd watch it drip off their noses and elbows, hanging for a moment on some corner of their body, catching the stage lights as it fell to the floor. It was positively swampy up there by the end of each night. People were always passing drinks up and that was perfect for

Vince. His idea of heaven was some place where he could play and have drinks delivered.

They were passing drinks to me too and I went overboard a few times but then decided to stay on the near shore. I played better with both eyes open. Enjoyed it more. Drunk drummers are not interesting.

Some people never seem to get drunk. I've seen Vince drink enough to kill a small animal but it would hardly slow him down. I've seen him throw back six shots of grain alcohol after drinking all night and still walk away talking. Four or five nights every week I'd see him drink at least a half pint of gin and never miss a note. In the Coco Mellow, where he had a pipeline to the bar, he only became inspired. We played some bone-crushing blues there. Pitiful, crying, sore throat blues that made everyone smile.

The band sounded so good there, and we had such a royal time being doted on, that it's almost easy to forget that the Coco Mellow was the same place where I came extremely close to dying twice in the same week. The first time was when I was fired upon by a pistol, the second time when a knife-toting drunk caught me standing by myself near the jukebox.

The gunfire incident, like most things, just seemed to sneak up on me. We were in the middle of a song and Vince was executing some double somersault flip of a riff on the guitar, his usual kind of fireworks during a lead, when—without my touching it—my left crash cymbal suddenly exploded and fell off the stand in pieces.

I was so stupid with shock I naturally kept on playing. I'd never had a cymbal up and break on me without at least being hit first. I didn't know they could do this, had never heard of such a thing. The song was a familiar one and not requiring much attention on my part so I was able to give all my thoughts to this broken cymbal laying at my feet. I should say also that the band was rather loud at that moment, so, in effect, the cymbal breaking and falling apart made no noise. The song continued on and I was getting ready to tell Vince and Dennis about it as soon as possible. Then an instant later, while I was looking right at it, my right crash cymbal raised up and splintered on me. My Lord, I thought, this really is the most peculiar night I've ever had. How could such a thing happen twice at the same gig? Have I been playing that loud? Am I drunk? Fortunately for us all, Dennis happened to be looking in my direction when the second cymbal cracked wide open, and stopped the song.

It was only then that we could hear the gun firing. I guess I would've sat back there and caught bullets for another minute or so if it hadn't been for Dennis. One of the patrons was upset about something and had chased a friend under a table where he couldn't get at him, so he was firing off his pistol in a random, Wild West fashion over his head, not noticing where it was pointed. The bandstand was rather high and seemed to be in the general direction of about half the shots fired. The club was divided into several rooms, and once we stopped playing you could hear all 300 bodies hit the floor. The bartender, a 400-pound fellow named Murvel who'd worked there for years, heard the commotion and came out from behind the counter wiping his hands on a towel, and in a very easy manner waddled over and took the gun out of the man's hand before tossing him out the door by the neck. Then he came up and told us to start playing again. Immediately after that Murvel sent up a tray of drinks. During our next break I checked the wall behind me and found bullet holes on either side of my head. Vince told me not to worry about it. "Motherfuck can fire guns at you all day, man. If it's not your time, you don't go."

The next day I was calmed down enough to start retelling the story and embellishing it. I moved the bullet holes closer together and increased their size from .22 to .38. I practiced on Leroy that evening and by Thursday I was pretty casual about the whole thing. I think actually I was grateful. Now I had a story worth telling. I'd waited years for this. Even Vince seemed to recognize my growing sophistication and listened to me tell it two or three different times, laughing and nodding and making faces like it was all true.

So I was starting to relax a little bit and feel more hip, rotating through the crowd during the breaks and telling my little story. I think, if anything, I was feeling somewhat bulletproof by then. I'd already made up my mind that if another shot was fired in my direction I'd be more blasé about it. "Yeah, man. If it's not your time . . . you know."

This attitude might have become a permanent part of my personality had it not been tested so quickly. I got over any notions of living a charmed life while standing next to the jukebox Thursday night. A very mean-looking fellow, half Indian and half black, with the most exotic Neanderthal face, came up to me and, with his hand in his pocket, leaned over and spoke into my ear.

I thought he was going to compliment me on my playing or something, but instead he leaned over and said, "I haven't stabbed a white boy in a long time." He said this like he was telling me there was a taxi waiting outside. Matter of fact. Just letting me know. My heart started crawling up into my throat and in behind my teeth.

I composed myself and tried to be polite, find some follow-up remark to this awkward entree. Me being the only white boy in the room seemed to personalize the remark maybe more than he intended. Maybe he was only looking for directions, asking if I knew of another white boy he might go stab. I nodded and said, "Really?" but it didn't come out sounding easy enough.

He was leering at me and was obviously quite drunk, one of those situations where I could hear him telling the District Attorney the next morning he remembered nothing at all. He was pressed right up against me and half the room was screaming and yelling behind him. I looked around for a familiar face I might communicate with but saw nobody. I scanned the floor and couldn't find Leroy. I remember this fellow's eyes as being Oriental looking and very close together with high cheekbones underneath a low forehead. Tiny eyes insisting that I pay attention instead of glancing around the room. He leaned even closer and said, "Yeahhh . . . " making it sound hungry, making it clear *I* was the white boy he'd been looking all over town for. His breath smelled like a graveyard after an earthquake.

By this point I was ransacking my brain for some clever remark that would put him off. I couldn't think of any Kung Fu movies I'd seen. I considered becoming an albino black for the evening but didn't think he'd buy it. I thought about pointing behind him and yelling, "Chuck Berry!" and then running for cover, but he seemed too slow on the uptake for that to work. I was fresh out of ideas and beginning to wonder seriously what it felt like to be stuck with a knife (which at the moment seemed about as unpleasant as anything could be) when a woman dancing behind the fellow bumped into him. He was so entirely drunk that he turned to see who it was (and maybe stick her for bumping him), giving me my opportunity to sprint in the other direction and the safety of the bar. I told Murvel the bartender, but it didn't seem to rate very high on his list of things to worry about, and so the subject got dropped all too soon for me.

With the exception of those two brushes with death, it was a relaxed and pleasant week for everyone. It was during that time I really started to feel a part of the band, the first week the tunes really started to gel. I began to relax finally and fall into their rhythms, their particular slant on the backbeat. An inspired week of playing for us— even without my crash cymbals. All the tunes found a pocket. Lots of fun on the bandstand. I could tell by the way Vince and Dennis were treating me that things had changed. I was introduced to the crowd two or three times a night over the PA and included in the jokes. Everything started to feel different. I was hitting triple rim shots after Dennis' jokes and even started playing without my cap and sunglasses.

Then, at the end of that week, Vince cooked up a little ceremony for me.

It was Saturday night, the room jam-packed and already yelling, when Vince brought Dennis over to me at the bar where I was hiding with Leroy. Vince ordered a round of drinks for us all. Both of them were smiling and dancing around, pumped up. Raising his glass to me, Vince said, "I gots the answer to all you problems, man. We talked about it and decided to vote you in. Here you are, man," and he handed me a card. It was a mass-printed, fill-in-the-blank piece of paper that said,

This card certifies that the bearer,
"MIKE LANKFORD,"
is a duly recognized and licensed
HONORARY NEGRO,
and is entitled to all rights and privileges therein.

Signed,
Alphonso P. Ebony,
President

Vince smiled and sidled up close. "Next time some motherfucker bothers you, show him this." And then Vince fell apart and started laughing. "Oh, man. You *honorary* now. Live it up!" I looked at the card again. It was the kind of thing you might buy in a racist grocery store in deepest Oklahoma, and they were presenting it to me as an award. Vince leaned his big toothless grin in close, shaking, unable to contain himself, coughing once or twice, hanging on my shoulder. "You honorary, man." Dennis too seemed to find the whole thing hilarious. "Yeah, man." He slapped me on the other shoulder. "We voted you in tonight. You got the card now. Mail it home and show you momma."

Even Leroy piped up, "Yeah, man. You hip now. For a white dude. Sound good too."

For that band, it was a warm moment.

Little Vince

I was always trying to get Vince to tell me about himself. In odd moments alone I'd ask him questions about who he'd played with and where he'd been, but these straightforward questions rarely produced straightforward answers. Everything came out of Vince from the side. Information had to be caught on the fly. If he gave up a fact about himself, it was only because it was part of a story he was telling about some funny little thing he'd done. He *seemed* to be talking about himself all the time, but that was a trick. He was in all the stories but didn't seem to be doing anything much but looking. Hard, biographical facts about Vince were hard to come by. I'd ask him an ordinary question, something like, "Hey, Vince, you ever stab anybody?" What I got in return was him flashing his cards and pulling coins out of the air for a while, telling me about three or four real interesting stabbings he'd seen, but never really giving up any yes or no information I considered useful. Not being the fastest person on earth, it took me six or seven months to notice he was doing this, but once I did it became infuriating. I'd try to corner him on little facts, nail him down, interrupting his stories by asking, "Okay, now. If *everybody* in that back room is doing this, does that mean *you* were doing this too?" And Vince would get a look of astonishment on his face like I was the stupidest white person he'd ever met in his life. "Oh man," he'd say. "You gots to tell this boy *everything*!" and then shake it off and go on with his tale—basically dodging the bullet and not answering my question. He did this so much, and I became so aware of it, that now his stories all seemed to me like little tales of deception. A little game of "Find Vince in this story." He was always buried in there, you were just never clear exactly where. I even suspected him of switching roles on occasion. All I knew for sure about Vince was that he was too extraordinary a player not to have *some* kind of history. I mean, if no one ever noticed *this* guy play guitar, then Chicago must be full of deaf idiots. And I knew it wasn't.

A person might wonder why I didn't just ask Dennis, since Dennis had known Vince all his life. That approach doesn't take into account all the subtle complexities of Dennis' and my relationship: Dennis didn't actually talk to me. Even after my place in the band was secured and he and I had stopped being polite to each other, he never said anything to me unless he had to. If I hung out with anyone it was Vince. And if Dennis hung out with anyone it was Vince. Dennis and I did not hang out.

So it was with considerable surprise one afternoon in Alliance, Nebraska, when Dennis offered to have breakfast with me. I'd just come out of my room and was passing through the lobby of this old hotel and Dennis was sitting on a couch with six or eight of the "permanents" who always lounged there watching TV. I announced, just in case anyone cared to know, that I was headed out to get breakfast, and Dennis jumped to his feet and said, "Good idea!"

I don't think I could've been more surprised if he shot an arrow into me. "You want to come along?" I asked.

"A man has to eat," he said, just like we had breakfast together twice a week.

So I ended up sitting across the table from Dennis in this small, downtown cafe. We were next to the windows and the snow outside reflected the sun all over the inside walls. Dennis had on his sunglasses but I had to squint to look at him. I kept waiting for him to say something that might indicate why he was there but Dennis seemed relaxed and only interested in company. He really acted like we'd done this twenty times before. He might even have been a little bored, looking around, waiting for something to happen, waiting to eat. Real casual. Dennis' version of cool.

We both sat there sipping coffee a moment, Dennis looking hip and me looking like I had salt in my eyes. The room was quiet. We were the only customers there at two o'clock in the afternoon. I couldn't be sure I'd ever have the opportunity again, so I popped my question. "Hey, Dennis, tell me. What was Vince like in the old days?"

Dennis looked me over a moment. In bands, a question like this can be very political. "What you want to know about Vince for?"

"Oh, I don't know," I lied, yawning a little bit. "Just wondering. You know he likes to talk. I figured it was probably all lies."

Dennis studied me a while longer. "I'll tell you this, he wasn't nothing like he is now. You think Vince is good? You like the way he sounds now? You should'a heard him when he was young. That's all I can say. Before the dope. Back when Vince was fucking four times a day and playing all night, he was the talk in Chicago. Everybody wanted to come hear Vince. Shit just pouring out of him. People come to figure out his sound. You know who his cousin is? Earl Hooker, that's who. Even when Vince was a little kid, Earl would get him up on stage. Vince was born good on the guitar.

"Even had himself a little band use to play out on the sidewalk in front of they house, catching quarters and such. They was like ten years old. Bo Diddley was in one of them little bands Vince had. You know, different neighborhood kids learning to play back then. Vince's daddy was a drummer."

"Oh, yeah? What'd his mother do?" I was trying to be crafty and draw him out.

Dennis smiled. "Do? She got by. Different things. Out on the streets, you know. Vince grew up with his grandma. A very spiritual lady. He didn't tell you that?"

"Oh, yeah, sure, I think he did. Of course. But what about those stories with B.B. and Muddy and all that he tells? Is he bullshitting me or what?"

"That's all true. Lots of people played with Vince, one time or another." Dennis was looking bored with the whole subject. I knew I should ask him about himself and learn what I could about Vince indirectly, but I kept up my straight-ahead approach and just waited. My face a blank. Squinting right at him.

"Yeah," he finally said, like there was nothing else to talk about. "Vince been around. But those guys was competition for him. They wasn't just letting Vince sit in, they was studying him—just like he was studying them. When he was young he was hot as could be around Chicago. Specially on the South Side, where all the action was."

"So what happened?" I asked, popping the big one and hoping he'd answer.

"Oh," Dennis looked around, not sure he wanted to get into it. "Lots of things happen."

For all his shortcomings, Dennis looked like Old Man Time to me just then. Most of those things that happened to Vince also happened to him. He looked at his fork and spoon a while and then said, "Mainly, it was Vince couldn't hold a gig. Motherfuck's had more chances laid on his feet than any ten musicians. Vince can turn gold to shit quicker than you can say 'Abracadabra.'"

"Really?" I said. "I hadn't noticed."

"Well, you don't notice everything. The whole time growing up Vince was kicked out of one good band after another, more than most cats get asked into. He just couldn't hold a gig. Start showing up late, showing up high, missing shit, forgetting arrangements. But he could play heads. If what you want to do is fake shit all night, then Vince's your man. But most bands want to work up a show and know which way things headed ahead of time. It's not that he can't remember it, he's good at remembering shit if it doesn't have to do with work, just that he don't care. Vince one of them dudes wouldn't know the club was on fire until his guitar was burning. That's *all* he knows about."

The waitress brought our breakfast and we both dug in. Dennis was turning into a fount of information. I couldn't believe my luck. I decided to play him like a fiddle and pepper him with more questions after the meal. Get him going once more. We had the whole afternoon in front of us.

Dennis ate the same way Vince did, like he was half starved. Dennis inhaled his eggs and bacon, then he eyeballed his pancakes and they disappeared under a withering gaze. I think he smacked his lips twice and then sucked up a bowl of grits and raisins. Then he had to have pie to finish off his breakfast and at the last moment included a side order of ice cream. Once his coffee cup was full again and he had a cigarette going I'm not sure you could have pried Dennis out of that chair.

With his smoking hand he prodded his sunglasses back on his nose and gazed in my direction. "You want me to tell you what a fuckup Vince is?"

"If you would, please."

"Vince is the goose what keep laying the golden eggs but got a bad habit of losing them. And there's only so many eggs in the goose. Vince knows that now; he didn't use to. You know why Vince got to stay on the road? Can't go back to Chicago? He'd be getting high in ten minutes back in Chicago. And he can't do that no more. Coke and heroin about killed him ninety times. Out here he's staying away from shit. Even Vince figured out you can't stay high forever. He still falls down though." Dennis rubbed his finger across the pie plate, gathering crumbs.

"Used to be he was falling down all the time. That's what fucked up his deal with Al Green, got him kicked out. Same with the Shirelles. He had two contracts motherfuckers just *laid* on him to record his shit, but he messed around and didn't get it done. Shit, half of Chicago won't even talk to him now. Used to be lot of dudes around town liked to have him sit in, just after a while nobody wanted him regular. He made pretty good money in the '50s in the studio making people sound good . . . when they could find him. Everybody liked him sitting on they albums, but that was all. And money is like poison to Vince, he just goes crazy."

It occurred to me I'd just heard Dennis' rationale for not paying Vince more.

"You seen them marks on his arms?"

I had seen them. Little nickel-sized circular scars, mostly on his forearms.

"Them's abscesses." Dennis made it sound like "absences." "Each one of them marks shows a time he was down and let things get bad. His arms is like a scorecard."

"Yeah," I said. "But he's also the best guitar player I ever heard. I mean, if he used to be even better, I don't know what to say. But he's fantastic now." I couldn't let the moment pass and not reassert my innocence.

Dennis had fallen into his Buddha routine and was giving me his "look of the ages" stare. "Don't mean a thing," he said.

"Playing's different after you been doing it forever. You young and frisky and think music the whole world. Vince thinks that way too, and look where it's got him. He's got no saving account, half his children don't know he's alive, and if it wasn't for me booking and keeping him working he'd be strumming his guitar behind a cup on the sidewalk. Vince is a hare brain when it comes to business."

"Oh, bullshit," I said. "If Vince wanted to, he could handle as much business as anybody else."

"You said the magic word: 'wanted to.' But I don't see him wanting to yet. What I see him doing is sitting up in the room right now dreaming on his guitar. Vince been drifting all his life. If Vince had a little business sense and got along with folks, 'stead of this cocky 'don't touch me' bullshit that's caused all his trouble, he'd have him some money and a place by now. Me, I'm going to retire here in a few years, take myself down to Florida. Vince going to be swimming on his own after that."

Dennis was working himself too much into the conversation for my taste. The wisdom of his retirement plan was not anything I wanted to hear about. I tried to lift up another part of the curtain. "So, did you guys mostly work around Chicago before getting with Sam?" Sam was our booking agent.

"Shit, no. Hadn't worked Chicago probably ten, fifteen years. Hadn't even been there in about ten. Used to book out of New York City, work mostly on the East Coast and down South. That was like . . . all through the '50s and '60s."

"So how'd you hook up with Dartboard Sam? No . . . wait! I don't care how you hooked up with Sam. Tell me," I had to think fast, keep Dennis on track, "what kind of crowds did you have, where did you play? Around New York?"

"In '59 and '60 we played the Apollo Theater twice. James Brown was on the bill. The Temps. Smokey was there and his miracle boys. We put on a hell of a show. About the only time I ever saw Vince pure nervous. Ask him about that sometime; he was shaking in his boots."

"Did he fuck up?"

"No. Shit. Vince don't fuck up on the guitar—it's just everything else he fucks up."

"What about down South?"

"We played all them little joints. What they call the 'Chitlin Circuit.' Worked lots of big houses too. Ballrooms around there. They's a radio station in Memphis used to play our tunes and we had a *good* following down South. Pussy good down there too, man. Some of them girls . . . damn! Sweet? I can't tell ya. Like buttermilk."

I jumped in quick, before he got off track again. "Did you play Atlanta?"

"Yeah, some big dance hall outside town. Worked there a lot. I remember the womens pretty fine around there too."

"What about, uh, New Orleans?"

"I like New Orleans. Nice town. They got women there too, you know. But don't talk to Vince about no New Orleans. He hates New Orleans and all the rest of Louisiana."

"Really? Why?"

"Oh, he don't like me telling this story. Vince stay mad at me enough without me giving him new reasons."

"Shit, I'm not going to say anything," I said, composing my face into a look of utter innocence. He had to believe me. I wanted to hear this story.

The waitress happened over and refilled his cup. Dennis lit up another cigarette, keeping a sun-drenched cloud around us there by the windows. He flicked an ash into his pie plate, smacked his lips, and looked back up at me.

"I don't go be telling you these stories to make Vince look bad. What happened to Vince could happen to anyone, only that it happened to *him*. You dig what I'm saying? Vince don't like history lessons. He'd like to forget all about this."

I nodded and looked right at him, all my tapes running at the same time.

Dennis stared around some more, stalling, then finally said, "We was playing a roadhouse out kinda the edge of town, near those swamps. Soul joint. I remember they had alligators round there someplace. Vince was standing outside smoking weed or something on break, and the local sheriff pulls up. Vince probably give him some lip and got hisself arrested. All I knows is he was gone when it come time to start again and I thought maybe he was out with some broad in the back of her car, you know? Then somebody say they seen him leave with the sheriff. We finished the set without him.

"By the time I got to the courthouse to see what happened they'd had Vince a couple of hours. They did a job on his ass too. Cracker motherfuckers. Coulda been me, coulda been . . . no, don't guess it coulda been you. But anybody else."

Dennis paused and I waited, making a low whirling sound.

"They worked him up good. Wanting to humble him, you know, fuck him up a little bit, show him who's boss? Did theyselves a strip search. Beat him around the head some. Poked a little stick up his ass. Made him sing. Fucked up his eye. He got steady high after that. Six or seven months he didn't even come up for air. Played a lot of guitar though. This about fifteen years ago. Round 1960 or thereabouts."

I was almost sorry I'd asked. It threw a pall over the conversation. I couldn't think of anything to say and Dennis seemed sorry he'd told me. "Don't you be telling Vince I told you, you understand? I mean, you don't be telling?" I assured him I wouldn't.

My First Stabbing

We were back at the Coco Mellow with Leroy and his gang about two months later. We were their star attraction that month. We'd probably covered fifteen states since we were there last, had a multitude of adventures, had seasoned as a band. There was a big hand-painted poster up behind the bar announcing our appearance. The bartender Murvel told me they booked four or five cheap bands that month in order to save money and get us for a full week. Vince loved the place and so did Dennis. And even though I'd nearly died twice there already, I too had fond memories and was glad to be back.

Tuesday night when we drove up to the club the crowd looked particularly large. Dennis had trouble finding a parking spot and we had to cruise in front of the place two or three times. Even with the windows of the van rolled up I could tell the jukebox was blasting from inside the club. Out on the sidewalk twenty or thirty people were standing around, mostly drunks and working women talking under streetlights, a few teenagers looking overly cool and prancing. Near one corner of the building an old man was bent over and examining the dirt. Across the street little kids played in the dust of someone's front yard. It was about 8:30. The street was lively but the Coco Mellow looked intense.

We finally had to park a block away and walk to the club. I was carrying Vince's guitar for some reason while he talked and chatted and waved his hands about nothing at all, filling up the night air. All of us were pumped and expecting a great evening.

As we turned the corner and approached the front of the club, I could hear a tremendous noise inside the place. It had to be a huge crowd, maybe our largest there so far. The jukebox mingled with yells and screams and under it all a huge humming noise like a beehive, the sound of hundreds of people talking at once. A sound that seemed much too large for the building. Every time someone came out the door it was like a pressurized tank leaking a little bit, jukebox music and wild shouting rushing outside for an instant and then being choked off, as though the place was about to burst. "*Man*," Dennis said. "Wish we was working for the door tonight."

We almost couldn't get inside. Dennis opened the door onto a wall of bodies and no one was able to move enough to let us through. If the room legally held 300 people, and I'd seen up to 350 in there before, there surely had to be 500 or more tonight. Plus three.

Dennis used me like a wedge, pushing me in first while I held

the guitar case up in front of me, jamming it between bodies and pry-
ing them apart while he and Vince followed in my wake. I don't know
how I got stuck in front. Probably another of my junior duties. The
room was longer in that direction than it was across and for a long
time it seemed I was just standing in the crowd jammed up against
people while being shoved from behind, everyone around me shouting and jumping, dancing straight up and down, yelling into each
other's face to be heard, and then turning and yelling at us once we
were recognized.

The whole place was hot, dark, smoky and loud as hell. Making
things even tighter were three pool tables with lights over them that
took up half of the space between the bar and front door. Along the
right-hand side was a row of booths decorated with duct tape. There
was a second room off to the left where the dance floor and bandstand
were. Both rooms had a low ceiling that made the place feel close; the
walls and ceiling painted black. After about ten minutes of "Excuse
me" and "Hey, anyone seen my pet snake?" I was finally able to make
a path for us to the bar.

The bar was packed too, buried under all the hunched backs of
people sitting there. I was drenched in sweat by then and needing
something cool to drink, but I couldn't see anyone working as bartender. Murvel was gone and so was his substitute assistant. All the
hunched-over people were nursing their drinks or rotating their empty
glasses, waiting like us, all except for this one fat woman who kept
turning around on her stool, legs spread to the limits of her dress so she
could touch the floor with one foot, shouting "Roger" over and over as
if it were the name of the whole room.

I'd begun to think that if I'd ever seen a party crowd, this was
surely it. While Tuesday nights are usually rather dull, each town is
different. There was a vibration in the air, more excitement than I'd
ever felt here before. My sense was that everything was shaping up for

a great evening. With a crowd like this, I could get up on stage and do nothing more than *start* a funky beat and the whole room would drop into a spasm. I was looking forward to it.

But the mysterious missing bartender was becoming a liability. As the youngest member of the band, I could still drink water and find refreshment in it, but Vince and Dennis had refined tastes. Vince, in particular, was becoming impatient and started talking in a lively way about the missing bartender. We waited and asked around but no one could give us the man's schedule. So after a while, because he couldn't get anything to drink, Vince wanted a cigarette and headed over to where he thought the cigarette machine was. Maybe not twenty feet away but he disappeared getting there.

Then, in the particular way of car wrecks and falling children, what followed occurred in an instant but seemed stretched out and in slow motion. I was standing by the bar and wondering what was taking Vince so long, when it seemed every person in the room suddenly shoved against me, almost like the building was tipped on its side. I was facing the other way and had to twist and push hard to even turn around and look. I traveled halfway across the floor and ended up in a corner, the fat woman screaming in my ear the whole way and various cigarettes burning me on the arms and side. I only stopped moving when I was heaved back against the wall and almost tripped on a Pepsi case that I had to step up on. It was because of that Pepsi case that I saw everything that happened. It looked like somebody was throwing beer bottles at Vince and that he was trying to duck and get behind the pool table while everybody else pushed back to give him room. There was flying glass everywhere. But when he stood up finally, it wasn't Vince at all but someone wearing an exact copy of his blue shirt, and this guy was yelling with veins popping up on the side of his neck. The whole room had become totally quiet except for the jukebox that kept blaring, but you could hear him yelling. Someone in my corner said,

"It's Hellfire Johnson! What's he doing here?"

The name fit him. He looked like pestilence and plague all mixed together. Maybe flood and locusts too. A big man, well over six feet, he had the look in his eyes of an oncoming train, a train with bursting boiler and eighteen smoking wheels. He did not look like a person you could easily hurt by just punching him in the stomach.

And someone even bigger than him, much taller and uglier, was ten feet away, grabbing more beer bottles off tables and slinging them one after another. The bottles were flying wild and breaking against the wall over people's heads or exploding off the floor, some of them hitting Hellfire on occasion. Hellfire skipped around and dodged a while, then finally put one arm over his face and went at this bottle-throwing giant. The big man then broke a beer bottle on the edge of a table to use as a knife, stabbing it at Hellfire's arm and making it bloody while he backed away from him.

I looked around for Dennis, thinking we should maybe get out of there but I couldn't find him; I couldn't have left anyway because the people were so tight in front of me. All I could do was watch for more flying bottles as the big man shoved glass into Hellfire's arm and Hellfire yelled at him stuff like "Nigger, Sombitch" while they stumbled around the circle that people made.

This little ballet went on for several seconds while they shoved and punched each other a bit more, and then the big man started waving a knife. I think someone handed it to him because he was running out of bottle to stab with, it breaking off way too quickly in Hellfire's arm and getting shorter all the time.

Hellfire didn't see it coming. The giant's arms must have been five feet long and he just reached in and slashed Hellfire across the belly. Hellfire stalled out for a moment, looking down at the expanding red mess across his stomach. Then Hellfire looked up and it was like the door of a furnace had opened.

They both lunged at each other and fell to the floor wrestling. This made it harder to see so I had to raise up on my toes. Hellfire didn't seem to be paying any attention to the knife but instead concentrated on choking the giant into a coma. They'd roll one way and then back another—freezing for an instant into a muscular lock, staring at arm's length, wrestled to a standstill—then rolling again, disappearing behind someone's head, then coming back into view. Finally Hellfire got the best of the big man and climbed on top of him, straddling him with his legs and making a popping sound when he hit him with his fist.

Hellfire got down to some serious choking, his back arched up like a cat's, his face down low staring into the giant's eyes. Nothing really moving, just vibrating, trembling for long moments. From where I was, the only visible part of the big man were the bottoms of his shoes; Hellfire was on top of him and the giant's legs pointed my way. Once in a while you'd see his feet jumping around as he was getting choked and one of his shoes came off. Then it seemed like Hellfire got twice as mad and started banging this guy's head on the floor. It was then I realized the big man wasn't waving his arms for help, but that he had a knife I couldn't see, and was putting it in Hellfire's back.

That was when, and I couldn't believe this, one of those dressed-up pimps in the crowd used his pool stick to tilt the light over the pool table outward like a spotlight so he could see the fight better.

Life was cheap in the Coco Mellow that night. Nobody made a move to stop the killing. Hellfire was squeezing the life out of that giant thrashing on the floor under him but now I could see the knife coming up every time it could and coming down on Hellfire over and over. There started to be little spots on Hellfire's back about the size of silver dollars, coming up slow and in different places like they had nothing to do with the knife, and then newer ones came up, and I could almost see the tiny cuts in the cloth that hadn't come up dark yet; and the whole time that giant kept planting the knife in Hellfire. I don't know how many times it went in and it didn't look like Hellfire was counting either because he was trying to strangle that knife out of the man's hand.

But choking is waiting and stabbing isn't, and eventually there were little dark circles all over Hellfire's back. He started slowing down too and for a long minute it just seemed they were trying to out-last each other. But the giant was the first to give. Regardless of what people said later, the giant gave first. I saw his feet roll apart and he looked like he was dead and when Hellfire saw there was nothing left to choke he started to let up. That was when people jumped in and pulled them apart, but it didn't make any difference by then.

When they pulled back on Hellfire he just fell and rolled away. I could see the giant's face then and it looked like the floor, it was so gray. Three or four men got under him and lifted him up like they were going to carry him out but instead they just dragged him around the room until he stumbled some and came to his feet and regained himself. Hellfire didn't even look over when they started that. He was breathing deep and looking at the ceiling, his shirt and pants and arms all red, but by the time the giant had come to and started to know what had happened to him I thought they might even go at it again. Hellfire ignored him. People waited and I watched and the big man got his senses back and kept looking over at Hellfire and finally was able to walk on his own and found his shoe and walked over to Hellfire and kicked him in the side, telling him to get up.

Hellfire just rocked a little bit and didn't blink, his eyes glaring just like he was still strangling and waiting but now without expecta-tion, looking and not looking, like something had come between him and the room. That's when everybody saw it, saw that Hellfire wasn't getting up, wasn't even breathing. People seemed to remember where they were and started talking all at once and gathering around the giant and only looking over at Hellfire to be sure he wouldn't gasp all at once and *still* get up. Leroy was the first to go over to him.

The jukebox was playing "Ain't no sunshine when she's gone." The record had a scratch and it was stuck playing, "I know, I know, I know, I know. . . ." This went on for ten minutes. I don't know if Hellfire was listening to the song when he died, but I wouldn't want to go out of this world with a stuck record in the background. "I know, I know, I know, I know. . . ."

That's when Dennis appeared out of nowhere and grabbed me by the arm like he was going to squeeze it in half and started pulling me towards the door saying something about us getting ourselves out of there before the police arrived. I started moving and Dennis didn't say anything and everybody was jumbling around at once, the room a mass of confusion.

Getting out was tough. Half the neighborhood was jammed up against the inside of the door, trying to get out. The other half of the neighborhood was jammed against the outside of the door, trying to get in.

By the time we were outside people were running down the street and we could hear the sirens somewhere getting louder. The air was cool and when Vince joined us we took a walk through the neighborhood until the ambulance and police left.

We started an hour late that night but the crowd was ready for us, most of them very drunk. I looked and there was a bloodstain on the wood floor but people acted like it wasn't there and walked right over it. There was a fresh intensity to their partying now. They danced like their feet were on fire, nearly wild with joy. And our playing was particularly fierce. Vince sounded monumental that night. We played an extra two hours and were reluctant to quit even at 3:00 A.M.

A Burning Tale

Traveling through darkest America we came across a run-down old Indian ballroom in Hubcap, Oklahoma called "Robert's Retreat" where I learned something new about myself. On our own we could never have found these places. We owed the privilege of working each one of these holes and dives to our booking agent, Dartboard Sam. And while I appreciated Sam at one level, most of the time Vince and I did nothing but bitch about him between ourselves.

There was plenty to bitch about. Sam had played, at some point during prehistory, with a few big bands and then retired into the agency business in Indiana. Sam was also head of the local musician's union, which I had to join. He owned a music store. His talent agency had been around for years. Sam appeared, on the surface, eminently qualified to book bands—except for one huge and glaring personal defect. The mind of a booking agent working over large distances must, of necessity, be a large mind, a mind divided into time zones and geographical areas, a mind containing mountain ranges and great salt lakes, and at the same time a mind as detailed as a county road map. The awesomeness of such a view would be a powerful thing and worthy of respect, if it existed. In Sam, it didn't.

For a man who had supposedly traveled widely, Sam hadn't the least idea where places were, or how long it took us to get there. I privately suspected Sam's concept of America must've been like a folded map where Denver rubbed up against St. Louis and the Mississippi River was only a few inches long. He probably booked off index cards and drank whiskey while he shuffled them around. Vince and I were forever telling Dennis not to book any gigs it took a rocket ship to get to, but Dennis wouldn't listen.

Vince was the one who called him "Dartboard." I never met the man. For me, he was a shadowy presence on the other end of a phone

line, someone only Dennis could talk to, and then only on Friday afternoons. I used to imagine Sam as this mouthy guy sitting in a cluttered
underground bunker office with no windows, rolling a cigar with his
brown moist lips, orchestrating the lives of hundreds of musicians
while bouncing them all over the U.S., cutting deals and trading favors
and switching dates, a large pile of index cards scattered over his desk
and two or three laying on the floor.

Once, I found myself standing alongside a snowdrift outside a
cowboy bar in Montana in February, looking at my hands covered with
bad mosquito bites. Town names became meaningless to me.
Bartenders started looking alike. The countryside rose and fell outside
the van's window, over and over, so much so I'd test it with my foot
before stepping out. My body clock during this time not only broke,
it wasn't even right twice a day. All I could remember of places were
the people I met there.

We traveled the circumference of the world, 25,000 miles, and
never left a sixteen-state area. We covered that and more about every
six to eight months, thanks to Sam, driving the old van in large vicious
circles, slapping on parts and twisting the bailing wire a little tighter
each time.

Which is how we barely got to Hubcap, Oklahoma and Robert's
Retreat, breaking down twice along the way. Robert's Retreat looked
ordinary enough from the outside, but once you were through the door
it was darker than the inside of a rock. Ceiling, walls and booths were
all black. Not shiny black, but soft bottomless black. Light absorbing
black. Even in the middle of the night, when you walked inside, the
room was so dark it seemed to pull the eyes right out of your head for
the first ten minutes. There *were* lights inside, but they were black
lights, those dark purple tubes that don't so much brighten an area as
radiate it. False teeth glow under black lights, as do certain colors of
clothing. Caucasian skin turns bluish green. The lights illuminated a

series of huge fluorescent spray paintings of naked women in various poses, paintings that seemed to float in the air over the booths against an endless background of darkness.

Directly above me over the bandstand was one large picture of a naked woman, small head, arms of different sizes and stringy hair, reclining on a hill and contemplating the charms of a Pepsi bottle she held down low. That was what you saw when you looked at the band: not musicians playing but rather this badly drawn fluorescent woman and her bottle, glowing just above my head. Other intriguing pictures were to be found about every five feet around the room, each floating in its own pool of black light.

The only white light in the whole room was over the cash register behind the bar at the other end of the building—where reality ruled. The stage did not have spot lights; we were surrounded on all sides by more black lights. One of the interesting things about black lights is if you're as dark as Dennis and Vince, you disappear, leaving instead an empty shirt and pants standing there holding a guitar or sitting behind the organ. For a place that booked soul bands, this was about the weakest idea I ever heard of. We probably looked like a one-man band with me glowing green in the middle while two shirts jumped around on either side, all underneath the deformed, naked, much brighter fluorescent woman.

It was an Indian bar owned by an old white guy named Robert. Robert looked like he'd personally tasted and gotten drunk on every juice known to man. In his seventies, he had weak little eyes that watered a lot and yellow skin that seemed to hang off him like an old bed sheet. His boy Junior ran the place.

Robert and all his official bar policies were badly racist. He had a No Blacks rule (exceptions always made for musicians) based on the premise that blacks and Indians fight too much. Mexicans couldn't go in there, and white people just didn't. You had to be some kind of

Indian, preferably Kiowa. Soul music was very popular and we were a big hit there.

Up until then, the only racism I had had to deal with was the small-time stuff like glaring looks and muttered grumblings that weren't directed at me but at Vince or Dennis. I'd learned to spot it in its ten thousand little forms and was starting to think this was one more subject I knew inside and out. I found it in the eyes of store clerks and in the way change was counted in cafes; I could spot it halfway down the block if Vince and I were walking downtown in Nebraska or Wyoming. I grew a sixth sense in that band that had an effective range of thirty yards—but apparently didn't work well enough in the dark. Maybe all those black lights scrambled my radar.

We had just come down off stage at the end of the first set. I went left around the dance floor and Vince and Dennis went right. Leaving the cluster of black lights around the stage I stepped into an impenetrable ink where I could pass next to a dead elephant and not know it was there. I could see the bar lights about sixty feet ahead of me and the flames from two gas heaters along the wall on my left. I used a handrail alongside the dance floor to guide me. Moving at a good clip toward the bar, I noticed a piece of flame seem to shoot out of the heater and then grow larger as it came straight for me. It was one of those "damnedest things I ever saw" moments when the laws of physics are suspended and you're never quite sure what to do first. I was still looking toward the bar, not quick enough to even turn my head, when the fire jumped out of the heater, made a long arc straight for me, and in half a second or less had burned through my shirt and right into my soft skin.

Then there was a guy in my face yelling "Nigger lover" and coming at me. I'm sure I yelled. I don't remember doing it but I'm sure I did. I had to. There was smoke rising off my chest. I could smell it in the dark. I put out my arms somehow and he bumped into them and fell backwards, stumbling into the group of men sitting around the gas heater. I think I yelled and I think I pushed him; I do know he ended up on the floor in front of the gas heater, waving a coat hanger that was still red hot. It took me a moment to figure out I'd been branded.

He thrashed around on the floor for another minute, yelling at me, but I can't be sure because I was bent over and having visions by then. Vince and Dennis came up, Vince with his hand in his pocket holding his knife. I never saw him pull that knife out the entire time I knew him, but he did get it ready a couple of times. And once was then.

Junior, Robert's son and main bartender, came up and saw (by virtue of the light from the fire) the huge hole in my shirt and the smoke rising off my chest, saw me dancing around in pain, saw the guy laying on the floor holding the still glowing coat hanger, and asked the dumbest question possible. "Did you burn him?" He said it in a way that made me think this trick may have been pulled before, like this guy had a reputation for getting drunk and burning people and I hadn't been warned. Junior made him give up the coat hanger and tossed him out. Suspended him from the bar for a week.

I had to go into the restroom to pull off my shirt and see how my branding looked, what kind of mark I was going to carry the rest of my life. He burned a backward "C" into me, the shape of the hanger's hook. Looked like the hoof print of a tiny mule that kicked me, only red and running.

Having that fresh wound on my chest made playing difficult the rest of the night. I was no longer in an artistic frame of mind. Instead, I was thinking about finding a blowtorch and returning the favor. It's surprising how much of your entire body movement is connected to that one pectoral muscle on the left side of your chest. Some people say that pain clears the mind. Pain tends to occupy my mind like an invading army. I didn't have one clear thought the rest of the night except to look out for people with neon coat hangers. My beat was unsteady and when I had to use my left arm very much I tended to speed up and lose the pocket.

Vince was sympathetic and during the next break told me about the time he was stabbed in the thigh by a woman who thought he was someone else. Pointing towards the door he said, "At least that old motherfuck meant it; I got stuck because I was wearing a hat and standing in bad light. Bitch apologized after she did it." Then he smiled at himself and chuckled a little bit, glancing over at me, wanting to laugh but holding himself back. It was his blues personality exerting itself again but I couldn't see that at the time. I wanted more sympathy. I really wanted a break from all these adventures I was having but there was no break in sight.

Vince, Me and the Devil

At first I thought a little worm inside would crawl its way to the surface and take over his personality, like some bad impulse woke up, some perverse suicidal mania that came over Vince about once every three or four months. But he insisted it was the Devil. He talked like he knew him well, like the Devil was a sneaky shit who'd walk into his life at odd moments and grab him by the neck and make him do wild things, which resulted in Vince either getting arrested or stabbed or pitifully drunk five days in a row, or made him score some heroin. More often than not, his devil preferred heroin.

Vince's seizure came to him on a Thursday in October after I'd been with the band nine months. We were working one of those dilapidated old ballrooms Sam found for us, this one on the outskirts of Dallas. I'd noticed Vince was making lots of friends that week and smoking weed out in the parking lot during every break, but I assumed he was just pleased to be away from those small towns and in a city once again.

Dennis had gone to the club early that evening to work on his amp. He was always rewiring his amp to get more power out of it. His whole rig looked like a ninth grade science project, with wires running every which way and duct tape on the outside and extra switches added on. I went by Vince's room early and caught him just as he was leaving to go somewhere. "You can come, man, but you got to be cool. Understand?" I said yes, but had no idea what he was talking about.

We walked a couple of blocks alongside the interstate from the motel to what turned out to be a whorehouse nearby. I found out on the way that Vince was going there to score some dope. I wasn't sure what kind and didn't care as long as I could tag along and not have to sit in that dreary motel room any longer.

Vince did all the talking going in the door and I just drifted with the flow, ending up on a couch in a small front room with a woman named Nona while Vince went into the back with a guy called Rosco. Looking closely at Rosco, I remembered seeing him at the club before, talking to Vince. Ten minutes later they came out of the back room bullshitting and shaking hands and being loud, both of them with bright eyes. The moment Rosco and Vince came back into the room Nona suddenly shifted gears and started telling me about her son, acting natural, after bitching continuously and in a low whisper the previous ten minutes about Rosco and his drug dealing and telling me he was drawing heat and making her business hard. She'd seen me at the club and liked the band and warned me to stay away from the hard stuff. I said, "Oh, it's not for me; it's for Vince." "Well, you gots to take care of yourself," she patted my hand. Then the door opened and she said, "And Desmond graduated *ninth* in his class at high school." "Whoa!" I said, a little late, noticing a scar on her arm that looked a lot like teeth marks.

On the way back to the motel Vince was humming and strutting and looking lighter than air. If he was full of the devil at that moment, he seemed fairly happy about it. What I saw was Vince with a fine focus in his eyes and a bouncy step, pretty much hopping all the way back to the motel.

I followed him into his room. It took him ten minutes of preparation to get down to business. Stuff had to be laid out, he had to find an extension cord, things had to cook. "Drag a chair over here, man. You can help."

| | |

I guess everyone has a dark side but at the age of twenty I'd not really rooted around in mine much at all. I was curious to watch Vince and learn something new, but I'd honestly never considered doing heroin myself. Even at the last moment, it was the furthest thing from my mind.

"Hey, man . . . I think Rosco done gave me some extra. I can fit you up with just a pinch, man. If you wants . . . little pinch."

Vince was being friendly and I knew that. The gesture really meant a lot to me. It was not empty or casual. Over the months he and I had actually come to be friends, started to think of ourselves as a team. For him to offer me a pinch of this or a drink of that was always more than just an offer; it was like breaking bread with him. Like he was saying, "My *real* friends? They got what I got—mine's theirs." Maybe it's just the power an older, wonderful musician has over a younger one. I rarely felt less than honored to be hanging with Vince, and when he made an offer of substance, more was going on than if I just *wanted* it. It was symbol, emblem, forbidden fruit and the blood of the cross. I said yes.

I also hated needles with a passion. Vince wanted me to go first, "So's there no screwups," he said. I agreed but was starting to feel sucked up in events and a little giddy already. Every time I said yes I moved closer to something I wasn't sure I wanted at all.

Vince took what I thought was a microscopic amount—really just a small fingernail dip of the brown powder—and dropped it into a cap off a Pepsi bottle. He added a few drops of water with the syringe, letting it mix and begin to bubble as it cooked over his lighter. He added some extra water after a while and stirred a little with the tip of the needle, making sure it was well mixed and ready to go. It all looked about as sinister as could be. When things were finally ready, he sat the cap down and wrapped the extension cord off Dennis' hot plate around my upper arm and told me to squeeze it tight. "Lean on that sombitch. One end in your mouth, then pull on the other. Lean on it hard. Got to get that blood in there to sit still so we can hit it."

I was fairly muscled up at that point of my life and when I made a fist, large, tubular veins stood up all over my arm.

"Oooh, weeee!" Vince said. "Man, I could do you in the dark. Wish I had veins like those! Tell you that for *sure!*"

Vince finally got the needle ready to go after thumping it a few times and squeezing a tiny drop out the end. Then he took me by the forearm and brought the needle down on the huge vein in the crook of my arm. About then I had to close my eyes.

I could feel the pressure of it going in and Vince said, "Loosen the cord, motherfuck." There was a long pause. I started to get curious about what he was still doing down there, so I opened my eyes.

Vince was drawing blood out and filling the syringe, then saw me looking and started to push it back in. I said, "Whoa, what's this?! Problem here?!"

"No, man. This called 'popping,' so's you get everything there is."

"Oh, good," I said. "Let's get it all, for sure," thinking to myself, I hope there wasn't a cockroach sleeping in this syringe last night, or licking the tip or whatever. I was deeply anxious.

Then there was a heat flash of about 200 degrees, and suddenly I wasn't anxious anymore. Vince finished and loosened the cord completely and that warm rush kept passing all over my body and it seemed to me like the most incredibly fine thing I'd ever experienced in my life. I took a deep breath and my IQ went up fifty points. I felt strong, I felt smart, and for maybe the first time in my life, I felt totally brave. Hell, I could've jumped right into a jet airplane and flown straight at the sun. Nothing, suddenly, was beyond me.

Then it was Vince's turn and he wanted me to hold the cord for him, probably because he couldn't bite it too well. He finished cooking up the rest of the stuff and getting ready. His shot was going to be ten times what mine was. He had to squirt it with water over and over to get that much cooked properly. He cooked and stirred and squirted so long I thought the stuff might be so hot he'd burn his vein.

Then he had me wrap the cord and draw down, "tighter than shit, man, lean on it!" I did, and in my improved and sharpened condition, probably squeezed too hard. I put all my drummer's muscles into it while Vince started slapping his forearm and bitching, looking for a vein. He had none that I could see. He had two or three long thin scars like gray threads that looked to come from being grazed by a sharp knife, and several dark lines of indistinct origin, and three or four small circular scars mostly on the forearm. Vince slapped and squeezed for a minute and then decided to go where he knew one had to be. "You gots to hold that mutherfucker *tight*, man. *Lean* on it."

He poked around with the needle until it seemed he was fairly confident and then drew out some blood. "There we are! Paydirt. You can relax now." He shot the whole business in, and then drew out a lot of blood and shot it all back in once again. That was it, maybe three minutes total.

"Turn loose the cord, motherfucker. Don't need it now." Vince leaned back in the chair and seemed to fall five or six miles through space. Like he was tumbling. Vince was relaxed to a degree that was unique for him. Really kind of thumped between the eyes. I'd seen Vince relaxed before but even dead tired and half asleep he was always a chatty person with a bright eye. Now, it looked like he was on some mind trip to China. His eyes were closed, and his breathing slow, mouth hanging open.

I gave him a minute and then said, "Hey, Vince. Got to get to the club. We only got twenty minutes until start time."

"Oh, yeah, man." He took a huge gulp of air. "The gig . . . gotta get to the gig." He roused himself out of the chair and went to the small bathroom for a cup of water. Vince filled a huge plastic sports cup with ice and water, drank off half of it, refilled it and he was ready to go. I grabbed his guitar and we were out the door.

I had run Dennis out earlier in the van so Vince and I could come later. We were almost late at this point and I'd have to drive fast to get us there. And I did drive fast but with only one eye on the road because of what was happening with Vince in the seat beside me.

He seemed to be exploding. I'd never seen anything like it. It can only be described as watching a human volcano erupt. Like seeing someone become supercharged, bursting with manic energy, compelled to move and breathe and talk and gulp water while sweating buckets. I think being confined to the van just made it worse. He was shifting around in his seat and looking three directions at once. Within minutes sweat was dripping off his ears. Furious talking, like it was building up in his mouth and he was spitting it out. His talk escalated into a torrent of clipped phrases punctuated by grunts or "Man!" or "Huh!" All his verbal mannerisms came to the surface, all the stresses and stretches in his speech jammed together in quick succession, one after another, like waves slapping on a beach. He'd jerk his shoulders up like his clothes were too tight or shoot his arm out like he was shaking something loose. Burning up.

His shirt turned as black just as if he were standing in the rain, and the more he sweated, the more he drank out of the giant cup. It was dangerous sweating, scary sweating. It made me think of heart attacks and seizures. He put his hand on the dashboard and left a wet handprint. Then he was jamming his foot into the floor like the van was too small and he was trying to stretch it out, talking the whole time, unconscious he was doing it. He was dragging sweat off his face with his hand, wiping it on his wet pant legs while hunching his shoulders and tugging on his shirt and shuffling his feet around, talking talking talking: "Shit! Oh man! I left my tie back in the room. Never mind . . . I don't need a tie . . . Fuck the tie, man. Motherfucker don't need no tie to play music. Ties are for sissies. Whores wear ties. Dennis wears ties . . . Ha Ha Ha . . . Oh man, that Dennis, he's a tie-wearing motherfucker. You got your tie on man? *Take* that thing off. We're not wearing any ties tonight, man. Fuck Dennis." On and on. Saying nothing, lighting cigarettes, slinging ashes all over the front. It was a cool night, late October, and Vince rolled down the window. "Man, you hot? I'm burning up. Must be ninety in here! Shit, mother-fucker melt in a place like this. You want to stop and get a Pepsi, man? I'm out of water, man. Pull in here and I'll buy us Pepsis."

I didn't stop. I told him he could drink an ocean once we got to the club but we were late already. He said he was drying up and about to die. He tried to crunch ice with his few teeth. He hung his head out the window and sucked in air. He fell silent for a minute and stared at the floor like he was back in China, and then snapped awake again and resumed talking. Those little trances came and went, never longer than a moment. The drive to the club might have been ten minutes, fifteen at the most, but Vince seemed to have burned up a week's worth of energy sitting in the seat, like a human humming-bird. I was afraid his heart was going a hundred miles an hour.

It was nine o'clock on the nose when we got to the club and we had to start immediately. Dennis was waiting on stage, his shirt glowing blue, staring toward the door when we walked in. I headed for the stage, thinking Vince was behind me but when I got up there he was nowhere to be seen. Dennis was full of questions and wanted to know why we were late. I tried to make excuses and got my sticks and stuff out of the trap case. I sat down and whacked a few notes on the snare to signal Vince "let's go." Vince, amazingly, was at the bar, bullshitting with a couple of women. Dennis said Vince's name once over the PA and Vince ignored him. I played a couple of fills but he didn't come. I told Dennis I'd get him and made my way the whole length of that long building back to the bar.

Vince was telling some long story about the time he'd played with Lionel Hampton and making it funny and using his usual charm but it wasn't working on the women. I don't think they knew who Lionel Hampton was and the bartender was getting impatient for the band to start. Vince was drinking big glasses of water and little glasses of gin and going like a sawmill, talking to the whole bar. I had to almost drag him to the stage. He was saying hi to people he didn't know and talking back over his shoulder.

Vince couldn't just plug his guitar in but had to mess with his amp, and then had to run his guitar cord around his strap a new way, adjust his mic stand, say hi to the audience, throw out a few riffs to limber up, take another drink of water, get a fresh cigarette going and drag a bar towel over his face. Then, ten minutes after nine, he looked at Dennis, did a little shuffle with his feet and asked, "You ready, man?"

Dennis was ready to spit. Dennis was doing nothing but cussing to himself at that point. Vince called out "Breezin'" by George Benson, an instrumental guitar song full of jazz riffs. And once again, probably for the ten millionth time in his life, when Vince started playing everyone forgave him. Or at least I did. It was *beautiful*. It was clean and tasty and strong and Vince was playing as if it were the very best song in the world. Compared to what I expected, you could almost hear the wind rushing into him, his focus was so tight. Like the eye of a storm. He was concentrating on his guitar in ways I'd not seen before. Ordinarily, Vince played his leads while singing or talking or looking around the room. Occasionally he'd play it behind his head or around his back, even playing riffs backwards sometimes while clowning around. He always made it look so easy, like only half his mind was needed to play something as simple as a guitar. But that night his guitar had all his attention. He milked it and stroked it and hugged it to him, choking it one moment and petting it the next, running up and down hills and playing those six strings like they weren't nearly enough for what he had to do.

And sweating like a hurricane too, blowing water left and right. It dripped off his elbows, his nose and ears, off any corner where it could collect, and where it couldn't collect it ran in streams to the floor. He dragged the song out, returning in some inspired way each time to an early bridge at the point we'd start the ending, building the song up again and finding in it fifty possibilities he had to work out. Finally, Dennis had to cut him off and end it for him. Vince had stretched the song out to almost fifteen minutes. I wish I had it on tape. The crowd went nuts.

The closest I ever came to actually slinging lightning bolts from the drum set came that night. My playing was something extraordinary. Listening to Vince, I didn't play over him but mostly kept time behind him, playing the song in my mind four bars ahead, knowing everything long before I did it, sorting and using my best ideas, floating on the back edge of the backbeat and hitting it hard. There's twenty different ways of keeping the same time, but God only does it one way and that's with a single omnipotent finger creating life at every stroke. The master of time doesn't *keep* time, he *makes* time, and that night I understood the difference. I was feeling so strong and confident that, for once, I wasn't following Vince at all, but making him follow me—follow me exactly where he wanted to go. It's complicated, but it was magical.

After the song was over I saw that the playing had relaxed Vince and slowed his breathing down. He wasn't jumping around any more and was talking less. He wiped his guitar off with the towel, then cleared his face and neck with it, then ran it down both arms and asked, "What next?" Dennis was looking at him with a quizzical expression, like "what got into you?" After we finished probably the best set we ever played—which went ten minutes overtime because Vince couldn't get out of "Bring it on home to me"—we took a break and Dennis wanted to talk to me. "Is Vince high? I know he is, but I want you to tell me. Is he high?" I told him the truth, or at least that half of it. "Man, you gots to keep him away from that stuff! If he gets started again we're going to lose him. Hell, he could die tonight!" Dennis put the heaviest spin on it he could and I felt blind and stupid and dripping with guilt. All I could think of was Vince dropping like a sack of rocks right on stage.

Musically, it was a great night, just damn near perfect. Dennis and Vince weren't talking but Vince didn't care. All he wanted to do was play. Dennis was grouchy and seemed to only sound flat, no enthusiasm at all. But you couldn't tell because there was so much Vince. And I pushed him for all he was worth. He burned bright that night. And for all the pushing I tried to do, it was him pushing me, jamming every song into a life or death struggle, playing like there was no tomorrow. Pure gorgeous. Over the night he played so many great riffs and sang such amazing songs—rich, powerful, pitiful songs—you could see his soul shining through, like he'd become a complete human being. For about six hours.

I guess my own soul was doing a little shining that night, so I wasn't the best judge of his playing—but it had *sounded* awesome. And after reflection things made more sense to me. I always wondered why a person would give themselves over to something like heroin, and now I knew. Heroin taught me that everything makes perfect sense if I just investigate it a bit. These people aren't stupid; they're being totally natural and immanently reasonable. This wasn't *just* getting high, this was like slipping into angel skin. I didn't know a human being could feel like this. I'd heard the antidrug rhetoric and believed it regarding heroin. I thought it was supposed to be entirely bad. Now I saw how truly complicated it was. How terribly complicated it was. Some things you don't want to know. The danger with heroin lies in waking up that one taste bud you didn't know you had.

| | |

The next day Vince slept until five and then was no good for anything. He'd ripped his voice, bruised his hands and was weak as a baby. Looked just awful. Like some bug had laid eggs in his eyes. He blinked away tears and grit, eyeballs so red it was painful to see. Mouth hanging loose, his nine surviving teeth covered with a white mucus. "Oh man . . . shit . . . whew! Did I have a good time last night!" Then he grouched around the rest of the day, bitching about one thing or another. That night he was unfocused and missed notes. Vince had burned up something in himself, something that would take several days to start back up again. Dennis wouldn't let him out of his sight until we left Dallas. Considering the rough way they had with each other, it was kind of touching.

I didn't suffer nearly so much the next day. I felt a little weak but was still functional. Vince looked bombed out.

I'd heard earlier Vince had a nickname, "Dancing Bear." That was his street name as a young man in Chicago. I think I heard that from Dennis and filed it away, thinking it didn't make much sense.

Vince didn't look like a bear and I'd never seen him dance until that one time he had a devil to dance with.

High Hair

I was getting a little numb by this point, my interest in the road starting to decline. The crowds all began to look the same regardless of how exotic the club happened to be or in what part of the country. Race, gender, region, whatever: it was just a mass of people that huddled around the bandstand. Each place we played we had our good nights and bad nights, but even the good nights were routine. My physical stamina was beginning to weaken as well. All my clothes smelled like smoke. My shit was runny from months of bad food. My outlook on the world began to suffer; I became jaundiced and poisoned.

Wide exposure to whiskey and drugs and sex and sin of all types had sharpened my vision concerning these things. I looked now not at the alcohol or any particular indulgence, but at the individual. *How* a person gets away doesn't seem important after a while. That he remains desperate to do so, *does*.

I find that most of my worst pictures of hell have been caught in reflection, out the corner of my eye, brief glimpses of a person's true nature, that awful craving some people have. Only occasionally does it happen otherwise. Only occasionally does a full blown, detailed example of ignorant blind hunger run amok just stand before you begging to have his photograph taken.

But everything and everyone imaginable will present itself sooner or later in front of the bandstand. Out in west Texas oil country in the late part of December that year, we were working in a country/rock bar called "The Jumping Bean." Sometime during the second set a man and a woman strolled into the club and sat at a table in front of the stage. They were a couple indigenous to country and western bars in west Texas in the early '70s. The man wore a turquoise suit with silver trim over a shirt with a high starched collar, dress boots with more silver trim, and his hair was combed high above his head in an exaggerated Elvis style. He was probably in his late fifties and seemed to be already half lit. His girlfriend wore her hair piled even higher than his in an imitation Dolly Parton style. Her dress was low cut and she wore spiked heels. Because of her smooth, fleshy, well-pampered extra pink skin, she looked like a fifty-year-old baby. You could describe them as seedy but that would be unfair to the seeds. I noticed the couple not because they stood out from the crowd, but because the man was obviously paying so much attention to the band and seemed to be talking about us to his date. Ordinarily, couples in clubs are either there to hustle each other, or they are married and want to get out of the house. This guy was animated and talked a lot so I knew he was hustling the woman. I imagined he considered himself a music critic and was expounding on the band's various qualities. Not that I cared, just that I noticed him doing it.

When it came time for us to take a break he was up at the bandstand immediately talking and introducing himself. I heard him say he'd had a record out a couple of years ago and had just come from doing a radio gig. As I had no interest in talking to him—based solely on his taste in clothes—I snuck off to the side of the dance floor and found a quiet place to rest. I ended up studying his girlfriend a bit from across the room, making myself depressed, imagining people cling together because they have to. It's never pleasant to see white knuckles in a relationship.

Once the third set started, Dennis told us we had a musician in the club who wanted to sit in. I asked him if he was talking about high hair sitting at that table over there and he said he was. "It's a bad idea, Dennis," I said. "We're going to sound bad."

"No, man. It's just one song. I talked to him; we'll sound good."

I looked and saw that high hair had his guitar case sitting beside him while he smiled and nodded at us. Letting strangers sit in is almost always a wrong decision. Usually it's wrong because they don't know the tunes or the band's arrangements and so will make mistakes and the whole band will sound weak. Even more often you will get an impostor who can't play at all and the song will be a disaster. Only occasionally will someone get up to play who is a quality player. But Dennis was a kindhearted person and hated to say no. Dennis considered himself a master of b.s. and—as a consequence—was bullshitted nearly all the time.

After two or three songs Dennis waved the guy up to the stage. I've seen scalded cats make a slower jump to their feet. No sooner was he under the lights than he had a microphone in his hand talking to the crowd. When I looked into his eyes and heard his voice I knew he was drunk. The first words out of his mouth were to thank "his good friends and buddies" in the band here in El Paso for asking him to play, as though we couldn't let such a rare opportunity pass without hearing some of his special magic on the guitar. He mentioned his record again—the title was something saccharine like "My Tenderness is All for You, Forever." I'd never heard of it. He had a boxy acoustic guitar hung around his neck that could never be heard without an electric pickup and so was obviously a prop. High hair then proceeded to tell the room that he had only just that day returned from visiting his good friend Waylon down in Austin. He said he always looked up Waylon when he was in Austin, suggesting that Waylon would be disappointed if he didn't. He also managed to mention his "good friend Willie." Then he mentioned "Buck" and "Charlie" and just about every other country music giant of the day. It didn't seem he knew any obscure people. Then he somehow brought up Nashville, then New York, and eventually got to California before he finished his next sentence. I looked over at Dennis and tried, by subtle nods and winks, to let him know our show was going to hell second by second.

"Let's play something," I said, to no one in particular. High hair took the hint and then began introducing the song. This too took him a while. He asked, in a quick aside to Dennis, if we knew a Johnny Cash tune that was a big hit at the time, "Ring of Fire." We did, so he then proceeded to tell the audience the personal story behind the song. Seems that Johnny had written it just for him. Sort of a personal tribute Johnny had wanted to pay him. An inside joke only the two of them knew. The more the guy talked, the less Johnny had to do with the song. Seems that high hair had been there when it was written, and had contributed a few verses, and the melody, and just about everything else, but he was such a generous guy he let Johnny take credit for the song. Then he mentioned that Willie was there too and always appreciated high hair's help when it came to writing his songs. He was about to launch once again into his personal, behind-the-scenes history in country music, when Dennis reminded him that now might be time for a tune.

We knew the song inside out and had probably played it a hundred times as a request. Dennis usually sang it. I counted it off and we started the intro. I immediately noticed that high hair was having a little trouble finding the beat. It was a simple train beat and right in front of him but he was looking all over for it. You couldn't hear his guitar out front so it didn't matter, but he looked at the rest of us like we didn't know what we were doing. As the first verse came up I was ready for anything. Seems high hair couldn't sing either. His voice was passable, in a low-grade fashion, but hardly anything you'd expect Johnny and Willie to listen to in their living rooms. But he *was* dramatic. He threw his head this way and that, twisted up his face for maximum effect, bellowed at the top of his lungs, and strummed his guitar like it was the crank that kept him going. He got high marks for energy but nothing else. If we hadn't known the song so well he would've pulled us all off the beat and confused the arrangement. He missed one bridge every time we crossed it. As it was, the band played with a grim determination all the way to the ending.

I expected Dennis at that point to thank the guy, get him off the stage, and let us continue with the set. But high hair was too quick. Even before the last note faded and the polite applause started, he was telling the audience they were too kind and that, yes, he would sing another song for them. Other than taking him bodily and slinging him into the crowd, there wasn't anything we could do. He started once again with his too professional, world-weary but deeply appreciative voice telling the audience that it was kind people like them who gave life meaning. I was getting deeply depressed and Dennis could tell I was about to stab the guy from behind with my drumstick and shook his head for me to lay off. High hair called out a Buck Owens tune and began telling the crowd some humorous anecdote about himself and Buck, when I counted it right over him and we began, cutting him off in mid-sentence. If anything, that song was worse than the one before. We were clearly getting too deep down his song list.

If he hadn't quit after that second song I was going to reach over and turn off the PA. It wasn't my job to call the breaks (that was Dennis') but I didn't know how long I could go on embarrassing myself with this idiot on stage. Fortunately he quit, but only after thanking everyone from the bartender to the doorman, with a "special" thank-you for his dear sweetheart sitting there at his table. He got down off the stage like he expected roses to be tossed at him and waved in his best Lyndon Johnson manner at the room as he walked back to his seat. It was a dispirited set we finished.

At the break I headed for the door outside to stand in the parking lot with the hookers and drug dealers and perhaps improve my impression of humanity. Look at a little comprehensible behavior for a while. I came back fifteen minutes later to start the last set and saw he had his arm around Dennis like they were sharing secrets.

During that final set I looked over periodically at him and his girlfriend sitting at the table and saw that the woman was becoming thoroughly embarrassed by the guy. He was drinking steadily and talking so loudly that occasionally I could hear him over the songs. Then, near the end of the night, I saw him slump and fall out of his chair. He'd drunk himself unconscious and hit the floor sound asleep. But the most astonishing thing of all (I had to sit up and look over my rack tom to see this) was that when he hit the floor his hair unfurled and slung itself out across the carpet, several large pieces coming loose, probably eighteen inches of it. He must have kept it hairsprayed in place but once he banged his head on the floor it all sprang loose and unraveled. It was so long people had to step over it to walk past. His head looked suddenly boney and little. The woman was mortified and just stared at him. People at nearby tables scooted their chairs away. He lay there a moment, eyes closed, mouth open, and then finally puked— slow and casual, it bubbling up and out of him like hot mud out of the ground. It was the doorman who came over finally to prop him back up and try to wake him but he was out cold. I think the girlfriend left in a cab. All I know is he remained propped there on the floor leaning against a chair for a good half hour. The last song we played that night was by his friend Willie. I thought about dedicating the song to him, but Dennis vetoed the idea.

Hell with the Lid Off

We continued on without even one vacation in the schedule, dragging our tired carcasses over one state after another, typically racing across Wyoming one afternoon, Missouri the next night. Months began to blur. I was so turned around and lost I couldn't have found north if I'd been magnetized and laid in a bowl of water.

It was springtime finally and the front of the van was an inch thick with bug bodies and disconnected wings and odd left legs poking up. It gave the van a two-tone look: beat-up blue everywhere except the front end, which was a reddish brown-white mix. Sometimes Dennis would have to scrub a spot in the dried bug juice to see out the front window. Usually, though, he'd wait for a rainstorm to clean things off. I used to hate rainstorms in that van during the springtime. As soon as you turned on the wipers, the windshield smeared over with a milky film and forced you to stick your head out the window to see. Or at least I would. Dennis would just stare into the milk until it cleared, endangering us all.

We came into Kansas City, Missouri during such a storm. It hit right at the city limits and left me with the impression that Kansas City was a confusing and obscure place. We were booked (by Dr. Dartboard) into a strip joint/lounge in a dark basement near downtown called "Cherry's." In my whole pantheon of bars and clubs, this place rested on rock bottom. It just wasn't safe to be in, for anybody. There was disease in the air, and bullets. Bad attitudes galore. No animating spirit like the Coco Mellow, no love of living in there at all. The room even looked dangerous, being underground and without many escape routes open. People died there all the time, though death didn't get mentioned much. Wasn't interesting enough. Too ordinary. It was that kind of place, sad and mean.

We were set up on a high stage with a ratty red curtain behind us and a dark red, sticky carpet underneath. On either side of the stage were go-go cages six feet off the floor and so close Vince could poke his guitar neck through the bars and bother the girls. Immediately in front of us and slightly lower, but still blocking my bass drum, was a third and slightly larger go-go stage with a permanent striptease going on.

I do not believe any of the girls had training as dancers. They all looked like women down on their luck and kind of hating it when men reached up with twenty-dollar bills. The newest dancers had the worst reaction to these sudden pokes and grabs and insertions. They had my complete sympathy. One of them, named Patricia, used a baton in her act and would stab people if they got *too* friendly. These women were all plenty nice when fully clothed, but on stage and under the lights they were expected to flop around and act like nymphos and follow the routine. You didn't want to look too deeply in their eyes while they were smiling and shimmying around.

That week Dennis hired a tenor saxophone player to sit in, a guy named Roy C. Apparently, the club's manager thought of saxophone music as strip music and required every band to have one. An old friend of Dennis and Vince's, Roy C had grown up in Chicago and the three of them had played in many bands together. It was like old home week. Roy C had just come off the road with Joe Tex and was living in KC with an old girlfriend and we were lucky to get him.

Roy C had a dapper look, manicured and polished. Each hair was right on Roy. He had a small thick mustache and quick eyes. He wore a suit and his tie was always expensive and perfectly knotted. His shoes were like an extra pair of spotlights on the floor. Shirts all looked brand new. Everything about Roy C was graceful and stylized. Restraint and decorum were his trademarks. He was one of those players who seemed relaxed even during the busiest tunes. Roy C didn't sweat. He looked like a banker next to Vince and Dennis.

The addition of a player that good expanded the band's sound and fattened us up considerably. My ear was so used to playing three piece that the saxophone sounded like a whole horn section to me, particularly on that very first song that first night. I think we opened with "I'm a Soul Man." We might have been two measures into the intro when the organ locked in, the saxophone screeched and Vince went double clutch—everyone saying, 'Hi, How are you!' We burned for about twenty minutes on that one, taking probably five minutes just to get to the first verse. And sounded like an orchestra. Dennis' singing was something immense.

As sour as I felt about a lot of things in my life right then, it was a privilege to play in *that* band *that* week. By the second night I'd turned into a stick-twirling fool. The three of them balanced each other perfectly. They knew each other's style, each other's influences, and conducted conversations on stage about the old neighborhood by trading riffs back and forth, riffs that for them had faces and dates. Vince would play some Muddy Waters riff and make it sound like a question, and Roy would answer in the affirmative, like, "Yeah, saw him last time I was in Chicago." Earl Hooker was discussed at length, I could tell that. Buddy was asked about. Willie Dixon was mentioned more than once, a lot of B.B. in there, but most of the references I didn't recognize. My grasp of sax players was too thin to be helpful. It was just blazing blues to me.

Vince was mostly restrained while playing with Roy. He gave him equal time. Vince only squirted in a huge way maybe every other song. Roy C would stand there holding his horn, nodding, grinning, listening to Vince, all while looking cool. He really lifted the whole band in terms of stage presence and appearance.

The strippers all seemed to like us. I was complimented on my beat several times. A good sense of rhythm is important to a stripper and they recognized in me an able fellow. I did my best. Still, I was more restrained than Vince or Dennis, who both worked the girls hard during and between breaks. The sight of all that naked flesh seemed to provoke Vince the worst. He liked to have long friendly conversations with the girls just as they came off the stage and before they had a chance to dress, finding some excuse for a brotherly hug or a little tickling. Until he got lucky a few days later, Vince had a badly cramped look and seemed distracted at times.

There were moments during tunes when I'd look out over the crowd, looking through the haze of smoke and between the spotlights, around or between the dancer's legs, looking all the way to the bar on the other side of this upholstered sewer, and think to myself, "this surely is the far back corner of hell." There was groping of some sort under almost every table. Men with nervous eyes and hands in their pockets. Sad, slow-moving whores patrolling up and down the bar, running their fingers across your back. Packages handed off in the rest room. No one wearing sanitary gloves. Our second night there I was cornered by a woman in a wheelchair who reached up and squeezed my pecker, causing me to damn near jump over her to get away. One of the bartenders who watched it all smiled later and said, "You don't want to get in a tight place with Linda after she's had a few. Bet she's hit on every guy in this bar. Surprised she's waited this long to go after you. Just tell her no and she'll leave you alone." I was not convinced.

I know she really wasn't a slut but a troubled individual, but that was the problem in that place: too much trouble in too small an area. Everyone there seemed to be desperate bottom feeders in one way or another. My response was getting out of hand. I have to take my grief in small doses or I get miserable. If the band hadn't sounded so good I probably would have slipped into a coma by the end of the week. Like everyone else, I ignored the large mirrors everywhere.

|||

Having Roy C around also turned those two or three hours after the gig into storytelling festivals where I sat at the feet of masters. Back in the hotel room, everyone lounging around, shoes off and ties loosened, Roy would pull out a joint and Dennis or Vince would drag out a bottle and something would be said that would remind someone else of a story and suddenly Vince was talking about bedbugs in prison down in Huntsville. Roy C would follow with a tale about two sax players he knew in Joliet who shared the same cell and challenged each other all day long. Dennis responded with a great story about a sax player who was challenged like that and was such a quick reader that he played a fly sitting on the page. But this only prompted Roy to come right back with a tale about a trumpet player who hit a note so high he lost his mind. "Hair turned white overnight. He got religion bad. Just like being hit by lightning, man, when it happens. He's preaching now, you know. Down in Oklahoma."

There'd be a pause and Dennis would reach over to take the top off the bottle while Vince started work on relighting the joint. I sat back in my seat and assumed my detached observer mode. Then a longer pause, "Oh man, that's nothing." Dennis would start in, having thought of something by then.

It was on one of those nights I heard the true story about Bad, Bad Leroy Brown, about how he was just a local pool hustler on the South Side who got shot and died of natural causes during an argument, and then some white boy comes along and writes a song about it. Everyone chuckled over that one, including me.

Into the late morning hours, just before dawn, the conversation would wind down and get serious. I probably learned more about music that week than at any other time. The three of them had all learned the same lessons, shared the same beliefs. The subjects late, late at night became Style and Sound and Identity. Talking about some piano player, Vince would always come back to the same point. "I'll say this about Oscar—car thief or not—he had his own sound . . . and that's what you got to have. Didn't nobody else sound like Oscar."

"You *got* to have your own sound," Roy C said. "That's it, man. If I don't know you by your playing, I don't know you. These wallpaper bands, man—that's what I can't stand. Just can't get behind that shit. I've got an on/off thing with a couple cats now, piano player and drummer, both *fine* musicians. No wallpaper in our band. Unique and sharp. Drummer particularly. He knows what you can't teach."

And Roy C let it drop at that. There was another long pause and I started to wake up and get curious. Roy was messing with a match and slowly digging in the ashtray. Dennis had his eyes closed and Vince was looking in the middle space. "Uh, Roy?" I finally asked. "What is that thing you can't teach?"

Roy looked up like this was a fresh question, one so simple he'd never think to ask it. He studied me a moment. "What's the special ingredient? You want to know Aunt Jemima's Secret Recipe?"

"Uh . . . yeah. If you could tell me." I was feeling luckier than at any moment in my life. Here it was, the philosopher's stone, about to be laid at my feet. Probably knock ten years off my development.

Vince refocused and then piped up. "The secret ingredient, *white boy*, is how much 'monkeyfuck' you throw in."

Roy laughed and Dennis woke up laughing too.

"Monkeyfuck?" I asked.

Roy calmed down and took me seriously. "It's that little special energy, that . . . twitch that makes shoe leather burn. What puts the twirl in the girl's skirt. It's being in the pocket and out of the pocket too, you know what I'm saying?"

"Don't confuse the boy, Roy," Vince said. "The drummer's job is to keep the fools in line. Leave the monkeyfucking to wild men like you."

"And you," Roy said.

I can't say how many hours I pondered this advice. I wear it now like a little knot of wisdom around my neck, like a medallion with those sacred words "Monkeyfuck" inscribed on one side, and Vince's smiling face on the other. It didn't speed up my development any, but now I knew what I was looking for, what lay at the end of the road, if I lasted long enough.

That Saturday night we tore down and said good-by to all the dancers and got paid and had a late dinner with Roy at an all-night restaurant before the three of us left town. We were off to Clovis, New Mexico for a week at the Cactus Club. A 750-mile trip. I missed Roy badly. We all did.

Romance

It happened to me the week we returned to Sterling, Colorado. We'd been there at least twice before—maybe three times, I'd lost count—working the same club, staying at the same hotel, eating at the places we'd eaten at before, the same local musicians coming out to hear us. We had first names for everybody, we had preferred rooms, set routines from the day we arrived. I'd like to say it was a homecoming for us, because that's what Dennis called it over the PA that first night, but it was more like being stuck on a Ferris wheel while the attendant is in the rest room. To paraphrase B.B. King, "The thrill was gone."

The town was buried under four feet of snow when we found it. After an incredible eighteen-hour drive up from Tyler, Texas, we went to the club first to unload and set up, the van parked between two snowdrifts, all of us walking around like mummies and smelling like a gym, then to the hotel for some rest. It was a sleepy, low-rent hotel in downtown Sterling only a couple of blocks from the club. The place was always three-fourths empty. The landlady lived in a room behind the check-in counter. She'd sit back there in an easy chair and watch TV all day and keep an eye out through the door for customers. I think her legs were bad because she walked with two canes. I never saw her come out into the lobby or any other part of the hotel; she lived pretty much in her room. The real work there was done by a young girl named

Jenny, who the old lady probably yelled for fifty times a day.

I had talked with Jenny before and remembered her well. It had taken me a while to know her because of her habit of never saying anything, and of staring at people like a moth stares at a spotlight. She was a boyish-looking girl with teeth that stuck out like guns from a fort. Her lips never touched when she closed her mouth so she swallowed a lot and wiped her chin. She could have been fifteen or twenty-five and was the one who cleaned the rooms. Jenny was kind of a presence in the hotel. I'm not sure she ever left the building. If you looked around, she'd always be somewhere. When I saw her again in the lobby, I said hello and she burst into her usual grin before showing us to our rooms.

I had always liked Jenny although I probably didn't think about her much. I always said hello to her because she was so enthusiastic about saying hello back, beaming at me and standing stock still. I assumed she acted the same way with everybody but I was never around to see. She had a deep horsy voice that did not go with her body at all.

Ordinary conversations with her generally did not occur. I'd not heard her speak a complete sentence yet. It was almost as if she were listening to her own private theme song all the time. Once each day she came to my room to clean but Jenny did not talk beyond a yes or no answer to a direct question. Typically, I'd just fish around for anything to say while she was there.

"So I guess it's a good deal, you living here. You like living here, where you work?"

"Yeahuh," she'd say into the sink and then grin.

"I know that I'd like it. Yes, sir-ree. Especially with the weather you got here. Just walk out your door and you're at work. And I imagine you meet a lot of people here, salesmen, families, oil field workers, beet farmers?"

"Yeahuh," she'd say again, and then start smiling from ear to ear.

She kept smiling until it turned into beaming, making no sense at all. I was a little disconcerted at first but, growing up in Oklahoma, I'd known many kinds of people and could talk to them all.

I discovered, through trial and error, that Jenny liked animal stories. So I told her about a dog I'd seen smashed by a semi in Nebraska and how the dog had been hit by the front tire and spun around and then headed right back in under the trailer to get hit again. I animated this with gestures and sound effects and made it as dramatic as possible. Jenny gushed and grinned and really seemed to enjoy this, so the next time I saw her I set fire to a cow and then dragged a cat behind a car. Most every day I had something for her. And when I ran out of narrative steam I substituted jokes, like the story of the three-legged pig. How was I to suspect that no one had ever talked to her before? There was no way of knowing she was having the time of her life listening to me. I sometimes think the world should come with warning labels. "Warning. This woman is having a significant experience. Warning." I was an innocent bystander in every way, only trying to be nice to a fellow human being, just trying to maintain myself at that level.

On Tuesday a blizzard hit and closed the roads in and out of town for two days. Cabin fever was rampant. The club had no business at all. There was so much echo in the room we had to turn our reverb off on the PA. We played for the waitresses and a couple of drunks and Vinny, the club owner, who developed a low, dark look whenever we came in the door. Vinny would have to pay us at the end of the week for music no one had heard. Something I'm sure he considered overpriced.

It was a week of seamless boredom. Everyone slept until one or two in the afternoon. Our only trips outside were to the cafe next door and to the club at night. There was a TV in the lobby that Vince and Dennis glued themselves to, but it was daytime soap operas, which I couldn't stand. I stayed in my room and read anything with print on it. I'd steal pillows from Vince and Dennis' rooms and then prop myself up on the bed and lay without moving while I followed the adventures of Elizabeth Taylor and the farm commodity reports. By three o'clock, Jenny would knock on my door. I always had to get up and answer it for her. In other hotels the cleaning ladies would just barge in and mumble if you were in their way. Jenny had to be invited. Then once inside the room, she was a nervous mess and giggled a lot. So I talked to relax her and unknowingly buried myself in an ever deeper hole.

By Saturday night we were ready to put Sterling behind us. We listened to the weather report on the radio and, finding no immediate blizzards on the horizon, decided to get a good night's sleep after the gig and start early in the morning toward North Dakota and Williston, Sam having naturally booked us in the deep north during the midst of winter.

The walk that last night to the club was frigid and silent. The first set was played to an empty room. The second set was played for a party of six who'd probably arrived on a snowplow. By ten-thirty we had the beginnings of a real crowd. Probably twenty-five people, driven out of their homes by the silence in town, had shown up and were being lavishly served by the tip-starved waitresses. Even Vinny had gotten off his bar stool and was seen walking around. Everyone started to perk up.

It was during a song in that second set that Vince nodded to me to look out at the crowd. He usually only did this if there was a fist-fight or stabbing or something else worth seeing. I couldn't find anything at all and had to look twice before spotting Jenny sitting at a back booth. She was sitting alone near a corner and looking at the band.

At the break Vince and I sat down with her, Vince saying, "Man, this is a hopping place. Hadn't seen this many people all week. We're doing good! How're you doing?"

Jenny didn't say a word but smiled at him and held onto her Coke can. Vinny didn't sell Cokes in cans so I asked her, "Jenny, can I buy you a drink?"

Jenny flinched and held her breath, then started to giggle, staring at me and then back at the table. My thought was that Jenny was being sociable, her night on the town. It was good to see a familiar face and I talked about the band and about traveling and whatever else came to mind, covering over the bad stuff. Then Dennis joined us and Vince was telling everyone about Atlanta and where he had played once and about seeing Shaky Legs sing at the Squat and Gobble Club. Vince was about to elaborate on Shaky Legs when Jenny spoke, quiet and just to me, her words hardly getting past her mouth, "You like me, my . . . my outfit?"

She had on a new jumpsuit that still had the large squares across the chest from being folded. Jenny held herself up straight and I said she looked really fine. I directed Vince and Dennis' attention to her new garb and they both oohed and aahed over it. She had on lipstick too and it had already rubbed onto some of her teeth.

The place looked almost full by eleven when we started to play again. We started with our big dance tunes, the hard rocking numbers, building some excitement in the crowd. Two or three times I looked over at the table and saw Jenny grinning and still holding her Coke can. I smiled and nodded my head at her. We pounded out that set with our best enthusiasm, and two cowboys wearing $100 belt buckles started whooping after each song.

When I sat down beside Jenny again she shrunk up, folded herself together for a moment, tense and focused. Then a waitress with pretty legs and a short skirt came up and leaned her thighs against the edge of the table next to Jenny, having to bend over and ask twice if Jenny wanted something because Jenny wouldn't look up at her. I ordered a gin seven, my drinking being a regular thing now and growing daily, and looked around the room at the crowd of about forty people. Vince and Dennis began talking about how Shaky Legs got his name and what women used to say about him. "Oh, man," Vince said. "When it come time . . . then his legs just take off! Like a fish flapping his *tail*, man. You know what I mean?"

There was a tug on my shirt and I looked at my shoulder to see Jenny withdraw her hand and smile at me. I waited to hear what she had to say but she just looked at me and smiled and after a minute I was ready to look at something else when she tugged again on my sleeve. I started to lean over when she lunged up—paused for a breathless second by my ear—and then snorted through her nose, giggling out of control.

I stayed leaning in her direction, like I still wanted to hear, but she whipped back around and locked in on the Coke can. Jenny was giggling hard against herself and could hardly breathe, flushed red, eyes straining out of their sockets, breaking a little sweat.

Then I saw that Dennis was looking at me, smiling and delighted, showing all his teeth. In our band, anything would go. We had no code of conduct. If she looked like a woman and came within grabbing distance, according to Vince and Dennis, she was fair game.

Jenny's breathing slowed down after a minute and she sat back in her seat. Now I felt embarrassed for her. Across the room people yelled at each other over the jukebox and a woman yanked her purse out of a man's hand. The waitress returned and I began drinking my gin.

Dennis kept smiling with a knowing look in his eyes. I ignored him and thought about the possibility that Jenny had never been in a club before.

I turned and asked her if she had a favorite song we could play. She looked up and over at me from the side while she thought of one. When she finally knew she turned in her seat and said, "Rolling," and then kept looking at me, deliberately, like she was making conversation now.

I had to think for a minute. "Oh yeah, 'Proud Mary'? That's one of my favorites too." Doing my best to be polite.

She was all expectation; her eyes widened and narrowed, as though thinking and looking at me at the same time. Then she tugged on my sleeve again, turning and coming up, drawing breath through her mouth, saying, "Ya'll sure good!"

She held onto my shirt for a second longer and then let go, turning back in her seat. The idea occurred to me that she might never have heard a live band before either, and that was why she'd come out tonight, because she'd met us at the hotel. I thanked her as I talked myself to my feet, saying I was sure glad she'd come out and that seeing how close the hotel was to the club she should have come sooner. It was time to start the last set.

We began with our 5/2 jazz shuffle, "Misty," for Dennis to do a talkover where he acted sentimental about our leaving Sterling and lied about all the friends we'd made there. Then he smiled real big for the crowd and acted like Elvis Presley, hamming it up over a significant pause and then said, "So ladies and gentlemens, until the next time we come to Vinny's Supper Club—and we all hope it's real soon—there is just one more thing I have to say—" and then he let out his best James Brown, leather-lung scream and we all snapped to a halt so he could shout, "I Feel Good." The three of us dropped into a wiggly little backbeat that brought the whole room out on the floor. That song led into the next, which led into the song after that. It was a standard medley for us and we played it with a high degree of precision. Lots of fast turns and tricky bridges I knew inside out. My sticks pretty much twirled themselves.

The place was heating up, requests came two and three between each song. Vince showed a red-blue reflection over his forehead and had large drops standing up on each side of his face. Dennis had a skunk mark up the back of his shirt—his trademark from my point of view. It was the first positive playing we'd done all week.

The songs were heating up. No one noticed when it happened, but the sound got important, more precise and felt. The individual riffs Vince brought out of his guitar began anchoring the music, making it surefooted and flexible, showing something emphatic and honest down behind, pushing and lifting, tossing in little flakes of monkeyfuck here and there.

And then, as always happens, when we stopped playing for the crowd, the crowd started listening. Late in the set, the dance floor jammed up and more people than we'd seen all week were bumping into each other, some smiling and others serious, dancing forty different styles and raising their hands into the air. Dennis took charge then and on cue we bridged into our handclapping, sing-along number, "Let the Sun Shine In."

The room was yelling when we finished and four or five people were at the bandstand right away with songs they wanted to hear. We only had time for one more and were already ten minutes past time to quit. Dennis ignored the requests and counted off, "A Little Help from My Friends," and I remembered Jenny's song too late to change. As the introduction was worked through I tried to look for her over all the heads and smoke but couldn't make anything out. Everybody was on their feet and every stage light was in my eyes.

It built slowly to the final chorus. All of us were singing, when the house lights came on. Then I saw Jenny against the far wall, the music and hollering all around her, awkward and fixed, looking out like someone on shore seeing a ship. Looking at me. I suddenly felt like hell and wondered how I got in these situations.

I knew at that moment that Jenny was going to follow me back to the hotel. I tried to think of what Roy C might do, or anyone else who'd dealt with this problem.

It was almost 1:20 A.M. before we had everything turned off and a waitress came up on stage to collect the glasses. Vince looked at the stage carpet for a guitar pick he really didn't need, trying to make it out among all the hundreds of cigarette burns and stains from spilled drinks. The jukebox was off and the room had emptied out except for one group of seven by the dance floor trying to get their arms into their coats. The waitresses were all at the bar counting money with Vinny. Everyone's face looked harsh and porous under the fluorescent lights.

Dennis got his coat from behind his amp and killed the stage lights. The three of us stepped down slowly to the dance floor, stiff and hot and heads ringing, with Vince talking about how tired he was and how glad he was we didn't have to tear down tonight. I was so sweaty I started to feel cool away from the lights. Jenny was still there and still looking, hadn't moved an inch. I walked over and sat down beside her again. The others went to collect the money.

"Say, I'm sorry about 'Proud Mary.' We got wound up and I wasn't able to get it in."

Jenny turned sideways in her seat, full faced, staring now like a moth before the sun.

"We do a big long ending on it and it really cooks. It would've been a good song to do."

Jenny looked confused for a moment and then gushed, "Oh, that's all right!" her voice even deeper now, ecstatic again and waiting for what I would say next.

I looked over at the bar and watched Vinny talk from up on a stool, his cigarette bobbing and him laying out his hands. Vince looked like he wanted to interrupt.

"I'll tell you," I said, only glancing at Jenny and then talking across the table. "This sweaty shirt is going to freeze solid walking back to the hotel. My coat won't make any difference at all."

Jenny waited and then tugged on my sleeve. I hoped she just wanted to see if it was wet. Then she tugged again like she wanted to tell me a secret. The jukebox was off.

I looked over at her, forced a smile and said, "Yeah?"

Jenny was almost giggling; she leaned a little bit toward me and tugged on my sleeve again.

Dennis was walking across the room toward us. I waited until he got to the table. "Vinny don't have the money tonight. Says we'll get it in the morning."

"Great," I said and stood up. Jenny waited a second and then got up too. Dennis looked over at Vince, still arguing with Vinny. "Screwball there is talking about calling Sam tonight. Vinny'll get the money; he wants us back. This blizzard wasn't our fault."

Vacuum cleaners came on in two different parts of the room. Jenny tugged on my sleeve with long steady pulls, just like ringing a bell, insistent, smiling just with her mouth now.

"Yeah," I said, leaning over.

She halted once, looking at me close, then her mouth moved over the noise of the vacuum cleaners, barely heard, "Ya'll sure good."

I was drawing blanks. "Tell Dennis; he works in this band too." Then I gestured to Dennis, hoping maybe she would like him instead.

Vince walked up, still looking ugly, still mad, started to speak but everyone was looking at Jenny.

Jenny looked at me and stuttered. I said it for her, "She thinks we sound good. She likes the band."

Vince stared hard at her. "That's good." Then he looked at me. "You know this good band is not getting paid, don't you?"

It was bitter cold outside and the snow was falling again. The sidewalk was lumpy with frozen footsteps and everyone walked fast with hands shoved in pockets, hunched up and blowing steam out our noses. It was completely silent, everyone's heads still ringing. Jenny walked behind for the first block, I heard her shoes crunching snow. Then she was beside me, walking like she was on an errand, lips pressed around her teeth, intense. I looked down the two blocks still to go and each looked half a mile long.

By the time we reached the hotel I broke from the pack with some mumbled excuse and headed up the stairs ahead of them. Once in the lobby I went to high speed and got into the hallway. My room was at the far end. As I hit my stride doors were starting to blur on both sides of me. Twenty more feet and I'd be safe.

"Moke?" It chilled my blood. I could hear her footsteps coming down the hall. My name seemed the call of doom. I was trapped once again. The fire escape was five feet away but it was a rickety old structure and probably wouldn't hold my weight. I drifted a bit further and stopped in front of my door, regretting everything around me, thinking I just wasn't right for this. She came up behind me and waited.

I started to say something, I know not what. I'm sure I dodged and weaved as much as possible, but Jenny could not be defeated. I talked myself dry but she just stood there, feet apart, looking straight ahead at my shirt, implacable, calm. Not looking up or trying to speak, she just waited.

I saw no way out. I was as cornered as if I were at the end of a tunnel. I expected her to start throwing in bits of burning straw to flush me out, laying on of hands and romantic declarations and such usual tactics.

She looked for a long time until she seemed to know what to do, and then raised her hands and put them around my neck. I could feel the little warm spots they made and I just felt all the more cold. Then she pulled me toward her, deadly serious now, turned her face and kissed me on the cheek. "Ya'll sure were good."

She turned and walked back down the hall, leaving me disjointed and sputtering for words. This is the condition of romance on the road: furtive, occasional, misunderstood, disquieting. One more thing I didn't want to know.

Death Stares Me in the Face

On the drive north out of Sterling, while passing between snow-banks six feet high on both sides of the road, we began experiencing van problems. It was one of those rare days of the year when even the natives of South Dakota, people probably suckled on icicles as babies, refused to go outside. The high that day was ten below. A crystal clear sky, no wind anywhere, sun shiny overhead, an apparently ordinary day in every way but for the fact that nothing moved. The DJ on the radio said that it was too cold to snow. I'd never heard of such a thing. I think that if we'd had a Texas fly trapped in the van and let him go, he would get maybe a foot out the window and then fall to the ground and break in small chunks. We were the only vehicle on the road most of the time. Occasionally we saw a snowplow. Not only was it enormously cold but it was a Sunday, the week before Christmas. We passed a farmhouse every few miles. The smoke from the chimneys reached two hundred feet into the air and steam fluffed out at different vents in the roof. It was so cold even the houses themselves seemed to waver like a mirage as they radiated heat. I saw no dogs in the yards. There were no birds in the sky. Nothing resembling life anywhere. And our engine starts knocking.

There are right and wrong times to have a breakdown. The very best time to have a breakdown is while you're coasting into the stall at the mechanic's garage. Next to that might be while driving past any gas station with the sign "mechanic on duty." It's not even so bad breaking down anywhere in town if you can afford a tow truck. Breaking down in the country is different. And breaking down in sub-zero temperatures in the middle of unpopulated territory is probably the worst. It's at moments like this you realize that the tiniest screw in the motor is all that stands between you and oblivion. Engines aren't big powerful things; they're lots of little weak things doing small jobs all tied together to one big result—in this case moving us across the frozen tundra. As soon as it started knocking Dennis slowed from forty-five to thirty.

"What's that noise, man?" Vince asked.

"It's the motor. Too cold outside." Dennis said.

"Too cold?! We've been driving for hours, why's the motor getting cold? That's not good."

Dennis didn't have an answer and for once I could see he was worried. "Hey, Dennis," I said from the back. "Maybe it's the lifters." None of us knew what lifters were but we were always talking about them like they were the main ingredient in the engine. Vince joined in. "Yeah, man. Sounds like lifters to me." Dennis was real sensitive about his lifters and didn't like them criticized. "They're fine, man. It's just cold; motor can't warm up."

Vince looked out the window and dragged off his cigarette. "Well, when do you expect it to warm up? I mean, we are driving north, man. It's not like once we get in North Dakota your engine is going to start running better."

Dennis didn't have any answers and eventually Vince stopped talking and we all fell to listening to the motor click and rattle. Then amazingly, after ten more miles, the motor seemed to perk up and put its trouble behind it. Dennis now declared that it was "warmed up." We climbed back to fifty-five and were sailing along once again. An hour later we stopped for gas in a little frozen burg called Custer and checked everything on the van we could. In its own peculiar way, the van seemed in ordinary condition. We kicked loose the huge chunks of ice from behind the wheels to lighten its load. The station attendant told us it was supposed to warm up later that afternoon, that there was a warm front moving up. We were all glad to hear it. "Yeah," he said, "supposed to get up around five degrees." "Five *what*?" Vince asked. The attendant smiled and looked suddenly cornered. He probably didn't meet many black people and didn't know when he was being bullshitted. "Five degrees on the thermometer," he said.

I personally couldn't feel the difference between ten below and five above. Prior to this adventure on the road, I considered thirty-five regular degrees to be remarkably few. Growing up in Oklahoma, I didn't really think temperature moved around much below zero. I used to think the negative numbers on a thermometer were just for show. Now I found out whole days could take place down there.

We loaded up on food and each bought a large coffee. The van was left running outside while we warmed ourselves by the office heater. The station attendant was a skinny man in his forties who looked like he'd grown up on gasoline, had gasoline in his blood. He was grizzled and had grease around his eyes and on his lips, ears full of it, hands looked like five-pointed hooves. A perfect miracle of filth. I saw chunks of food in his beard as well as lint, string, and something else I couldn't identify. He had a perpetual runny nose which he would snort back, and it sounded like someone draining a swamp each time he did it. Then he'd swallow, or chew, depending on his mood. Occasionally spit. He mostly chewed while we were there.

"What's the quickest route to Williston?" Dennis asked.

"Williston? North Dakota? Well, if it was me, I'd probably take 385 north to 85. Only road I know that goes there. Unless you want to visit Montana. You on vacation?"

As one of his leadership duties, Dennis had to do the talking at times like this. "We book out of Indianapolis. But Vince and I's from Chicago. We're musicians."

"Him too?" pointing at me.

"Drummer," Dennis said dryly.

The attendant eyed me over, as though he'd never met a drummer before. Then he smiled and seemed to enjoy this notion of a white drummer in a black band. I could read his mind and stared him down.

"Yeah, 85 will take you right to Williston. They like their roads straight in North Dakota, but they keep their signs small. Watch out for 85 and you'll be okay." We thanked him and got back in the van. We drove for another half hour at various speeds and eventually moved into the warm front. We knew this because it began snowing. And it appeared that the further north we got into South Dakota, the warmer it became, as the snow kept getting faster and heavier. Eventually we moved into what South Dakota must think of as their tropical zone, and found ourselves in the worst kind of blizzard. Then the sun set. Dennis figured we could reach Williston in four or five more hours.

After a while things were getting ugly inside the van. It didn't help that Vince had his bottle out. We were moving only 25 MPH and couldn't see ten feet in front of us. The snow blew laterally from right to left, nudging the van into the opposing lane and causing Dennis to hunch himself over the wheel and bitch up a storm.

Then it got worse, leaving each of us to wonder out loud just how bad weather could become, and what the hell was going on anyway? The wind was driving hard now into our right side, a steady, constant shriek like it was coming out the nozzle of a machine, pushing tons of snow. Loud whistling sounds came off all parts of the van. Then, just when I thought it couldn't get any stronger, it would gust and shove the van two feet to the left. It was like being in a frozen hurricane.

Every ten minutes someone would think to ask if this was still 85. It was impossible to tell. For all we could see, we could've been heading up someone's driveway and wouldn't know it until we drove into his barn. On the radio the DJ kept saying, "The roads are impassable. Stay at home. Blizzard Alert!"

Finally, Dennis said he knew we were on the right road because we were still headed north. Vince asked him how he could tell and Dennis said he had a built-in compass. This was news to me. I'd traveled with Dennis for almost two years now and had heard nothing about this built-in compass. He said he could tell true north from northeast or northwest, that he could lay a beeline straight north and not vary one degree left or right without immediately knowing it. He said it was an instinct he was born with. Then Dennis told a long story about being down in the sewer system in Chicago as a child and in an old tunnel they didn't use any more. He said it was pitch black and the tunnel twisted back and forth and that anyone else would have been lost but that he had a solid fix on north the whole time and found his way out. Vince looked at him and said, "I remember that! You was lost! You was crying for your momma when you come out that hole. I don't remember you saying nothing about no 'built-in compass.' You weren't talking no 'built-in compass' when you came out that manhole. You was just built-in *scared*. That's all." Dennis got mad and said it wasn't that way at all and they managed to get ten or fifteen minutes out of the subject before it was dropped.

They argued their way over the next four or five miles, rotating through a variety of subjects, and then a remarkable event occurred: there was a turn in the road. It caught Dennis so by surprise he was hardly able to keep the van out of the snowbank. But worst of all, there was another road in the other direction, a road we saw at the last instant, a road we did not take. We realized at that point it wasn't a turn in the highway so much as it was a fork in the road. And we'd gone left. There was no way to know any more what road we were on. Typically, there was no sign to tell us, or if there was, it was buried. Everything became equally possible.

As is always the case, there was an immediate division of opinion about which fork we should have taken. Dennis, because he was driving and had made the turn, said we were on the correct road. Vince, suspicious of anything Dennis did, was convinced we should be on the other road and wanted to go back and look. I came down in the middle, which is to say I was out in the field somewhere between the two roads and didn't know which one to take. Pandemonium ensued. Vince proceeded to call Dennis a "pig-headed asshole" and "dumber than a rock" and other choice items. Dennis talked right over Vince, calling him a "drunk idgit." I stayed quiet and contributed nothing to this bloodbath. Dennis rendered the discussion moot as he kept his foot down the whole time, even speeding up to solidify his position. After several minutes he'd won his case, or at least the decision about which direction to go.

Vince was convinced that true north was veering off to our right and that we were now headed for Montana. A road map was found and, unfortunately, a fork showed up on 85. The only problem was it was too far north still yet for us to even be there to miss it, at least according to Dennis. Dennis began saying at this point that he'd been aware all along of that "other" fork but wasn't going to worry about it until we got there, which he said would be another two hours. He said that Vince was confusing a dirt road for the main road and that he, Dennis, had followed directly along where the road wanted him to go, so he knew we were still on the highway. Vince reminded him of the incredible high-speed turn he'd made to keep us on this "main road" and if he hadn't made the turn we'd have gone straight and be on the real main road. Then Dennis mentioned his built-in compass again and told us not to worry.

I looked at the map and tried to figure the distance we'd come since Custer. It was impossible to tell because our speed was uneven and I wasn't even sure what time we'd left. Given all those variables, it would have taken a team of experts in mapology to plot our position. About the best I could do was point to the area north of Custer and say we were "somewhere in here." And that was assuming we left town on the right road. Given the possibility that we were further north than Dennis thought, I calculated from the one known fork in the road where we might be and looked for what towns were coming up. Then

I found another fork much further south, a little insignificant fork just north of Custer we should have passed long ago but that now I couldn't remember passing at all. The more I thought about it the worse it got. I plotted every possibility that occurred to me and found six different parts of the state we might be in at that moment.

If Dennis was right, there was a town ahead in the next ten to forty miles called Deadwood. I showed everyone the map and we tried to figure how long it would be until we reached the place. After twenty miles Dennis was still reassuring us we were on the right track. After thirty miles Dennis was showing doubts and Vince made an unnecessary reference again to Dennis' built-in compass. Dennis shot back that "I knows what I knows and you can't say nothing about it." Then he accused us both of ruining his speedometer. I began to feel totally lost.

At that moment, as if to make the whole evening picture perfect, the engine began knocking again. This silenced them both. Like a soft tapping heard inside a coffin, it stalled out the conversation. "Oh, man," Vince said. "I don't *believe* this."

A quick look out the window showed nothing in the way of human settlement either in front or behind us. I knew we were in one of the least populated states of the country, and I feared we were in one of those pockets of that state where there was no population at all. I'm not sure I could see even fifteen feet in that blizzard. We had not passed another car in over an hour and the radio announced that parts of 85 were now closed due to drifting snow.

The knocking became louder. Dennis wanted to slow the van down and see how far we could get, hoping Deadwood was still up ahead. Vince wanted to speed up and cover as much ground as possible before it broke completely so we could at least *coast* a while, he said, be *somewhere*. They started arguing about this new subject and the knocking became still louder. The engine was really hammering itself by this time. I thought we should find a place to pull over and just run the motor for heat until we figured out something, or another vehicle came by, but no one was willing to stop. We limped along banging and hammering, sounding like some kind of industrial plant having a spasm. When it became obvious that if we continued we would soon need an engine transplant, Dennis slowed down to a crawl, unable to just stop, having no option other than to keep going at any speed. But the van wouldn't have it. At slow speed it would hardly pull itself at all and started coughing and shaking badly. Then there was some kind of loud pop and the engine just died altogether and we eventually drifted to a complete and total dead halt on the road.

Everyone was quiet and sat facing forward in their seats, Dennis with his hands still on the steering wheel, everything as if we were still moving. No one wanted to admit we were stuck and in a bad way. We sat like this for several minutes until the wind howled again and drew my attention outside the van and I realized we were a roadblock for the first snowplow coming down the road. In this blizzard they wouldn't see us until they had pushed us a mile. I was the first one to speak, "We got to get the van off the road or we'll get smacked from behind." There was no disputing the point. We were a sitting duck. No one wanted to go outside.

As soon as the doors were opened the gale-force winds completely emptied the van of heat and blew snow in on the amps. Everyone together started cussing. It was the bitterest kind of cold, an unearthly cold that seemed to weaken the bones and suck breath out of the body. Vince and I got behind the van to push and Dennis shoved from the driver's door so he could steer. Getting outside the van and pushing showed us one thing we did not know before: we were facing up a hill. A hill so steep we couldn't push the van forward at all. But we tried, just to show how confused we were. Even with our best effort we could only keep it from rolling backward. I walked up and told Dennis we'd have to find a place behind us to park the van. Dennis was becoming despondent, he said nothing, snow was piling up on his shoulders and head. He could only nod in agreement even though he hated to back up and wouldn't be able to see where he was going. I walked back down the hill to find a place and immediately lost sight of the van. After a hundred yards I came across a hole in the snowbank that might be the entrance to a small road and I figured that was good enough. I walked back and told Vince and Dennis about it and we rolled the van backwards to the place with Dennis weaving and scraping both snowbanks.

We climbed back in, shaking badly, listening to the wind outside. When the big gusts came along they would lift the van and rock it. Then I had to get out again to take a piss, standing only a few feet from the van and totally blind in that blizzard. Once back inside my hands were completely numb and my feet had disappeared. I was wearing a medium-thick army coat. Vince had a short leather jacket he always wore. Dennis had a heavy sweater and down vest on. We decided to ransack our suitcases and put on whatever we could. When we did start talking again it was about the likelihood of a highway patrol car or plow coming along and rescuing us. We were all certain it would happen soon.

Within thirty minutes Vince and Dennis both were huddled around the engine cover for heat and I was in back wrapped in my bass drum blanket and curled into a ball. We hadn't seen even one snowplow yet. Vince and Dennis were passing the bottle by now and were still human enough to offer me some but I turned them down. I'd heard somewhere that whiskey lowers your body heat while making you feel warmer and that people froze to death while drunk and didn't even know it. If I froze to death I'd want to know it, if only to finish off this whole experience. Vince kept up a low-level complaint. "Goddamn! I can't believe I'd come with you in this ratty old van. Piece of junk like this breaks down twice a day, and you want to drive it to goddamn North Dakota." Cough, shiver. "Motherfucker would have to be ignorant to go anywhere with you." Shudder from head to foot. "We're going to lay out here and get fucking pneumonia and be sick for a year all because you're too cheap to get a mechanic to fix this thing." Teeth rattling and steam coming out his nose. "Shit!"

I expected at that point that I would die. After a couple of hours we all thought we *were* dying, but it wouldn't happen. I told Vince and Dennis that I'd read about people freezing to death and that it felt like sleep coming on: you would first get drowsy and feel a willingness to stop fighting, and then a certain sense of peace came over you before you passed out and crystallized. About four o'clock in the morning we were all convinced death had come. Especially Vince and Dennis, who had emptied their bottle. Every few minutes one of them would shake himself awake and take a deep breath to make sure he still could, then lay back down and start dying again. I was so drowsy I had to push my eyes open and flip from side to side to stay awake. I don't know when I stopped, I only know I was dreaming about heaven and imagined it to be a place of beautiful scenery and unusual shapes—when an air horn went off outside the van.

I was bolt awake and sitting up. Vince and Dennis both raised their heads. We couldn't see a thing. All the windows were covered over with snow. The inside of the van was a freezer. "Waz that?" Vince said, half asleep, clouds coming out of his mouth. Both of them tried to sit up but acted like they were in body casts and just rolled to the side. The air horn went off again. Soon there was a knocking at the window and the door opened. "You'll have to move this van; I've got a road to clear." We were saved.

Dennis began explaining our predicament and the man went back to his plow to radio for a tow truck. Vince stretched himself awake—popping all over—and then got out to pee. From outside the van I heard him say, "Well, fuck me senseless." I followed him out the door and what I saw nearly knocked me flat. The road we were on was right at the edge of a gigantic cliff. We were in a tourist pull-over spot. Below and above and all around us was the wildest picture of rugged scenery. We were surrounded by huge rock spires a hundred feet high with snow-covered tops looking like enormous ice-cream cones. Off to our left I saw a frozen waterfall. All along the horizon were towering broken mountains. And about three feet in front of me and two hundred feet below were beautiful jagged pointy rocks in various shapes and designs that I would've landed on if I'd stepped over that little cable and off the edge last night. I hadn't known I was pissing off a two hundred foot cliff; I'd thought I was pissing into a ditch. It was the strangest, most dramatic landscape I'd ever seen. Vince turned to me and said, "We're in the Rocky Mountains. Probably in fucking Idaho."

I went to the plow and asked the man where we were. He looked at me a moment. "Well son, you're in the middle of the Black Hills National Park." I asked where that might be and he informed me it was still in South Dakota, only a few miles outside of Custer.

Dennis had crawled out by then and was looking around him like he'd woken up on Neptune. I went back and informed everyone where we were. Dennis' built-in compass was in disgrace. Vince and I both raked this subject back and forth over the coals for several days after that, and then made it a point to insert the word "compass" in random sentences for weeks to come. I also looked at the map and ascertained that if the van hadn't broken down, we would have gone another hundred miles on that road and not found one stop sign or lighted window.

To deliver the final blow to Dennis' reputation as a pathfinder, the tow truck that hauled us away came from Custer and was driven by that same snot-chewing fellow who had given us directions some twelve hours before. He showed us where we'd turned wrong. Vince smiled and smiled when he saw it was the fork in the road. That was the only bright moment in an otherwise dismal trip that seemed to go on forever.

Give Me a Break!

I played with Salt & Pepper for well over two years and eventually became so physically exhausted, so badly turned around, so blunted to all the depravity and misery everywhere around me, that I decided maybe a nice small town college campus might look good for a while. Either that or end up in the Home for the Disoriented and spend the rest of my life with old airline pilots and bus drivers.

My nonmusician friends—those who had stayed at home and lived quiet lives—could not understand this decision to leave the band and give up my exciting life. I'd made the mistake of writing people and describing different little experiences I had—dressing things up and colorizing the stories on those dull afternoons in hotel rooms— only to discover I'd painted myself into a corner. I returned home to huge disapproval, my friends thinking I was a fool to give up such a dreamy, idyllic, fun-packed existence. I wanted to say, "Don't you people know how to read a letter?" Whenever I'd mention one of the numberless old drunks with lungs that whistled in two octaves while he wheezed and coughed, spraying me with alcoholic spit and hanging his arm around my shoulders while calling me Ringo, my fool friends would think this was somehow unique and interesting and encouraged me to meet other such characters. They believed with all their heart that this was an adventure and I was an idiot to give it up. To a few musicians I attempted to explain, but even they were unable to understand.

I told the complete truth about Dennis, but my moron level friends insisted on thinking he was "vivid" and that I could still learn a lot from him. Whenever I'd mention Vince and his self-destructiveness, people reminded me he was a master musician and an amazing find. When I tried to explain how nasty clubs were night after night and what it meant being around desperate, unhappy people all the time, they would wave this away as a nuance and "point of view," something I shouldn't let bother me. They'd read the magazines and they thought they knew what I'd been doing, insisting on their damn ignorance. I resorted to my worst, most gruesome stories, trying hard to disgust people, but their eyes only lit up and they wanted to hear more. Nevertheless, I had no choice but to quit. I knew in my bones I had to. Like a sailor coming home after years at sea, the stories were a lot more appealing than the life. I did not feel that being jaded and world-weary was as educational as some people thought. I was twenty-three years old and felt forty-three.

But at the bottom of it all, the music had died on me. Especially those last three months. I could put up with a lot, but not that. At first there were occasional nights when I'd get up on stage and realize I did not want to be there. Vince would be acting like a clown and Dennis would just seem impenetrable to me. Every song I played that night was played mechanically. No heart, no interest at all in what I was doing. I was just making sound. Putting square pegs in square holes. It's funny that the more familiar a song becomes, the more alien it becomes after a while. Things break down into their component parts. You atomize. All those notes in the air around you could just as well be bouncing balls—nothing coheres. The tunes lose their glue. This is what's called 'burnout.' Near the end, it became such a mindless routine that sometimes I'd wake up in the middle of a song and not know its name or even how the melody went—and I was *playing* it. Complicated parts too. On nights like that I could've propped up a magazine on a stand next to me and read the whole thing by the end of the set. Everyone has off nights, but my off nights started bumping into each other. And it wasn't just me. Sometimes the whole band would be sounding weak and occasionally during a song I would glance up and meet Vince's eye and feel him failing in some way, unable that evening to play up to what he heard in his mind, and there was nothing I could do. I had nothing left to give, and besides, I knew by then he was utterly locked inside his own head. Every soloist is, finally. What I desperately needed was a vacation, but Dennis was too greedy, and for Vince it was too dangerous to take a week off. So they kept playing and I eventually had to pull out.

Still, leaving the band was hard. Vince was my friend and I knew I'd never see him again. And I'd never sounded better in my life. It's one of those immense ironies that you can sound technically great and not care in the least. Playing six nights a week with musicians that good had given me a punchy, clean quality I much enjoyed, and a reasonable ability to improvise. I could keep up with Vince, and Vince could spin ideas all night when the spirit was on him. But I was running on automatic. My body had been trained. My hands were thick and callused, my arms large and rippled, my legs looked like tree trunks. Nobody messed with me. I was in shape and hated to give that up, but I'd lost my reason to stay. Nothing seemed meaningful to me anymore. Add the wheezy alcoholics, the sad looks, the bad food and everything else—the decision to leave got made almost without me.

So I returned home and found myself treated like a killjoy, a party pooper, an antiromantic, someone who refused to taste life deeply. I didn't care. They didn't know what they were talking about. I sat in eventually with a few local bands but couldn't work up any interest and ended just picking a couple to work with for the occasional money. I was outplaying, overplaying, playing circles around everyone. There was no pleasure in this either. Every musician in town tried to steal me into his band but I had learned an awkward truth: being the best musician in a local band is not really any fun. Being the star in a mediocre band was a delusion I was no longer suited for. I would much rather be a good player in a great band, than the best player in a merely good band. I'd been exposed to quality playing and could not go back. Instead, I just played for the money every other weekend, treating my drum set like a large cash register, caring less and less as time went on. I'd sit in with whoever had a gig and do whatever I could to spiff up their sound, but then leave the job counting my money and really not thinking about anything else. Listening to all those young white guys sing left me feeling kind of empty. I got more into school and out of music and over the next couple of years my interest in playing cooled down and eventually disappeared into a small frozen block I left in the back of the freezer.

My drums were left behind when I moved to Iowa to attend graduate school. I left them in my mother's attic—just where she thought they'd end up all along. And they remained there for the next fifteen years, with one short-lived exception. My mother fell in with a bunch of retirees, three or four of which decided to start a little band and play dance music at the retirement village. They had everyone they needed except a drummer. My mother said she had a set of drums at home and this got her into the band. Suffice it to say I had a friend come by and get the drums down and set them up for her and show her a beat. Then I gave her verbal encouragement and little drum lessons over the phone from Iowa. The band got good enough eventually to pick up a second gig at the other retirement village across town for their monthly shuffle.

I also tried to help my mother pick a name for her band. Her choice was "The Melody Makers" but I squashed that. The guitar player, a man named Tex Harris, preferred "The Hip Cats" and I said I thought that closer to the mark. My suggestion (which she promised to take back to the band for consideration) was "Uncle Wiggly and his Stray Bullet Band." I also mentioned "The Raging Jalapeños." She promised me she would bring them both up at their next practice, but with my mother you could never tell.

So I buried myself in books for a few years, made friends with Shakespeare and Donne and Faulkner and García Márquez. I moved so far away from music I didn't even plug in my stereo for months at a time. During the furthest of those years I hardly ever heard a song unless it was by accident over at a friend's house. I'd moved to the country and was enjoying the peace and quiet. All of my musical instincts had died. My burnout was complete. When occasionally I did encounter a performing musician, I couldn't look at him without seeing through his machinery to all the levers and switches he was pulling. It seemed to me that knowing too much about a subject will ruin it for you, as my playing ruined music for me. During those fifteen years I probably didn't go into three clubs. If I happened to be somewhere and hear a tune I used to play, it might bring back faces and places to me, and perhaps the air would seem to get a little smoky and stale for a moment as I reminisced, but these were fleeting moments and never raised any nostalgia in me. My musical years began to seem like another life finally, a previous life. If someone were to cut me in half and count my rings, those playing years would be much closer to the middle core than the outside bark.

There's a simple test one can apply to ex-drummers to see if any residual rhythm remains in their system. I call this the "Turn Signal Test." Watch any ex-drummer while he waits at a traffic light in a quiet car, his turn signal clicking away like a metronome. If he is alive to his calling, that steady click . . . click . . . click . . . will begin filling up for him and getting complicated. A person can play any rhythm imaginable between the clicks of a turn signal. His fingers will fall in with the pulse and he will begin to keep time and cut time and rearrange time and jazz up that turn signal until it sounds like a Brazilian orchestra. There is so much potential rhythm in a turn signal you can exhaust yourself finding it, or be called awake by the driver behind you. My turn signal, needless to say, remained silent for almost fifteen years.

‖ EPILOGUE

So when, in the late '80s, the whole country suddenly got nostalgic about old rock'n'roll, my first thought was, "Well, this makes no sense either," followed quickly by, "Oh, they're resurrecting the old myths, telling themselves fairy tales about their own lives, rewriting the past. American innocence and all that. I've seen this before."

Then I forgot about it again and was going along minding my own business, leaving society alone and no longer trying to improve things, living peacefully with my cat, listening to the birds chirp and the corn grow, when one of my friends started tacking too close to the national wind.

Willy is one of those enthusiastic, curious types who always seems to have half a dozen projects going at once. Unlike myself, Willy *finds* things to do. And one of the things he found to do was drag his old bass guitar out from under the bed after twenty years and start himself a golden oldies band. Like the proverbial turtle dropped on a rock which sets off an avalanche that causes a tidal wave that wipes out Tokyo again, Willy's newfound mania for playing music and "getting down" eventually affected me as well.

Another story of being bushwhacked by life: I was relaxed and comfortable and lounging in my nest whenever possible, when Willy started developing this preternatural glow in his eyes and talking to me about his band at every opportunity. If they had a good practice, I heard about it. Had a good opening set at the gig, he called and told me everything that happened. Having lunch with Willy had become an ongoing monologue about how *fabulous* it was to be playing music once again. "I feel twenty years younger, man. Damn near bulletproof. Rock'n'roll *is* the fountain of youth." He kept inviting me to their jobs and I kept refusing.

Willy's reversion to adolescent behavior did not inspire envy in me. I had no interest in acting like a teenager again. Elvis no longer seemed like a god but rather like a guy who didn't handle his life very well. All this dancing around and going nuts in large crowds seemed just silly. In other words, I'd become an old fogey. And liked it. Considered it the apex of wisdom and was not looking to have my mind changed.

Then my good friend Willy laid a trap and I fell into it. He arranged to have a birthday party for himself, his forty-first, and then got his wife Wilma involved in the planning. Wilma was much harder to turn down than Willy and I ended up having to go to his damn birthday party and sit there listening to his damn band while watching Willy jump around the stage like Ponce de León.

Then—as I should've expected but somehow didn't—late in the fourth set, just about the time I was ready to get up and leave, Willy got on the mic and said something I wasn't listening to and then suddenly was introducing a guest star. I was actually looking around the room to see who it might be, when Willy called out my name to come up on stage.

"No!" I yelled out. "I'm not coming." I could only figure Willy must've lost his mind, overcome with enthusiasm again. Getting me up on stage was to invite disaster. Why was he doing this?

As happens in these situations, there was automatic applause and people started yelling and the whole room went manic for a minute and my choices got real slim.

"Okay . . . fine. *Damnation!*" I said and got to my feet. Climbing on stage I told Willy, "If you'd given me fair warning I would've worn my fool's cap and clip-on ears." Willy dismissed this remark and I got settled in behind the drums.

The guitar player asked me if I had a choice of tune to play. A guy about my age, he had a kind and friendly face but clearly did not know the gravity of his question. "Anything," I said. "Make it short."

Willy counted the song off. They'd picked one of those Creedence tunes that always show up at times like this. I came in on one and broke a sweat almost immediately. Halfway through the first verse—just as I knew would happen—muscles started screaming all over my body. My arms seized up and my right leg seemed to be losing its mind. I was in a panic to even keep the tempo. All of the interior rhythms in the song were invisible to me, all the tricks of playing notes against each other were lost. Hand maneuvers that were once second nature, now were tangled knots. By the second verse I was totally exhausted. I tried to resurrect my old instincts, drag back up to the surface vital bits of old drum knowledge, rooting around in my psyche in a reckless and desperate fashion for about two full minutes. For me, it was like being peeled and dipped in salt water.

The song, of course, was a dead loss. Once we finally stopped playing and I laid down the sticks there was a cool reality in the room. The crowd gave only polite applause, like you'd give to a little girl who dropped her baton six times. The musicians were all fiddling with their instruments, looking at the floor, taking deep slugs off their beer. Only Willy was still smiling, and then made one of his obscure jokes. "Hey man, when the bear comes out of his cave, he always takes a big shit, first thing. Happened to me too."

"Yeah, well, Willy, I owe you one. But this bear's not coming out of his cave." I was grinding my teeth all the way home.

The next day, though, I was driving in the car and turned on a music station for no particular reason. There was an old Aretha Franklin tune I really liked. I did the same thing the day after, and then just never turned off the radio again.

Then I saw a variety show on TV that featured a band and was disturbed to find myself perspiring slightly after their song was over. A little later I woke up to find myself standing in a park and listening to a reggae group while I was late for a meeting. It was as if my tongue was tasting something my brain refused to recognize.

And it only got worse. Jingles from hamburger commercials

began circling my head, leaving me disoriented and anxious. Day after day I found my prejudices shifting around, my poles reversing on several subjects. Before long I was slapping the edges of tables again and banging on the steering wheel. By the time the fever was fully upon me—some six weeks later—my turn signal woke up and started jamming. I could feel the old circuits re-energize, like seeing ancient canals fill again with water, like dusty sails flapping to life. I was thinking rock'n'roll. And it was Willy's fault.

Then their drummer eventually had a baby and wanted to spend weekends at home and I was recruited to take his place. It took very little persuading on Willy's part. I had my drums shipped up on overnight express and spent the next couple of weeks trying to get in shape and separate my left side from my right once again. Everything had fused together over the years. I didn't separate very quickly, but it did occur, and launched me on a series of recovered memories and examinations. I hauled out a stack of old records and listened day and night. I made practice tapes and wore them out. I started simple and let things resurface on their own, like shaking and releasing air bubbles out of an old underwater wreck. If nothing else, the physical exercise alone started to brighten me up.

I tried to put out of my mind everything I'd learned about the music business and prepare myself to find romance once again. And the romance was there, bits and pieces in the songs, just where I'd left it, but something had changed. These weren't really the same songs, even though they sounded the same—and occasionally, in the beginning, even got my heart throbbing in the same old way. At our first old codger practice, I rediscovered that quite certain and genuine joy of thumping the same beat with other people, of playing *together* again, a tribal feeling I could hardly remember it was so old. After a couple of practices, after I was firmly in the band and my chops started to come back, I too started walking around and breathing extra deep, looking in a penetrating fashion in and around things, using words like "hip" and "cool" once again.

They were called the "Love Muffins" and I hated the name. Someone's wife had picked it and I resolved to retitle the band as soon as I had the political pull to do so. We practiced once or twice a week at the guitar player's house in his fancy basement studio, working around everyone's schedule at work and softball games and PTA meetings and other grown-up functions. I got to know all the wives and kids. I became familiar with secretaries who would pass me through to "Mr. Cronour" so he and I could schedule a band practice. Everything about this group was deeply middle-aged. It had about it a huge aura of fantasy and guilty pleasure, and it literally dripped with nostalgia. I continued to feel a little bit silly, but I also had to admit how good it felt to have that pulse working inside me once again.

We were four thick-bellied, slow-moving men, grinning a lot and playing the old hits. Our practices had a sense of geriatric enthusiasm that I noticed right away, that not-quite spontaneous activity that seemed a little too intentional, a little too deliberate, a little too consistently happy. A little like weekend golf. At the most obvious level we were clearly faking it, playing air guitar with real amps there for a while, but the fakery seemed a necessary step in cranking ourselves up and getting in the mood for the real moments of music making when they occurred. At least once every two or three practices I could convince myself this was all worth doing—we'd slip into a moment of unabashed joy and everybody started swaying together and stomping the floor and I'd think, "Yeah! This is it."

But all the old problems were there as well. I tried to avoid them. I saw politics played. Personalities had to be massaged and petted, conflicts resolved, little power plays averted. Willy worked double overtime on all this. The other two prima donnas in the band required regular soothing and ego boosting and Willy did the work of keeping them happy. I couldn't do it. Didn't have the stomach for it. Our guitar player, a nameless soul of large dimensions but minuscule talent, a mortician during the day, had a bug about playing the tunes "exactly like the originals," allowing no variations or creativity to creep in. Our keyboard player, longtime friend and cohort of prima donna number one, the owner of a retail store and otherwise a rubber stamp on two legs, always agreed with his old friend. Willy was open to suggestions on how to play things but overall, the tunes were treated like Egyptian mummies. The better we started to sound, the colder the tunes got.

An odd combination of present moment playing in the past tense, I tried for the longest time to figure why these old tunes felt so weird to me. Tunes like "Gloria," which had only sounded one way since I first heard it, suddenly sounded rosier—domesticated and enshrined. Tamed. Gloria was someone's unruly daughter now. Nothing is ever the same the second time around, I knew that, but this was *essentially* different. It wasn't the kids running loose, it wasn't the wives looking bemused and encouraging, it wasn't even the oddness of the four of us shedding our daytime identities and hopping around like fools. It was my vague impression, early on, that the songs we were playing were supposed to sound like echoes somehow, were actually, in our minds and hearts, being replayed, reproduced, resurrected. We didn't seem to be *making* any music of our own. My half-articulated but slowly growing sense was that I was caught up in an act of homage. And it felt bad. Or at least different and unmusical to me. All I really wanted were those moments of pure gush and flush where the tunes came alive for an instant, while everyone around me seemed to be dusting off glass cases in their silly museum.

But that was under the surface, not anything I talked about. I was having a good time mostly. Finally we got out of the practice room and started playing little gigs around, dragging our entourage with us. The tunes were all big hits. The dancers, mostly in their thirties and forties now, loved us. We had our moments of lifting the room, and being lifted along with it, but the whole thing remained hugely complicated in my mind.

It was also profoundly exhausting. Amazingly so. I'd finally walk in the door after a gig about 3 A.M. or later, trailing clothes behind me, stagger to the bed and just topple forward. Ignorant, dreamless sleep. Motionless sleep. I'd wake up ten or twelve hours later in exactly the same position as when I laid down. Eventually, one of my lids would involuntarily relax and start to inch up and I'd gaze at the sheet for a minute, let the brain snap on, gaze a bit longer, and then realize I still felt totally fried. My eyes would be dry, my mouth sore, my hands stiff, throat raw. Both my legs felt like I'd rented them out to some marathon runner who, in turn, loaned them to everyone else in the race. My right shoulder would be rusted shut and my ears still ringing. And when finally I'd raise up and attempt to get out of bed and put two feet on the floor, I had the rare opportunity to count every joint in my body as it snapped and popped into place. I hadn't remembered playing being this hard before.

It usually took me a couple of days to get over a gig. I'd spend the first half of the first day gulping coffee and pushing buttons on the remote control, getting pissed off at politicians on Sunday talk shows, occasionally shifting my position on the couch to keep the blood circulating. Later that afternoon I'd attempt to get out and take a walk, stretch all the muscles and inhale fresh air, but half the time I'd get outside and there'd be some kid on a bike I'd have to dodge at the last minute, or a dog barking suddenly in a bush while I was right beside him, force-firing all the old synapses and making me jump. On days like this I felt like I had palsy and rheumatism both. Acres of dull pain. The second day would be marginally better and by the third day, if I drank a lot of fluids, I'd be walking upright again and responding to situations.

My body was like a thing apart, like a dowdy old uncle I had to invite to the party and who ended up—somehow—at the head of the cha-cha line. Everything seemed slow and sluggish. I had to wait for him continually. He was always in the way, losing a shoe under the table or getting his tie in the dip. Damned old middle-aged fool. I was frustrated out of my mind with all the good ideas I was throwing out in songs, only to see not one of them implemented by my body in time to do any good. It seemed impossible to make a spontaneous move any-more—or at least do so and be satisfied with the result. The tunes eventually got cleaner and snappier at the same time they became even more canned and artificial and scripted. My discontent started to grow wings.

I put about nine months into it. What I'd call a fair test. The band started working pretty steadily and my muscles gradually reac-quired some tone. My playing improved slowly but there was little light, only heat. I had a clip-on fan blowing the whole time on stage. We worked the same two or three beer joints Willy could talk us into. Then he started getting enthusiastic about booking too and before long "Dynamite Ranch" (our new name; Willy picked it after lots of arm-twisting from me) became one of those local dozen bands that played the local dozen bars.

I ambled along in this unresolved state, not yet knowing what I was going to do, working hard to even sound decent and not sure I was making it. Everyone else was highly enthusiastic about the band. Wives helped out whenever possible. We had fancy artwork posters, a band logo, someone arranged to have T-shirts made. A couple of wives started wearing poodle skirts and penny loafers and flouncy blouses to the gigs and I about puked.

The whole experience might've passed uneventfully and been forgotten but for the night we worked a fairly new place in town called "Memories." A veritable pit of regret and loneliness, it was decorated in memorabilia from the '50s and most of the patrons dressed either in leather or some other costume. We did the head shakes on Beatles' tunes and got the yells, we did the pouts and the hokiepokie too and the audience responded in turn. A standard-issue bar band doing the standard thing on a Saturday night for an ordinary crowd somewhere out in the midwest. For all the world it seemed to me a scene of charades and pretenders, everyone carrying baggage and acting out, half the room probably in a recovery program or thinking about it, and here I was leading the parade once again. Or at least stuck too near the front. We were in the first verse of "Tutti-Frutti"— a tune I didn't particularly like—when the last petal fell off the flower. I looked around me with bare naked eyes and realized I didn't have a reason to be here.

I scanned the dancers, watching them as they bumped into each other and stumbled through their steps, desperate to have a good time and trying way too hard, people clinging to each other and laughing too loud, individuals coming in and out of view in the small spaces between my cymbals, rotating around in the speckled light and looking like fish in an aquarium.

Then, just before we got to the second verse, just when I was finally convinced I'd never be surprised again—an idea came to me, and I was surprised. I shook my head once and it occurred to me I might be totally wrong about everything, *completely* full of shit, that perhaps my thinking had been gummed up and distorted for years when it came to music.

Not a big idea, kinda obvious really—if I'd been married my wife would've told me—but it came to me why I've always had this adversarial relationship with working gigs, why I could never be entirely happy with my own playing, why I was my own worst enemy most of the time. Why I avoided the whole music scene for fifteen years. Simply, obviously, I was as guilty as everyone else when it came to seeing music as more jacked up and glorified than it truly was.

I'd never seen things clearly. As a youngster I was always thinking ahead and seeing every situation I was in as temporary, living for the dream, the future. Now, I looked around me and all I saw were people glancing backward, regretting, dreaming of the past. And here I was in the middle of it still, reacting one way or another, being drawn out, constantly pulled.

I understood suddenly that looking forward or backward was really only looking away from what was in front of me the whole time. Stripped of past and future both—of politics, sex, culture, age, business, the expectations of others, my own expectations, everything else that I've attached to it—music is a damn simple proposition. Always was. The *only* reason to play rock'n'roll was for the hell of it. I guess I'd been over-thinking things.

This idea settled on me and I eventually relaxed and dropped into the swingingest rhythm probably put to "Tutti-Frutti" since Little Richard first did it. I became as mindless and open and spontaneous as a sixteen-year-old boy. I swung the shit out of that song. Swung it and lifted it and had skirts twirling all over the room, my blood surging, heart thumping, starting to fall in love all over again.

The golden oldies band didn't last much longer but it didn't matter. I found another band, a country band, and had a great time with them too. Then I branched off for a while and played old swing music from the thirties and forties. And loved it. I'm thinking now about finding a jug band. See what that's like. Or maybe an old blues band. There's nothing like playing the blues.